Praise for the
Linda Reilly

"A very fun cat-centric novel, along with strong writing, fun characters, and a crowd-pleasing finale." —*Kings River Life Magazine*

"I thoroughly enjoyed this puzzler of a mystery. Reilly cooks up a perfect recipe of murder and mayhem in this charming cozy." —Jenn McKinlay, *New York Times* bestselling author

"Smart, sassy, and a little bit scary. Everything a good cozy should be!" —Laura Childs, *New York Times* bestselling author

"Foodies and mystery lovers will come for the red herrings and stay for the cheese." —*Kirkus Reviews*

"Masterful misdirection coupled with a pace that can't be beat, Linda Reilly has grilled up a winner for sure!" —J. C. Eaton, author of the Sophie Kimball Mysteries, The Wine Trail Mysteries, and The Marcie Rayner Mysteries

"A well-crafted and fun start to a new series! Carly and her crew serve mouth-watering grilled cheese sandwiches while solving crime in a quaint Vermont town. Plenty of twists and turns to keep you turning the pages and guessing the killer to the very end." —Tina Kashian, author of the Kebab Kitchen Mysteries

"A delightful and determined heroine, idyllic small town, and buffet of worthy suspects make this hearty whodunnit an enticing start to a decidedly delectable new series! This sandwich-centric cozy will leave readers drooling for more!" —Bree Baker, author of the Seaside Café Mysteries

Books by Linda Reilly

Grilled Cheese Mysteries

Up to No Gouda
No Parm No Foul
Cheddar Late Than Dead
Brie Careful What You Wish For
You Feta Watch Out

Cat Lady Mysteries

Escape Claws
Claws of Death
Claws for Celebration
Claws of Action
The Girl with the Kitten Tattoo

Deep Fried Mysteries

Fillet of Murder
Out of the Dying Pan
A Frying Shame

Apple Mariani Mysteries

Some Enchanted Murder

You Feta Watch Out

A Grilled Cheese Mystery

Linda Reilly

BEYOND┬PAGE
PUBLISHING

You Feta Watch Out
Linda Reilly
Copyright © 2024 by Linda Reilly
Cover design and illustration by Dar Albert, Wicked Smart Designs

Beyond the Page Books
are published by
Beyond the Page Publishing
www.beyondthepagepub.com

ISBN: 978-1-960511-95-9

This book is dedicated to Charles Dickens, without whom the world would never have experienced that cherished tale of forgiveness and redemption known as *A Christmas Carol.*

ACKNOWLEDGMENTS

It is nearly impossible to thank everyone who contributed to this mystery. To my editor, Bill Harris, thank you for your encouragement and for being such a joy to work with. Amelia Koziol, thank you for your insight on the inner workings of a theater. Any mistakes or inconsistencies are mine alone. Wendi Murphy, chef extraordinaire, what a treat it was to have you prepare Grant's feta appetizers for testing. They were far more delicious than if I had made them! Maybe we can have them again soon? Judy Jones, for always being there to brainstorm with me. Judy, your faith in me kept me motivated on those days when I doubted myself. And to my dear friend Terry Palys, who came up with the title *You Feta Watch Out*. May Santa fill your stocking with everything your heart desires.

CHAPTER 1

FROM THE SPEAKERS HIDDEN WITHIN THE WALLS OF THE FLINTHEAD
Opera House, the soft strains of "God Rest Ye Merry Gentlemen" faded to
silence. Bells began clanging, a strident sound that grew louder with every
second.

Eventually the ringing waned, and a low cloud of dense fog rolled across
the stage. From it arose a ghostly figure. At least eight feet tall, it appeared to
hover for several seconds in midair. Then the fog dissipated, and the figure sank
slowly to stage level. Garbed in gray, his waistcoat in tatters, the actor dragged
his black boots across the floor. In his oval face, his eyes were so dark they
might have been coals. A kerchief was tied around his head and jaw, as if that
alone was keeping the skull intact. A chain made of cash boxes, steel purses, and
other assorted symbols of money surrounded the figure's waist. From there it
trailed off behind him like a heavy metal train.

Carly Hale sat mesmerized by the theatrics. She could almost believe that if
she reached out with one hand, she could touch the spectral vision who was
portraying Jacob Marley. That's how close he seemed.

It helped that she was seated dead center in the second row of the opera
house. It would be prime seating for the average ticket holder, but as today's
performance was only a dress rehearsal, there was no charge to those who'd
received special invitations. Balsam Dell's police officers, firefighters, and town
employees had also been invited. It was a special thank-you from the Carpenter
family—founders of the opera house—for their service to the town.

Norah Hale, Carly's sister and the significant other of Nate Carpenter,
rubbed her cashmere-covered arms. "Amazing costume," she whispered loudly.
"I'd swear it was a real ghost."

Carly gave her sister a glare. Norah was famous—infamous, really—for
talking during movies or any other sort of performance where silence was
expected. One time, when they were kids at a Disney movie, Carly pushed a
handful of popcorn into her sister's mouth to make her stop talking. Norah's
already loose tooth had come tumbling out. Their mother had not been amused.

Onstage sat another figure. Bony and gaunt, he cowered in a small chair,
wide-eyed and shivering with fear.

Ebenezer Scrooge.

"How now! What do you want with me?" Scrooge beseeched.

"Much!" Marley bellowed.

Carly sank back into the plush seat, thoroughly engaged by the
performance. She'd been looking forward to this day for weeks. Her bestie,
Gina Tomasso, had landed a minor role and was thrilled to pieces. As one of a
trio of carolers, she'd already sung at the opening of the play.

1

But something in Gina's expression during that short scene had been off. Her face had been taut, her gaze focused downward instead of toward the audience. Her voice had started strong but ended faint. It's not something most people would have noticed, but Carly knew her friend well.

A case of nerves, that's all it was, Carly told herself.

Marley continued his eerie rant, but something was awry with him, too. He stumbled over words. At one point he paused, as if struggling to remember the next line.

Carly squirmed in her seat. Norah shot her a look, but this time kept silent.

Hushed whispers filtered through the opera house.

With a sudden shriek, Marley tore off his kerchief and threw it to the floor. "I can't work like this," he growled. "How can I remember my lines when I'm stuck working with a bunch of amateurs?"

For a moment he stood and gazed out at the audience. Then a woman wearing low heels and a black pantsuit came out from behind the curtain and scurried over to the actor. The two spoke in low, urgent tones, and then the woman raised her hand and pointed stage left. Or was it stage right? Carly could never keep them straight.

The clomping of Marley's boots echoed through the opera house as he stalked off the stage.

Carly looked at Norah, who merely shrugged her shoulders. The woman who'd spoken to Marley moved to the front of the stage, her hands folded primly in front of her. "Ladies and gentlemen, I am very sorry, but we're going to be taking a break for at least thirty minutes." Her voice shook a little. "Please help yourselves to snacks in the front lobby. I do apologize for this unscheduled interruption." With that she retreated behind the curtain from which she'd materialized.

The overhead lights went on. Murmurs rose from the audience.

Carly sat back in her chair, her mouth agape. "Who was that?"

"That was Hannah Collier, the director," Norah explained. "I can't imagine what she's feeling right now. It was her decision to cast him in that role."

"She must be mortified," Carly said, feeling bad for the woman.

Carly watched in dismay as people began leaving their seats, their voices growing louder. "Who was that actor?" she asked her sister.

"I told you about him, remember?" Norah rolled her eyes. "That was Prescott Lennon, but he prefers to be called *Prez*. A blowhard if I ever met one. He's been causing trouble since rehearsals started last week. He . . . he singled out a few people in particular to bully," she murmured, then winced at Carly. "I'm afraid one of them was Gina."

Prescott Lennon. The name sounded vaguely familiar to Carly. A minor actor from way back when—an actor who never seemed to land any important roles.

"That's terrible," Carly said. "This is the first I've heard of it. Gina never said anything to me."

Then again, Gina had been so busy Carly had barely caught a glimpse of her all week.

Carly was the owner of Carly's Grilled Cheese Eatery, a popular restaurant in downtown Balsam Dell, Vermont. Gina, who she'd known since grade school, owned a specialty stationery store that was growing by leaps and bounds.

At that moment, the person in question climbed over the seats in Carly's row and plunked onto the empty seat beside her. "I think I'm going to drop out," Gina said dismally, swiping at her heavily rouged cheeks.

Carly reached over and gave her friend an awkward hug. "Why? What happened?"

"Prescott Lennon happened. He's been sniping at me all week. Yesterday he said"—she swallowed back a sob—"he said I was a local hack with a hen-scratch voice who couldn't sing her way out of a chicken coop! And he said it in front of *everyone*. And then he started up again this morning."

Carly pulled a pack of tissues from her tote and gave them to Gina.

"Thanks." Gina dug out a handful and blotted her eyes. "Do you think I should try to talk to him? I really don't want to drop out."

"That's up to you," Norah said. "But considering who we're dealing with, I doubt it will help." She reached over and squeezed Gina's hand. "Don't feel bad, okay? It's not you—it's him. He's just an awful person. And you are not dropping out," she said firmly.

"But why is he getting away with treating people like that?" Carly said darkly. "Can't they replace him?"

Norah motioned for them to follow the other audience members, who were trickling into the lobby. The promise of snacks had drawn them like moths to a flame.

"It was Hannah's idea to cast him in that role," Norah explained, leading the way out of the row. "Believe it or not, he wanted to play Scrooge, which is a far more substantial role. No way could he have memorized all those lines. Hannah told him it was Marley or nothing."

"How did Hannah end up directing the play? I mean, why this opera house? Doesn't she live in New York?"

Norah shouldered her way around a slow-moving couple, forcing Carly to do the same. "She and Nate know each other from way back. Long story short, a few years ago she formed her own theater company. She has a lineup of actors she chooses from to perform in various plays. All local venues, but supposedly she loves her job. Hard to figure how she makes a living at it, but she's married to a rich guy now, so it's not like she's hurting for money."

By the time they reached the foyer, it was jammed with people. Many of the actors had joined the audience members. Carly thought she saw old Fezziwig sharing a laugh with the Ghost of Christmas Past.

People mingled and chatted over miniature pastries and holiday punch as if the unscheduled break was a typical event in the world of theater. Carly recognized several of the town employees, along with a few of the police officers.

"Hey, there's the grilled cheese lady!" a young officer joked. Carly laughed and went over to wish him a happy holiday.

The foyer itself was a spectacular room—a wide oval graced with three spiral chandeliers hanging from the cathedral ceiling. The walls were adorned with massive tapestries depicting scenes from famous operas.

A few years earlier, Nate's family—all opera professionals—had purchased the dilapidated Flinthead Farm on the outskirts of Balsam Dell. With the help of an architectural team deemed to be a collaboration of "sheer genius," the farmhouse was transformed into the magnificent Flinthead Opera House. The undertaking had been staggering, but the result was a building that combined the modern vibes and technology of current-day opera with remnants of the original farmhouse.

Carly had only been inside the opera house one other time. It was the day Norah's beau had helped rescue her from a desperate killer.

Norah nudged Gina with her elbow. "I think Hannah wants you. I see her threading her way toward us."

"Gina, there you are, thank heaven," Hannah breathed. "I've been trying to find you."

Up close, Hannah Collier was a striking woman. Somewhere in her late forties or early fifties, she had flawless, almost translucent skin, her silvery blond hair worn in a 1950s-style French twist. She reminded Carly of a fashion model from an earlier era.

Gina introduced her to Carly. After politely offering Carly her slender hand, Hannah tugged lightly at Gina's caroler robe. "Gina, I'm worried about you," she said in a low voice. "I could tell you weren't yourself up on that stage. May we talk privately?"

Gina's face fell. "Su . . . sure, of course." A touch of panic in her eyes, she followed Hannah down one of the corridors that branched out from the foyer.

"That didn't sound good," Carly said.

Norah squeezed her sister's arm. "Don't worry. Hannah's a capable woman and a super-nice one at that. She can handle whatever the problem is. I'm going to see if I can find Nate. Maybe he has a clue what's happening."

"Go ahead. I'll meet you back in our seats."

By that time, people were making their way back into the theater. Carly had almost reached the doorway nearest her row when she heard a familiar voice call her name.

"Hey, Carly! Wait up."

Don Frasco, publisher of the town's free newspaper, scooted up behind her. His ginger-colored hair had undergone another transformation. Gelled at the top and short on the sides, it was one of his more stylish looks. His sweater was another story. Bright red, it was emblazoned with a neon green Christmas tree that had actual blinking lights.

"I thought I saw you earlier," he blurted. "Do you know what's going on? What's the holdup about?"

"I know as much as you do, which is nothing. Are you taking photos?"

He scowled. "I've been forbidden from taking any photos at the dress rehearsal. But I took plenty out here while people were stuffing their faces. Got some great shots. Hey, can I sit with you?"

Carly sighed. Don could be a chatterbox, and today he sounded wound up. But she had to admit, on more than one occasion, their combined efforts had helped bring a killer to justice.

Besides, the seat next to hers had been vacant, so she couldn't really say no.

"As long as you don't talk during the performance," she warned him.

He twisted his fingers over his lips in a key-in-lock gesture. "Got it."

Norah hadn't returned. Carly reclaimed her own seat and Don plunked down beside her. She glanced at her phone. Almost forty minutes had gone by since the play was halted.

"How come Ari didn't come?" Don whispered.

Ari Mitchell was Carly's fiancé. He and Gina's beau, Zach Bartlett, were spending the afternoon in search of two perfect evergreen trees, one for Gina's apartment and one for Carly and Ari's home.

Carly started to respond when Norah rushed into her seat from the opposite side. Her face was flushed. "I found Nate. He's furious at the holdup. I guess he read *Prez* Lennon the so-called riot act."

"So the performance is still going to happen?" Carly asked, growing impatient.

Norah shrugged. "The actors are ready. They're just waiting for Hannah to give the go-ahead."

Noises drifted from behind the curtain. Carly hoped it was a sign that the play was about to kick into gear.

She was tucking her phone into her tote when a piercing scream made everyone gasp. Heads swiveled, trying to pinpoint the source. Carly's heart jumped in her chest.

Something about the voice . . .

In the next instant, several audience members leaped off their seats and made a mad dash for the lobby. Carly recognized two of them—one was a police officer and the other a firefighter.

Norah and Don sat frozen in confusion, as did most of the remaining audience. Anxious whispers rose from the seats.

5

Fear gripping her insides, Carly tapped Don's knee. "Don, can you get up? I need to find out what's happening."

Before he could object, Carly stepped over his legs and stumbled her way out of the aisle, mashing the toe of someone's leather boot in the process. "Sorry, sir. Sorry," she mumbled, then flew out the rear door.

In the elegant lobby, chaos was erupting. Several people were hurrying down a corridor as if their shoes were on fire. Their footsteps echoed off the travertine floor. Two others, a man and a woman, both in uniform, were gathered around one of the players. From the color of the player's robe, Carly knew it was one of the carolers. It was the voice that chilled her to the core.

Gina.

Her legs feeling like pudding, Carly squeezed between them. Gina was shaking uncontrollably, her face buried in her hands. When she saw Carly, she broke into heaving sobs.

"Gina, what happened? Are you all right?"

Gina shook her head vehemently. Her stage makeup, blended with her tears, gave her a macabre look. "No, I'm not all right. I . . . I found him in his dressing room. I'm pretty sure he's—" She choked out a strangled sob.

Carly shook her friend gently. "It's okay, Gina. Just tell us who you found."

Gina's eyes widened, and she grabbed Carly's arm. "J . . . Jacob Marley," she stammered out. "Jacob Marley is dead!"

CHAPTER 2

JACOB MARLEY.

Prescott Lennon.

"Carly, we'll take it from here," the man said in a low voice.

It was then that Carly realized who he was. Ian Gregory was a local police officer who frequented her eatery. He was a huge fan of her Zesty Pesto grilled cheese.

Ian guided Gina gently by the arm and led her to a chair that rested between two tapestry wall hangings. The woman in uniform followed in his wake.

He spoke to Gina in a calm voice. "Miss, we don't want to jump to any conclusions just yet. Help is on the way. An ambulance should be here at any moment. Right now, I need you to take some deep breaths, okay? Can you do that for me?"

Gina nodded and tried to follow his instructions, but her breathing was ragged.

The woman, slender, with tight blond curls and sharp blue eyes, stooped down in front of Gina and took her shaky hands in her petite ones. "You're Gina, right? You made my sister's wedding invitations. They were gorgeous, by the way. I'm Cindy Little, the town's newest police officer. Officer Gregory and I are going to find a private place where we can all chat, okay? Meanwhile"— she turned to Carly with a meaningful smile—"your friend is going to fetch a hot cup of sweet tea for you, aren't you?"

"Um . . . yes, right," Carly said, realizing she meant her. At Gina's frightened expression, her heart sank. "It's okay, Gina. I'll be right back. I promise."

As Carly left in search of hot tea, she heard the wail of sirens drawing closer. What had happened to Jacob Marley, or rather, Prescott Lennon? Had the stress from being ordered off the stage given him a heart attack?

She quickly found the room off the main corridor that served as a mini café of sorts. Some of it was self-serve. Several people milled around, some buying snacks from vending machines. At the rear was a door labeled *Restrooms*. A girl who looked no older than seventeen, reindeer antlers bobbing on her head and earbuds jammed in her ears, stood behind the counter. She removed one of the earbuds when she saw Carly approach her.

"Hi, I need a cup of hot tea, please," Carly said. "And a bunch of sugars?"

"Sure, no prob." The girl plopped a tea bag into a paper cup, then added boiling water from a pot resting on the burner in front of her. She handed Carly the steaming tea and a handful of sugar packets. Carly paid with her debit card.

The girl leaned over the counter, her lavender-tinted eyelashes fluttering with curiosity, "Hey, what's the deal with all these people running up and down the hallway? Isn't the play still going on?"

A woman standing near a candy machine was thumbing away at her phone. "I can tell you what's happening," she said. "My fiancé just texted me, he's one of the firemen. Jacob Marley is dead. I mean, *really* dead. They found the actor who plays him deceased!"

The teenager's jaw dropped. "OMG, are you *kidding* me? Then—" She broke off abruptly, her young face flushing pink.

Carly nearly dropped the cup. "Then *what?*"

The girl's face flushed. "Never mind. It's nothing." She averted her gaze and busied herself wiping down the counter.

Carly wanted to press her further, but then a glut of people strode into the café, three of them wanting coffee. At the self-help counter, she hurriedly put the tea together and popped a plastic cap over the top. By the time she'd returned to the lobby, the front doors were wide open. Two EMTs were jogging inside, wheeling a stretcher.

Seemingly out of nowhere, Hannah Collier appeared. "Follow me!" she instructed the EMTs, squeezing ahead of them. Her high heels clicking, she led them down the main corridor.

Carly glanced around. The lobby was becoming crammed with people wanting to know what happened. There was no sign of Gina and her companions.

Shoot. Where were Gina and the officers?

"Come with me," a voice behind her instructed, cupping Carly's elbow.

Moving swiftly, Cindy Little steered Carly away from the clamor and down a different corridor. After a series of confusing turns, they entered a doorway labeled *Dressing Room 7*.

Inside the room, Gina was seated on a tufted love seat. Ian Gregory was sitting on a plastic chair tapping away at his cell.

Carly handed her friend the tea. "Careful, it's steaming hot," she cautioned. "Are you okay?"

"No, I am *not* okay. Can you drive me home? Please!"

"Ms. Tomasso," Ian Gregory said gently, rising to his feet, "as I explained, you're not free to leave just yet. I promise, we'll get you out of here as soon as we can, okay?"

"But I need to call people," Gina cried. "They're going to be looking for me."

"I'm sure your friend will be glad to do that for you," Cindy offered with a pointed look at Carly.

"Um, yes, of course, but can't I stay here with Gina?"

"I'm afraid not," Ian said. "One of the detectives will be in here shortly. He'll want to ask Gina a few questions before she's released."

Released. Carly cringed at the word. It made Gina sound like a prisoner.

She bent over Gina. "Listen, I'm not going to leave the building, okay?

Whenever you're ready to leave, I'll be waiting for you in the lobby. I promise."

"Okay," Gina said shakily. "Will you call Zach?"

"Of course. I'll take care of everything."

A horrible feeling gripped Carly—the familiar sensation that something had gone terribly wrong, and that Gina was caught in the middle. She thanked both officers for their kindness to her friend, then flew out the door before they could see the panic in her eyes.

The corridor was oddly silent. Almost as if this part of the building was soundproof.

Carly started to retrace her steps back to the lobby when she realized she was lost. There were no signs pointing to the exit, no doubt because this area was off-limits to visitors. The turns had been so confusing she wasn't sure whether to go right or left.

She turned left, hoping it would lead her to the lobby. She passed a row of dressing room doors, each one numbered.

Which begged the question, where was Prescott Lennon's dressing room? Didn't Gina say that's where she found him? But why would she have gone there in the first place?

Carly reached another intersection of hallways. She thought she heard voices drifting from her right, so she followed the sound.

When she finally reached the lobby, she blew out a breath of relief. The sight of people milling about was strangely comforting. Those deserted corridors had given her the willies.

The police were trying to corral everyone into orderly groups, but it was turning into a monumental task.

Carly squeezed around a pair of women who were talking in hushed tones.

"If I'd known I was going to stand around all afternoon," one of them griped, "I'd have gone to the mall instead."

"No kidding," the other one muttered. "I still have a gazillion toys to buy for the grands."

Recognizing them as town hall employees, Carly smiled politely and scooted past them. She needed to find a quiet place to call Ari. He and Zach were together, and she could relay the message about Gina to both.

"Carly," someone called sharply from behind her.

Uh-oh. She knew that voice.

Chief of Police Fred Holloway strode up beside her. He was looking more relaxed these days, a change Carly attributed to his recent marriage to Valerie Wells, her eatery's grill cook. The two practically glowed when they were together. It was a match made over grilled cheese, and Carly couldn't have been more elated.

"Hey, Chief. Kind of a zoo in here, isn't it?"

Casting his glance around the lobby, he ran a hand through his thick gray

9

hair. "I got a text from one of my sergeants," he said in a low voice. "I understand there's been a death."

"I'm not sure if it's been confirmed," Carly told him, though the chief's statement and his grim expression signaled that it had been. "An ambulance arrived a while ago. Ian Gregory and another officer whisked Gina and me into a private room, so I didn't see if it left or not. After I got tea for Gina, the officers made me leave. Gina's so distraught, Chief. I'm going to wait here for her so I can drive her home."

Holloway fixed her with a meaningful look. "You should go along home, Carly. One of my detectives is coming by to question Gina before the state police get here. She could be here for some time."

Carly sagged. That wasn't the news she'd hoped for. "But why? It wasn't a suspicious death, was it?"

"Right now, I can't comment on any of it. What I *can* do is see that you get out of here without waiting in line to give your contact info."

Carly pulled in what she hoped was a calming breath. "I appreciate that, but I promised her I'd wait here for her. Ari and Zach are out looking for Christmas trees, so I have to let them know what's happening. Meanwhile, my sister abandoned me. I don't have a clue where she is." She felt frustration bubbling inside her like a geyser about to erupt.

Holloway signaled to one of the officers stationed at the entry.

The officer, somewhere in his forties with a round face dotted with perspiration and a protruding belly that stretched the limits of his uniform, was at Holloway's side within seconds. "Yes, Chief," he said briskly.

Holloway snapped instructions at him, assured Carly she was in good hands, and went off down the main corridor.

"I'm Ted Quinto," the officer said with a kind smile. "Sorry you had to get trapped in this mess." He spoke into his radio, and within a minute another officer came by, wrote down Carly's name and contact info, and escorted her back into the theater to retrieve her coat.

"I'm sorry, miss," this latest officer said, "but we have orders to see you safely to your car. The chief promised to call you the moment Miss Tomasso is allowed to leave. You'll be able to pick her up at the front door."

Carly felt like a beach ball being bounced from one person to the other. Was she ever going to land somewhere so she could call Ari? There was still no sign of Norah. And where had Don Frasco disappeared to?

The temperature outside had dipped below freezing. The officer who'd seen Carly to her car waited until she'd started her engine to head back into the building.

Carly had no intention of leaving. Somehow, she'd figure out a way to get back inside the opera house.

While her engine warmed up, she called Ari.

"Hey, sweetie! Wait till you see the tree—" he started to say.

"Ari, listen. Something has happened," Carly interrupted. She gave him a quick rundown of events, ending with Gina's status as a semi-prisoner.

"We're leaving now," Ari said in a tight voice. "Stay safe in your car, okay?"

"I'm going to try to get back in the opera house," she said. "Don't worry about me, okay? My phone'll be with me. Love you!"

She clicked off before he could voice an objection.

Now, how to get back inside.

There was no sign of the ambulance. Had the actor been transported to the hospital? From the section of the building where the dressing rooms were, she wouldn't have heard the siren. Police cars—some unmarked, Carly surmised—were clustered around the entrance to the opera house. From what she could see, only official personnel were being allowed inside.

She needed a plausible excuse to get back into the opera house.

Carly was contemplating her plan of attack when someone banged on her passenger-side window. She jumped and gave a little shriek. A young man with a halo of tightly curled black hair was waving at her. "Hey, you're Carly, right?" he yelled through the glass. "Can I hop inside? I'm freezing. I'm a friend of Gina's."

The last thing she wanted was to let a stranger into her car. She also didn't want a friend of Gina's—or anyone, for that matter—to freeze to death outside.

One hand curled around her cell phone, Carly popped the lock. The man slid onto her front seat and slammed the door shut. "Thanks! My brother's picking me up but he's not here yet."

"Who are you?" Carly demanded. "How do you know me?"

He gave her a crooked smile, then blew into his cupped hands to warm them. "Oh, sorry. I'm Malachy Foster. Gina talks about you all the time. Plus, I ate in your restaurant a few times and I saw you there. Man, your Smoky Steals the Bacon is epic! Anyway, Gina and I are in the play together. Well, sort of. I'm an understudy, but . . . well, I think that might change now."

"Oh?" A queasy feeling settled in Carly's throat. "And why is that?"

His mouth twitched. He looked at her through solemn brown eyes. "Because I'm Prescott Lennon's understudy. I'm next in line to be Jacob Marley."

11

CHAPTER 3

AT THAT MOMENT, A CAR WITH A FAILING MUFFLER ROARED INTO THE parking lot.

"Oh, good. That's Shaquille." Malachy swung open the car door. "Thanks for letting me warm up in your car! Tell Gina to call me, okay? I couldn't find her inside."

Before Carly could utter another word, he bolted from the car and waved down his brother, who was cruising the lot looking for him.

Carly let out the breath she was holding. Could this day get any crazier?

She needed to get back inside the building. Maybe Norah could help—if Carly could find her, that is.

She tapped Norah's cell number on her phone, but it went to straight to voicemail.

Gahhh.

Where are you? Call me! she texted her sister.

In her rearview mirror, she saw a black pickup pull up behind her. Relief surged through her like a tidal wave.

Ari and Zach tore out of the truck at the same time, and Carly got out of her car. Ari grabbed her in a hug and pulled her close. "Are you okay?"

She nodded, but poor Zach looked frantic. "Carly, what happened? Where's Gina?"

"Inside, with the police. Gina apparently found Lennon's body in his dressing room, but that's all I know. The chief promised to let me know when she was free to leave."

Zach looked baffled. "I'm confused. Weren't you all at the play?"

"We were, but there was a problem." Carly explained about the actor's onstage meltdown and the unscheduled intermission.

Zach swore under his breath. "I've gotta find Gina."

"They'll probably stop us at the door," Carly warned. "We'll have to think up a good excuse why we all need to get inside."

She locked her tote in the car and slid her cell into her jacket pocket. As all three were trooping toward the opera house, her cell buzzed. She pulled it out and glanced at the readout. "Wait up, guys, it's the chief." She tapped the phone. "Yes, Chief?"

After listening for a minute, she jammed her phone back into her pocket. "Let's go. Gina's being released. She'll meet us at the front door."

With that they picked up their speed.

Gina was standing just inside the lobby door. Officer Cindy Little stood at her side in a protective manner. When she spotted Zach, Gina burst into tears, and she threw herself into his arms. "They're letting me go," she choked out.

"But I have to be at the police station first thing tomorrow morning to be interviewed. I guess they decided I wasn't a flight risk," she added with a scowl.

Flight risk?

A sinking feeling landed like a boulder inside Carly's gut. Did that mean Lennon's death *was* suspicious?

Without warning, a woman with bleached blond hair and an overabundance of makeup tromped over to Gina and waved a manicured finger in her face. "So the cops are letting you go, huh, lady? Well, mark my words, it won't be for long. My poor husband is dead because of you. You're gonna be spending your Christmas in jail!"

Gina's face went deathly pale. "What are you talking about? I didn't do anything."

With the speed of a rattlesnake, Cindy Little looped her hand around the woman's arm and steered her away from Gina. She spoke to her in hushed tones, which seemed to have a quieting effect on the agitated woman.

"I'll take her." Another woman had sidled up alongside the blond. Her straight black bangs sweeping her eyebrows, she slipped a tattooed arm around her friend and said, "Come on, honey. You need some food and some rest. This whole day's been a nightmare. The police said we can go, so let's get you back to the hotel."

The blond sniffled into a tissue and nodded. Without even a backward glance at Gina, she allowed herself to be escorted in the opposite direction.

"Can we go now?" Gina begged. "I'm so tired."

With a sympathetic smile, Cindy said, "Absolutely. Go home and get some rest. I'm afraid tomorrow's going to be a long day for you, Gina."

Zach wrapped his arm around Gina's waist and tugged her toward the exit. "Come on, sweetheart. Let's go home."

They all started toward the door, but Carly backtracked a few steps and went over to Cindy. "Officer, who was that woman who screamed at Gina?"

Hands on her hips, Cindy rocked back on her heels. "That was Honey Lennon, Prescott Lennon's wife. She's taking her husband's death very hard. She's been crying her eyes out since he was . . . found."

Carly nodded. There was so much she didn't know, but now wasn't the time to ask. "Then I'm sorry for her loss, Officer. But she's wrong about Gina."

Ari and Carly followed Zach and Gina into the parking lot. The temp had dropped into the twenties, and the sky was growing dark. They'd decided that Zach would drive Gina in Carly's Corolla, while Carly hopped inside Ari's pickup.

"You got trees," Carly said. She'd noticed them in the bed of the pickup.

"We did. Couple of beauties, too." Ari reached over and squeezed her hand. "It's going to be okay, honey."

Honey.

It was an endearment Ari used often. At that moment, the word only brought Prescott Lennon's wife to mind. What was it about Honey Lennon that bugged Carly?

She tried picturing the woman's face, though she'd only seen her those few seconds when she was railing at Gina. Shoulder-length hair bleached to the color of straw. Cheekbones accented with expertly applied rose-colored blush, the tone a perfect match to her lip gloss.

Hazel eyes, hard and accusatory.

Stop it, Carly chastised herself. *I'm being petty because she attacked Gina.*

Still—

Wait a minute—that was it.

Cindy Little said that Honey had been crying her eyes out since her husband's body had been found. But if that was true, why had her makeup looked picture-perfect?

• • •

Gina's apartment was directly above Carly's Grilled Cheese Eatery. Location notwithstanding, both women were usually so busy with their respective businesses that their "bestie" time had dwindled to a few hours a week.

As for the apartment itself, nearly every bit of décor was a throwback to the 1960s. Gina's mom, who'd passed away when Gina and Carly were in middle school, loved everything about that decade. Gina believed her mom was smiling down on her, approving of every accessory she'd chosen for her apartment.

In the kitchen, Gina dropped onto a vinyl-covered chair at her Formica table. Her dark brown curls were askew, her face drawn with fatigue. Her kitty, who she'd adopted several months prior, leaped onto her lap.

"I know, KitCat. I missed you, too." Gina hugged the black cat, kissed her snout, and set her down to gobble the gourmet kitty tuna Zach had put out for her.

One glance into Zach's green eyes told Carly how worried he was. Somewhat reserved by nature, he seemed at a complete loss as to what to say or do next. He tried urging Gina to eat, but she only shook her head.

Carly shooed everyone into the living area adjacent to the kitchen. Then she pulled Gina's pink speckled teapot from her cabinet and went about making a strong pot of tea. While the fragrant tea bags steeped, she cobbled together a tray of wheat crackers, cheddar squares, and red grapes.

Zach and Gina had claimed the burnt orange sofa, while Ari and Carly took separate chairs. After swallowing a mouthful of tea, Gina reached for a cracker and broke off a corner. "I should have quit days ago," she said bitterly. "Being a caroler was supposed to be fun, not a chore. That horrible man"—she quickly crossed herself—"disliked me from the moment he set eyes on me."

Carly pushed the tray closer to her friend. "Did you share your concerns with Hannah?"

Gina nodded. "She tried talking to Lennon several times. Problem was, I wasn't the only one he bullied. Some of the younger actors—all women—got a taste of his nastiness, too. And you should hear how he spoke to his own wife! Rude, condescending—" She shook her head and gulped back a mouthful of tea.

What an unpleasant man, to say the least, Carly mused. "Gina, I don't want to upset you, but this is important. Do you have any idea why his wife would think her husband was dead because of you?"

Gina swallowed the miniscule bite of cheddar she was munching. "Probably because it was me who found him. Honey's the type who attacks first and asks questions later. Know what some of the cast members call her? Honey *Lemon*, because of her sour personality."

Ah, that was interesting.

Carly hated questioning her friend this way, but she knew the police would press Gina far more aggressively when they interviewed her in the morning.

"Gina, why *did* you go to his dressing room?" Carly asked quietly.

Gina dipped her gaze toward her lap. "It sounds dumb now, but I was going to suggest a truce. You know, exchange apologies and bury the hatchet, so to speak?"

"What if he refused?"

"Then I'd revert to plan B."

"Which was?"

"To back out of the play. Which I really didn't want to do."

His brow creased with concern, Zach finally spoke. "Sweetie, I wish you had told me all this before," he said, squeezing Gina's hand. "I'd have gone over there and given that joker a piece of my mind, if you get my drift." He raised a curled fist.

That got a tiny smile out of Gina, and she squeezed his arm. "I know you would've, but it was something I needed to deal with on my own."

Carly sensed Gina was holding something back, but now wasn't the time to prod. She looked exhausted from her ordeal. She needed to get a solid night's sleep.

After they finished what they could of the snacks, Carly put everything away and tidied the kitchen. Zach quietly asked Ari if he could leave their tree in his pickup, at least for the time being.

As Carly and Ari were leaving, Carly hugged her friend. "Gina, is there any reason why the police would think Lennon didn't die of natural causes?"

Tears filled Gina's large brown eyes. "No reason, unless you count the chain of cash boxes wrapped around his neck."

CHAPTER 4

THE CHAIN OF CASH BOXES.

An unwanted image of the prop wrapped around Lennon's neck had woven its way into Carly's dreams. She'd awakened with a start to find both Ari and Havarti, their little Morkie, gone. Bless Ari. He'd taken the dog for his morning walk so that Carly could snag a few extra minutes of sleep.

She rubbed her eyes, then took a moment to indulge her senses in the sight of their newly decorated bedroom. Five months earlier, she and Ari had bought Joyce Katso's two-family house, where Carly had been renting the second-floor apartment. She and Ari had renovated the house, converting it back to the charming one-family home it had been decades earlier. A kind and generous woman, Joyce had sold them the house at a price that'd made it affordable. After the rehabbing was complete, Carly and Ari moved their living space to the more spacious downstairs.

Joyce had moved to a senior community where top-notch care and gourmet meals were part of her everyday routine. Her former caretaker, Becca Avery, was earning her LNA certification. Becca hoped to eventually find employment in the facility where Joyce was now a resident.

When she was living with Joyce, Becca had also checked on Havarti during the day. She'd refused to accept payment. Instead, she'd enjoyed the soup and sandwiches Carly plied her with in return for her dog-sitting services.

Luck was with Carly when she found a professional pet sitter who was willing to take over for Becca. Her fee was reasonable, and Havarti adored her. She stopped by twice a day to check the dog's food and water supply, and to take him for a walk—or let him run in the yard. It was a relief to know Havarti was being cared for while she and Ari were at work.

Carly jolted upright as the events of the previous day crashed over her. The first face that popped into her head was Gina's. In a few hours, she'd be undergoing a police interview. Carly had endured the same experience on more than one occasion. She didn't envy what her friend was about to go through.

After showers, a quick breakfast, and hugs for Havarti had been accomplished, Carly and Ari headed to work. Ari, an electrician, would be spending his day doing some wiring upgrades at a local hardware store.

When Carly arrived at the eatery at a little after eight, Gina's car was gone. Carly parked her Corolla behind the building and unlocked the back door.

She flipped on the lights and turned up the heat a few degrees. After plunking her coat, gloves, and tote on the seat in one of the booths, she made a beeline for the coffee machine.

While she waited for it to brew, she checked her phone for any messages from Gina—or anyone connected with the disastrous events of the day before.

The only message was from Norah.

Sis, sorry I abandoned you yesterday. Nate hustled me out of there and made me go home! I'll make it up to you. It was trailed by a series of hearts and sad-face emojis.

Which still didn't explain why Norah hadn't at least texted her the day before. Carly sighed and shook her head. Norah had her quirks, but Carly loved her to the ends of the universe and back.

She was pouring herself a mugful of coffee when Valerie Holloway—who'd been Valerie Wells when Carly hired her—unlocked the front door and entered the eatery. Valerie peeled off her sky-blue parka and knitted mittens, hung them over a hook on the front coatrack, then hurried over to where Carly sat on one of the counter stools. "Hey, girl, you doing okay?" Her topknot bounced a little when she slung her arm around Carly.

Carly forced a weak smile. "I'm fine, just so darn tired."

Valerie prepared coffee for herself, then scurried around to the opposite side of the counter. "Fred didn't get home till after ten. Between the audience, the actors, all the stage helpers, and the musicians, it took hours for the police to take down everyone's names and information so they could be released."

Carly set down her mug. "I really appreciated Fred getting me out of there fast yesterday—and for letting Gina go home when he did."

The chief hadn't always been so accommodating. In the past he'd been at odds with Carly over her involvement in local investigations, specifically murder investigations. His marriage to Valerie had mellowed him considerably.

Valerie's love for her new hubby shone in her eyes. "He's so caring and wonderful, isn't he? Not that I'm biased," she said, her cheeks flushing pink. "But I don't envy poor Gina. The state police will be interviewing her today." She opened the minifridge beneath the counter and pulled out a package of frozen homemade biscuits. "Biscuit today?"

Carly shook her head. "No, thanks. My stomach is still revolting from everything that happened yesterday."

The bacon and cheese biscuits were a treat Carly created for herself after she first opened the eatery. They'd helped get her through the busy mornings when she was still working alone. At the time, her grill cook, Grant Robinson, worked afternoons part-time. Her server, Suzanne Rivers, worked from eleven until three.

After Grant became their full-time grill cook, he improved the morning biscuits by experimenting with different cheeses. Thinking of him brought a lump to Carly's throat. Although her current staff was her own personal dream team, she still missed Grant so much. He'd left three months earlier to attend culinary school in Boston. She saw him at Thanksgiving, but only for a short visit.

With a sigh, Valerie returned the biscuits to the freezer. "Maybe I'll skip, too. With all the holiday eating coming up, I should save the calories."

The front door swung open, and Nina Cyr—Carly's assistant manager—popped in. In her usual style, she was a burst of color. The sight of her bubbly employee always made Carly smile.

Nina had joined the staff in midsummer, after a chance visit to the eatery demonstrated her skills at serving customers. With Grant's departure on the horizon, Carly had quickly offered her a job. Not a day went by that Carly regretted her choice. Not only was Nina an efficient and genial worker, she also designed and baked the eatery's buttery cookies, which were wildly popular with customers.

Nina pulled her bright green beanie off her super-short canary yellow hair, then stashed it in a pocket of her neon orange jacket. She left it all on the front coatrack. "Hey, guys," she greeted her coworkers.

Valerie poured her a mugful of coffee, and Nina dropped onto the stool next to Carly. "I heard about what happened yesterday, but the only details I got were from the news."

Carly gave her a recap of the disastrous events of the performance that was so abruptly cut short, and everything that happened afterward.

Nina's wide-set green eyes grew even larger. "Well, first, I am so sad for that poor actor. Even if he was unlikeable, he didn't deserve to die. And then Gina, having the bad luck to find him. I can't even imagine what she's going through right now."

"She's being interviewed this morning at the police station," Carly said anxiously. "I can't stop thinking about her."

Nina reached over and rubbed Carly's forearm, her pixie-like face awash with sympathy. "I am so sorry your friend has to go through this. We all love Gina, and we're here for her. And if you need to leave for any reason today, I'll work as late as you need me to."

"Thank you, both of you," Carly said hoarsely. "I can't imagine running this place without either of you."

They all brought their coats into the kitchen and hung them in the closet designated for employees. Carly tried to focus on kitchen tasks—thawing tomato soup on the commercial stove, preparing the salad from the recipe Grant had created, frying enough bacon to last through the day—but Gina kept slipping into her thoughts.

Shortly after ten, Carly was slicing a block of cheddar when Suzanne pushed through the swinging door. "Hey, you're early," Carly greeted her with a smile.

Suzanne hung her things in the closet, then helped herself to a slice of cheddar. "I'm starving. Josh's school project bit the dust this morning when he was trying to squeeze it into a grocery bag. By the time we cleaned up the mess, I had about three seconds left to eat breakfast and drive him to school."

"Aw, poor kid. What was the project?"

"A shoebox with a scene from *Robin Hood*. He even made tiny arrows out of Q-tips. It was adorable." Suzanne's gaze went all melty. "I felt so bad when he accidentally squashed it. I'm glad we'd taken good pics of it so we could show his teacher."

Josh was Suzanne's only child. At nine going on ten, he had multiple interests, but the archery club was his favorite.

"Anyhow," Suzanne said, leaning her elbows on the work counter, "I heard about yesterday's fiasco, so I came in early to get all the deets."

Carly told the story again, this time cutting to the highlights. "Bottom line, Gina found the body, so she's now being questioned by the police."

With a roll of her eyes, Suzanne helped herself to a bottle of apple juice from the fridge. "Un-freakin'-believable. It's like the cops have tunnel vision. If the guy was such a jerk, there must be a dozen people who'd have been glad to pop him off."

Suzanne's blunt declaration notwithstanding, her words held some truth.

Carly transferred the cheddar slices into a square container and snapped on a lid. "I'm sure the police will have many more suspects once they ramp up the investigation."

Fingers crossed and the sun still rises.

With everyone pitching in, the dining room was spotless and ready to open by eleven. Nina turned the *Closed* sign to *Open*.

• • •

The eatery filled up almost immediately. The freezing temps, along with the huge evergreen wreath Carly had hung on the front door, were attracting more customers every day.

Over the past summer, they'd had a teenaged helper, Ross Baxter, deliver meals to some of their best customers. It was Ross's grandmother who'd suggested his startup business, which he'd dubbed Fab Food on Wheels. With so many elderly folks unwilling or unable to order food online, Ross had created a tidy little business for himself. Now that he was in college and his service shut down, Carly was forced to use another delivery service. It was pricier, but in the long run the extra business was worth it.

At the front of the restaurant, next to the refrigerated beverage case, Carly had set up a small table over which she'd thrown a red tablecloth. On it she'd placed a faux Christmas tree, about two feet tall. With its colored lights and macramé star at the top, it was the first thing customers noticed when they entered the restaurant. Carly, Valerie, Nina, and Suzanne had each contributed a few ornaments, giving it a personal touch.

The restaurant hummed with the sounds of low chatter and an occasional burst of laughter. The scent of melted cheese, crispy fried bacon, and tangy tomato soup all blended into one olfactory delight. While Carly was pleased with so much business on a Monday, a typically slower day, she found herself checking her cell every five minutes for any word from Gina.

It was a little after one thirty when Gina finally called. Carly's relief was short-lived when she heard the tremor in her friend's voice. "Hey, I'm home. Can you come upstairs?"

After letting her coworkers know she was taking her lunch break, Carly grabbed three frosted sugar cookies, tugged on her jacket, and hurried upstairs to Gina's apartment.

The door was open slightly, so Carly let herself in, closing it behind her. Tissues in hand, Gina was sitting at her kitchen table, her eyes puffy from crying. She looked as desolate as Carly had ever seen her.

"Gina, what happened?" Carly gave her a quick squeeze and set down the cookies in front of her.

Gina bit off the frosted green hat of a merry elf, chomped it, and swallowed it. "Thanks. I needed a fat-slash-sugar fix. I can't stay long because I'm jammed with work at the shop, but I wanted to tell you what happened."

"Can't your helper take over for the day?" Gina's employees changed so often that Carly didn't recall this one's name.

"Not without her having a panic attack. And I just got a large order for wedding invitations that's going to take me till the next Ice Age to complete. All the rehearsals this past week wreaked total havoc on my schedule."

Carly poured them each a glass of spiced cider and sat down opposite her friend. "Where's KitCat?"

"Sleeping on my bed, poor little sweetie. I think I made her nervous with all my crying." Gina sniffled.

"Gina, it's going to be okay," Carly soothed. "Whatever happens, we'll get through it together, I promise. Why don't you start from the beginning?"

Gina sucked in a breath that rattled in her throat. "It all started when Prescott stormed off the stage yesterday. I knew he must've gone to his dressing room, which is in a different section from what you saw yesterday. The so-called stars"—she made air quotes around the word—"are in a different wing. I really was ready to quit the play, but I didn't want to." She let out a breath. "I thought, maybe I could try offering him a truce. You know, a 'let's play nice and get along' sort of thing. Or maybe he could just tell me why he hated me." Her lower lip quivered.

"Gina, no one on this earth hates you. From everything I've heard, that man didn't like anyone."

"Anyway, I dilly-dallied for a while, then decided to take the plunge. When I got to his dressing room, I knocked lightly and called out his name. I even said 'Prez,' which is what he liked to be called." Gina's dark brown eyes misted.

"Take your time," Carly said gently.

"When I called his name again and he didn't answer, I opened the door a crack to see if he was there. So *stupid* of me." She swallowed. "And that's when I-I saw a black boot sticking out from behind the full-length mirror." She paused for a long moment.

Carly reached over and took Gina's hand, a silent encouragement to continue.

"Something about it looked wrong," Gina went on, "so I went all the way inside. Prescott was lying on his back. His eyes, they just . . . stared at the ceiling. I called his name a few times, but he never moved." She blew her nose loudly into a tissue. "That wasn't the worst part. That . . . that chain, the one with the cash boxes, was wrapped around his neck." She sucked in a loud sniffle. "When I saw that I almost tossed my cookies, but I managed to run out of the dressing room and scream for help."

The scream heard round the opera house . . .

"Gina," Carly said gently, "when you were in his dressing room, did you touch anything?"

She looked at Carly with a haunted expression. "No, nothing . . . but there's something else, and it's bad. This morning, the police got a preliminary report on the fingerprints found on the chain. Only two sets of prints were on it, the prop master's—his name is Curt Blessings—and mine."

Carly gaped at her friend. "But . . . how?"

"A few days ago, before one of the rehearsals, Curt was in the prop room. He was digging the props for the play out of a big box. As luck would have it, I happened to walk by when I heard him cursing. I peeked in and asked if I could help with something. Turned out the Jacob Marley chain was a tangled mess. Not only did I fix the jumbled chain, but I rearranged some of the cash boxes to give it a more dramatic effect. That's what I get for helping people," she spat out.

"But you explained that to the police, right?" Carly said.

Gina pressed her lips into a thin line. "Oh, sure, I told them. But when they asked Curt about it, he hedged—big-time. Claimed he wasn't sure if I touched the chain or not. Evidently, he'd been forbidden to allow anyone into the prop room who wasn't authorized, so my helping him turned out to be a big no-no."

Carly sagged in her chair. "How did he get hired?"

Gina polished off the elf cookie and reached for a reindeer. "Supposedly, he has a good reputation. Plus, he lives locally, and I guess he hasn't worked much lately. He told Hannah a little extra cash for the holidays would be a big help. She's so kind. I'm sure she wanted to give him a break." She bit off an antler and munched it between her teeth.

"But Gina, he needs to tell the truth. Maybe they should give him a lie detector test."

She shrugged. "I can't force him."

"I meant to ask you," Carly said, remembering something else. "When we were standing in the lobby during that intermission, Hannah Collier came over and said she needed to speak to you. What was that about?"

Gina drooped in her chair. "She knew I was thinking of dropping out of the play. She wanted to beg me to stay. She said I had the strongest voice of all the carolers, and that it wouldn't be the same without me."

Carly's heart broke for Gina. She'd been so excited to be a caroler. She'd wanted it so badly she was willing to make peace with a tyrant—at least for the duration of the play.

Carly wanted to ask about Honey Lennon's accusation that Gina had caused her husband's death. But in light of her friend's current state of mind, it probably wasn't the best time. Then she remembered something else. "Gina, I forgot to ask you last night. Do you know a Malachy something? I can't remember his last name."

Gina sat up straighter and her eyes brightened. "Sure. Malachy Foster. He's a third-year drama student at the college. Super-nice guy, really talented."

Carly gave her a recap of her encounter with the young man. "He told me to tell you to call him. He also mentioned he was the understudy for the Jacob Marley role."

"Yeah, he is," Gina confirmed. "He's also one of the guests at old Fezziwig's Christmas Eve party. Some actors play a dual role." Her face suddenly froze. "Wait a minute. Oh, sweet kittens in a caboodle. If they don't cancel the play, he'll end up being Jacob Marley!"

CHAPTER 5

THERE WERE SO MANY OTHER QUESTIONS CARLY HAD WANTED TO ASK GINA. If Prescott Lennon had been so utterly disliked, the list of people who'd wanted him out of the picture should be growing faster than dandelions in a summer rain.

Unfortunately, Gina had insisted on rushing off to her stationery shop, What a Card. She worried that her current employee—a recent junior college grad named Taylor—would panic if more than three customers browsed in the shop at the same time. Taylor was the third assistant Gina had hired within the past six months. The prior two hadn't worked out, for reasons Carly never quite understood. She had her fingers crossed for this one.

After checking to see that things were running smoothly in the dining room, Carly went into the kitchen for a quick bite of lunch. Suzanne followed on her heels, tossing her apron into the laundry bin as she headed for the closet.

"It's time for me to bail," Suzanne announced, snatching her coat and purse from the closet. "Remember, I told you I have a meeting with Josh's teacher at two?"

Carly had completely forgotten. "Yes, you did tell me. Good luck at the meeting. See you tomorrow."

Suzanne gave her a quick hug. "Hang in there, girl. Later!"

Carly waved, then threw together a small salad for herself. Grant's recipe—a blend of field greens, dried cranberries, crumbled goat cheese, and sunflower seeds—had grown in popularity since the eatery had begun offering it.

She sat at the table in the kitchen and dug into her lunch. One thing she was thankful for, the police hadn't held Gina on suspicion of murder. *Yet.*

Didn't that mean they didn't have enough evidence to support such a charge? And what was the deal with the prop manager, Curt Blessings? Did he seriously think the police were going to believe that he didn't recall if Gina had touched the chain?

Maybe Curt Blessings should be at the top of the suspect list, not that Carly had started one. But if the police didn't land on the killer soon, she would have to do some nosing around.

After rinsing her salad plate in the sink, she washed her hands and returned to the dining room. It was shortly after two, and about half the booths were occupied. The light chatter of customers enjoying their meals was a balm to Carly's soul.

A woman sitting in a booth about halfway to the entrance suddenly spotted Carly and waved a slender arm at her.

Carly ambled past the booths, greeting patrons as she passed. When she reached the woman who'd waved at her, she realized that it was Hannah Collier.

Linda Reilly

Seated opposite Hannah was a stylish gentleman with neatly coiffed silver hair and a ready smile. His silk-lined scarf was draped loosely around his neck, and his wool coat rested partway off his shoulders. Mugs half filled with hot chocolate rested on the couple's table.

"Hannah, how nice to see you," Carly said.

Hannah pressed a hand to her sweater-clad chest. "Oh, I'm so glad you remembered me," she said breathlessly. "We didn't exactly meet under the best of circumstances yesterday, did we?"

"No, we didn't," Carly agreed. "Yesterday was a bit . . . chaotic."

"Gina has been raving about you and your restaurant, so I simply *had* to eat here. It's even more delightful than she described."

"Well, thank you. I'm quite partial to it myself."

Hannah touched a manicured hand to her companion's arm. "Carly, I'd like to introduce you to my husband, Douglas. We've been married for six whole months! Still in our honeymoon phase, as we like to say." She giggled and her pale cheeks flushed.

Douglas smiled warmly at his wife and then rose. He took Carly's hand in his firm one, his hazel eyes beaming. "It's a pleasure to meet you, Carly. We are both so impressed with your establishment."

Carly smiled at the word *establishment*. It elevated her casual eatery to a whole new level. "Well, thank you. That's a kind thing to say. Have you ordered your food yet?"

Douglas sat down again. "Oh, yes, that charming young woman with the short blond hair already helped us. We're waiting for our Alvin's Panko Perfections to be delivered. Such a marvelous idea, coating the tomato slices in panko first and then grilling them! How creative you are."

"I'm afraid I can't take credit for the recipe," Carly confessed. "The dad of my former grill cook came up with the idea. He was helping us out one day when we were short-handed, and a new grilled cheese was born."

Carly remembered the day well. Grant and his dad, Alvin Robinson, had been at odds over Grant's choice of profession. A gifted cellist, Grant had been under constant pressure to pursue a career in classical music, as both his parents had. But that day, observing his son doing what he loved best—feeding people—Alvin underwent a transformation. He "saw the light," as he put it, and gave his blessing to his son attending culinary school.

"That's a great story," Douglas said, and then his lips curved into a frown. "After the morning Hannah and I were forced to endure, being here is like heaven."

Hannah blinked. "The police, they were so . . . intense," she said tightly. "They interviewed us separately. It was not a good experience."

Now that was interesting, Carly thought. Had the police pressured Hannah to give them evidence against Gina?

24

Something else occurred to Carly. If anyone could supply intel about the various players, it was Hannah. As director, she'd be familiar with the backgrounds of the actors and have a handle on their personality traits.

A mom and dad came in just then with three little ones. Bundled in puffy jackets, the toddlers were all talking at once. Nina's hands were full delivering orders, so Carly excused herself and seated the group.

After she got them settled in a rear booth and gave their orders to Valerie, she went back to the Colliers' table. The two were eating their sandwiches with blissful expressions. Carly was trying to dream up a plausible excuse for meeting the Colliers someplace other than her eatery when Hannah unwittingly solved her dilemma.

"Carly," Hannah said, after dabbing her lips with a paper napkin, "We saw in the playbill that your restaurant is one of the sponsors of the play."

Carly was surprised they'd noticed. She didn't think anyone looked at the ads in the back of the playbill. The half-page ad Carly bought had been a bit pricey, but it was the least she could do to support her sister and Nate.

"So," Douglas said, picking up the thread, "we would love it if you would join us for tea at the Balsam Dell Inn tomorrow afternoon."

Carly'd recently seen an ad in the *Balsam Dell Weekly* that the inn had begun serving a fancy tea on Tuesday and Thursday afternoons. She'd never been to one, but she'd heard through the grapevine it was an experience not to be missed.

"We've already reserved a table," Hannah added, "but I'm sure they can squeeze in one more. Please say yes."

"Wow," Carly said, "that's such a lovely invitation. May I ask what time your reservation is for?"

"Three o'clock sharp," Douglas announced, his hazel eyes twinkling. "Rumor has it that's when the best food is served."

Three o'clock was perfect. The eatery would be in its midafternoon lull. Carly was sure Valerie and Nina wouldn't mind if she left for a few hours.

Carly smiled at the pair. "I accept your invitation. I will meet you there at three."

The plan agreed upon, she treated them each to one of Nina's holiday sugar cookies. Douglas opened his wrapper and took a large bite. Hannah slipped hers into her silver purse.

As the couple was leaving, Hannah leaned close to Carly. Her lips quivered slightly. "I know Gina didn't kill Prez. She would never do something like that."

Touched by the woman's raw emotion, Carly gave her a brief hug. Hannah's belief in Gina's innocence was a massive relief. Not that Hannah had any influence with the police. But at least she knew an innocent person when she saw one.

"Dear, we should be going," Douglas said, slipping his arm through

Hannah's. "I need to stop at the drugstore, remember? I need my drops."

"That's right," Hannah said, looking suddenly flustered. "Carly, we'll see you tomorrow at three. I'm so glad you'll be able to join us."

After the couple left, Carly's suspicious mind kicked into action. Hannah had practically begged her to have tea with them at the inn. Was she genuinely grateful for Carly's support of the play? Or was there a hidden agenda lurking under that polished demeanor?

Either way, it would give Carly a chance to question Hannah further.

• • •

It was after five o'clock when Don Frasco strode in. Valerie had left early, and Nina was clearing the booths of dirty dishes. Only a handful of customers remained, and they were chatting quietly among themselves.

Judging from his harried expression, Don hadn't had a good day. He grabbed a can of root beer from the refrigerated case at the front of the restaurant, then slid onto a stool at the counter.

"Take your coat off, stay a while," Carly joked, noting his sour expression. She went behind the counter and plopped down a clean glass in front of him.

"Nah, I'm not gonna stay long."

Nina swooped behind him with a playful smile and ruffled his gelled auburn hair. "Hey, guy!"

"Hey," Don mumbled, his freckled cheeks turning cherry blossom pink. He popped open his root beer and emptied it into the glass.

"Want a bacon and tomato sammy?" Carly asked him. Don did *not* do cheese.

"Nah, thanks anyway. I ate a PBJ in the car. 'Course, it was half frozen." He gulped back a long swig of root beer.

"I wondered where you disappeared to yesterday," Carly prodded. "Did the police make you leave?"

"They did, after I gave them my contact info. Like they don't know me by now," he grumped. "Anyway, it turned out to be a blessing in disguise. When I got home, my kitchen was flooded. Freaking mess like you never saw."

"What happened?" Carly asked, sincerely concerned.

"Water pipe under the sink burst. My landlady was skiing with her son, so I had a devil of a time reaching her. I had to hunt down a plumber myself. On a Sunday. During a Patriots game."

"Well, that stinks," Carly said. "Is it fixed now?"

"Yeah, to the tune of a hundred ninety bucks. Which amount I'm deducting from next month's rent, whether my landlady likes it or not." His pale brown eyes sparked, and a sly smile slid across his face. "I do have an interesting tidbit, although I don't know if it's related to the murder."

Carly's ears perked up, and she rested her elbows on the counter. "Do tell."

Don took another gulp of his root beer. "So, get this. The plumber told me he got called to the opera house on Saturday to fix a clogged toilet. Someone tried to flush something that didn't make it all the way down. Ended up being a black plastic bag, the kind you can't see through. Before Larry could check the contents, the head custodian there took it from him and told him he could leave. Sounds weird, doesn't it?"

"A plastic bag," Carly repeated, her suspicious mind cranking out possibilities. Her first thought was that someone had tried to dispose of drugs. She didn't like to think of illegal drug dealing in Balsam Dell, but she wasn't naïve enough to think it couldn't happen.

"Then, get this." Don was animated now. "When Larry was on his way out, he saw a cop car parked out front. Two cops were heading inside as he was leaving."

"Hmmm. Was it a public bathroom, or in someone's private section of the building?"

He shrugged. "I'm not sure. Larry didn't elaborate."

Another mystery in the Flinthead Opera House? Carly wondered. Was it connected to Prescott Lennon's demise?

"I'm surprised you're not all over this," Carly said wryly. "You're usually like a bloodhound with a juicy story."

He scowled. "I tried, believe me. The cops all gave me the brush-off. Don't they get that it's my job to report the news?"

"I'm sure they do," Carly said, trying to soothe his ruffled feathers. Don was known to be a pest of sorts, despite his having helped solve a few local crimes, including murder.

Carly was a teenager when she first met Don. His mom had called and asked if she could babysit him for an afternoon. He'd screamed bloody murder when she tried to make him a grilled cheese. After that, he clomped over his mother's dining room table in his cowboy boots, creating permanent gouges. Carly got blamed for the entire debacle, and—thankfully—was never asked to babysit him again.

She could honestly say that he'd matured since then, though he tended to be a complainer.

Don finished his root beer in a few long swallows. "I gotta run, but the reason I came over is to share some pics with you."

"From yesterday?"

"Yup."

Carly scurried around the counter and dropped onto the stool beside him.

He pulled his cell from his pocket and began tapping at it. "It's mostly a jumble of faces, but I thought I'd show them to you to see if anyone looked out of place."

"I'm not sure how I'd know that," Carly pointed out. "The only cast member I know is Gina."

"Just look, okay?" He gave her his cell.

She scrolled through the photos, but each one was pretty much a sea of faces. She thought she spotted Nate in one of them, but the image was tiny. "Well, I recognize a few people, like the women who work at the town hall. Some of the police officers, too. Can you send these to me so I can view them on my laptop?"

"Of course. Don't I always share?"

Carly shot him a look. "Was that a hint?"

He shrugged. "Just an acknowledgment that you and I have a history. As I recall, we managed to sideline a few dastardly characters by working together." He waggled his eyebrows like an old-style villain.

Inwardly, Carly groaned. She couldn't deny that he was right.

Nina came up quietly behind Don and tapped his shoulder. She handed him a sugar cookie. "I made this one specially for you."

Don stared at the cookie. It was a face with hair exactly like his own, the eyes nearly the same shade of auburn. "Is . . . is this me?"

"Sure is," she trilled.

"Nina, that's unreal," Carly said with a chuckle. "It's adorable."

"Uh . . . thanks, Nina," Don mumbled, his cheeks burning crimson.

Nina's soft laughter floated over the eatery. "You're welcome. I'm so glad you like it!"

With that she retreated toward the kitchen, humming "Jingle Bell Rock" all the way.

Avoiding Carly's gaze, Don hurriedly texted her the slew of photos he'd taken. "If you see anything we should investigate, let me know."

He left so fast it was a miracle he didn't trip over his own boots.

Carly turned her attention to the photos. Don had snapped twenty or so, taken from various angles as he ambled around the lobby. Some faces reflected confusion. Others looked bored, or simply annoyed at the delay.

She'd been right about seeing Nate in one of them. Because of his height, she spotted him right away. He wasn't in the lobby, though—he was at the far end of the corridor that led, she was almost sure, to the "star" dressing rooms.

When she enlarged the image, the anger in Nate's expression was tangible. The photo was a Live one, meaning it revealed a few seconds of movement and sound when she held her finger to the phone. While the ambient noise of the crowd muffled the words, the snarl on Nate's face spoke volumes as he gripped the upper arm of a man—a man in a tattered waistcoat.

Jacob Marley, aka Prescott Lennon.

CHAPTER 6

CARLY STEPPED FROM THE FOYER INTO THE LIVING ROOM OF THEIR NEWLY renovated home. The enticing aromas of cinnamon, nutmeg, and a hint of orange peel curled around her, tickling her senses and lifting her spirits.

"It's good to be home," she said to Ari, wrapping her arms around his neck. She'd just shed her outerwear and given Havarti a kiss on the snout, saving the man she loved for last. "Did you have a good day?"

Ari grinned and pulled her close, planting a kiss on her lips. "The best part was coming home to you, but I did have a decent day. I managed to finish the wiring upgrades at Quayle's Hardware. Best part was, the owner's wife stopped in with cranberry macadamia cookies, and she insisted I bring some home to you."

"Well, I won't pass those up." Carly patted her abdomen. "Though if people keep plying us with holiday treats, I'll be able to fill in for Santa Claus at the community center without using any padding."

"Not a chance," Ari protested. He lifted her left hand and kissed her ring finger. "Every time I look at this ring, I get excited all over again about our summer wedding."

Carly smiled down at her hand. "Yeah, me too. The moment Christmas is over, we need to start doing some serious planning."

They'd chosen Carly's engagement ring back in July—a sparkling marquis diamond flanked by two small emeralds. After a terrifying experience with stolen gems only a month before that, she wasn't sure she wanted the emeralds. But green was her favorite color, and the ring was exactly what she'd dreamed of.

"I feel bad that we never had time to have an engagement party," Carly said wistfully.

When she and Ari had first announced their intentions to a houseful of invited guests, they'd promised to host an official party after the home renovations were complete. The reno work, however, had dragged into Thanksgiving week. By that time the holidays were fast approaching. And though the downstairs was picture-perfect, the upstairs still needed attention.

Ari slipped an arm over her shoulder. "I know. Me too." He kissed her temple. "Maybe after the new year we can have an informal open house. Nothing fancy. Just a gathering of family and friends."

"Now that," Carly said, "is a great idea."

She ambled over to their new electric fireplace and held out her hands to warm them. Atop the oak mantel was the source of the delightful aroma—a set of three burning candles, ranging in size from four inches high to eight. At the far end of the mantel sat a handmade wooden sleigh, filled to the brim with pine cones and tiny wrapped boxes.

"I see you brought the tree inside." Carly went over to the front window to admire the balsam fir Ari had purchased at the local tree lot on Sunday. The shape wasn't perfect but close enough, and the piney scent was heavenly.

Our first tree in our new home.

"I know we're not decorating it till tomorrow, honey," Ari said, slipping an arm around her waist, "but I thought bringing it inside would save time."

"I'm glad you did. Mom and Gary are looking forward to trimming it with us tomorrow."

"And I'm looking forward to your mom's mini turkey pot pies."

Every year on the day after Thanksgiving, Carly's mom, Rhonda Hale Clark, used leftover turkey to make miniature pot pies in individual crocks. She froze them immediately so they could be enjoyed whenever anyone was ready for turkey again. For Carly, it was like having Thanksgiving dinner all over, only better and easier.

"I opened two bottles of wine," Ari said. "There's another one in the fridge if we need it. I wonder what Nate and Norah are bringing for dinner."

Carly shrugged. "Norah texted me this morning but didn't mention dinner." She gave Ari a worried look. "Shoot. I hope they remembered they're supposed to be here."

The invitation to Nate and Norah had been extended several days earlier. Norah had accepted but insisted on bringing the food, asking only that Carly and Ari supply the wine.

"I'll text her a reminder," Carly said. "Why don't you put on that cable station that plays the holiday songs?"

"Ah! Good idea."

She shot off a quick text to Norah: *Still coming for dinner tonight?*

When she didn't receive an immediate response, she freshened up in the bathroom. After that she changed into a forest green sweater and black leggings and stuck whimsical reindeer earrings in her ears.

When the doorbell rang, Carly blew out a relieved breath.

Havarti at his heels, Ari went to the door and ushered Nate and Norah inside. Nate looked slightly stressed, but Norah's crimson-lipped smile was brilliant. She handed Carly a bright green gift bag stuffed with sparkly tissue, then bent to give Havarti a few light pats on the head.

"Thank you!" Carly said and hugged her sister. "You didn't need to bring anything. Well, except for the food." She laughed and set the bag under the bare tree.

Nate, who towered over Norah by nearly a foot, held up an insulated carrier. In his other hand he held a large brown paper bag. "Speaking of which, can I take this stuff into the kitchen? Everything's nice and warm."

"Follow me," Ari said.

Havarti trotted after the men, no doubt hoping to share in whatever goodies Nate was toting. He'd had his own dinner earlier, but in his doggy world there was always room for more.

Norah removed her red wool coat, revealing a curve-hugging LBD accentuated with a red cashmere infinity scarf. Her chin-length blond hair was styled to perfection. Much as Carly adored her sister, she had to admit feeling a twinge of envy at Norah's simple but classic elegance. It also seemed a bit dressy for an informal family get-together.

"We had the caterer who does our après opera parties whip up some scrumptious goodies," Norah said. "Wait till you taste her quiche!"

That was another thing about Norah. No matter what she ate, none of it stopped along the way to add some padding to her hips.

"Good," Carly replied, "because I'm starving, and I love quiche." The small salad she'd had for lunch was a distant memory, and her stomach was beginning to rumble.

When Nate and Ari returned from the kitchen, Ari took their coats and scarves and hung them in the closet.

"Not to rush things, but since the food is warm, shall we go ahead and have dinner?" Carly suggested. She could already taste the creamy quiche. "The dining room table's all set."

"I'm in," Ari said with a grin.

As if on cue, Havarti curled up in his fluffy new bed in the corner of the dining room. With everyone pitching in, the meal was ready within minutes. Nate had even brought along a wicker basket for the sliced crusty bread. He rested it next to a crock of herb-seasoned butter.

Ari poured wine for everyone. As they all sat down, Nate's face began to relax. He identified the offerings. "We have a traditional quiche Lorraine, a broccoli-tomato quiche, a crisp romaine salad, and roasted sweet potatoes." A smile widened his face. "I'm saving the dessert for last—it's a surprise."

"Man, this all looks fantastic," Ari said. He dimmed the overhead light, a vintage art deco ceiling lamp resembling the petals of an open rose.

Everyone helped themselves, and the feast began. Carly was tempted to bring up Prescott Lennon's murder, but it wasn't the appropriate time.

Norah accepted a sliver of veggie quiche from Nate. Narrowing her eyes, she skimmed her gaze over the table. "Carly, aren't these Mom's dishes?"

Surprised at the sharpness in her sister's tone, Carly swallowed a bite of her sweet potato. "Um, they are, yes."

Nate gave Norah an odd look, then slid a forkful of quiche Lorraine into his mouth. Several moments of silence passed. Carly hoped it was because everyone was savoring the delicious meal.

Once everyone had eaten their fill, Ari recruited Nate to help clean up the table. "How about we let the gals relax while we do kitchen duty?" He winked at Nate, who took the hint and leaped off his chair.

While dishes clinked in the kitchen, Norah sat stonily and stared into her wineglass.

"Norah, are you upset because Mom gave me the dishes?" Carly quietly asked her sister.

Norah blinked. "Mom promised me the china would be mine one day. And then I come over here and see it on your table!"

Carly went over and sat beside Norah, slipping an arm around her shoulder. "Norah, look at these dishes. They're not Mom's china. They're similar, yes, but they're from a cheap set of stoneware she picked up at a consignment shop a few summers ago."

Norah's cheeks flushed. "I thought they looked a little . . . colorful. Sorry, my mistake." With that her eyes filled with tears.

Carly squeezed her sister's shoulder. "Norah, what's wrong? This isn't about dishes. What's really going on?"

Norah shook her head. "Nothing. It's just . . . yesterday was such a horrible day." She lowered her voice to a half whisper. "Nate is blaming himself for what happened, but he doesn't want to talk about it either."

"Why does he blame himself?"

"He thinks he should have checked out the players' backgrounds more thoroughly, made sure no one had a checkered history." She sniffled.

"Does he normally do that?" Carly glanced toward the kitchen, then back at Norah.

"No, because he knows the opera people. This was unusual, leasing the venue to a small theater group. The thing is, he knew Hannah Collier from way back. She was his middle school music teacher. He had faith in her judgment."

"I didn't know that."

"He was so excited about having *A Christmas Carol* at the opera house. He loves Dickens, and it's one of his favorite stories." She pinched a tear from her eyelashes. "Let's talk about something else, okay? I don't want Nate to hear us."

They switched to small talk. By the time the men returned to the dining room, Norah was admiring the wallpaper pattern, the way the pale white roses were miniature versions of the art deco ceiling light. Joyce, the former owner of the house, had loved the pattern. In deference to her, Carly and Ari agreed to leave the wallpaper in place.

"Everyone ready for dessert?" Nate asked hopefully.

After the huge meal they'd consumed, Carly wasn't sure she could squeeze in an ounce of anything sweet. But she didn't want to hurt Nate's feelings, so she issued an enthusiastic "Yes!"

Nate rubbed his hands together and grabbed Ari's sleeve. "Come on."

Minutes later, they returned to the dining room. Ari set down a tray of coffee fixings. Nate's face beamed brighter than a blazing fire as he set the dessert in the center of the table.

Carly sucked in a breath. "Is that a yule log?"

"It sure is. In French it's a bûche de Noël. This one is a chocolate sponge cake rolled around a layer of vanilla pudding spiked with hazelnut liqueur. You can get creative with the fillings—some chefs use cream—but this one's awesome."

"It's amazing," Ari said. "How did they make the mistletoe on top?"

Norah shot up her hand. "I can answer that. Those are sprigs of rosemary tucked around fresh cranberries, dusted lightly with confectioner's sugar."

Nate leaned over and kissed her. "A perfect description. Now let's slice up this bad boy and have ourselves some dessert!"

• • •

After everyone was stuffed, they retreated to the living room. The soft glimmer from the flickering candles cast a cozy glow over the room.

Nate and Norah took the sofa, while Carly and Ari sat in opposite overstuffed chairs. From the television came the sound of Elvis crooning "Blue Christmas." Nate hummed the tune in his stunning tenor voice but didn't sing along.

Havarti leaped onto the sofa and gazed up at Nate with his soft brown eyes.

"Come on," Nate said with a laugh. "There's plenty of room on my lap."

Havarti wiggled his tail end and then clambered onto Nate's legs, curling up on his corduroy trousers. The dog looked as if he'd landed on a cloud and was staring down from heaven.

"I'd love to have a dog," Nate said, rubbing Havarti's ears. "But we travel too much, and it wouldn't be fair."

Norah shot him a look that said, *Don't even think about it.*

Uh-oh, Carly thought. Was Norah and Nate's idyllic relationship showing a few minor cracks? They'd been inseparable for over a year, with no signs of strain. Carly hoped this wasn't the beginning of a rift between the two.

Carly moved to what she hoped was a neutral topic. "Nate, how's your family doing?" She knew that both his dad and his sister had roles in every operatic presentation performed at the opera house.

His face lit up. "Great, and thanks for asking. Dad is seriously psyched about doing *The Magic Flute* in January. It's already sold out. Can you believe it?"

"I hope you saved us tickets," Ari noted with a chuckle.

"You bet we did. Family always comes first."

Norah kicked off her black velvet heels and shifted her legs onto the sofa. "I have to say, you've done an amazing job with this place, Carly. When you first bought the house, this room looked to me like a 'little old lady' parlor. But

33

you've made it into a cozy, warm, comfortable, *open* living space. And a very welcoming one, at that."

If there was any sarcasm in Norah's tone, it hadn't been obvious. Her compliment had sounded genuine, which tickled Carly to the core.

"Thank you," Carly said, smiling at Ari. "We both had a hand in decorating and choosing the furnishings. Luckily, we have similar tastes. Well, except for the print of the poker-playing dogs Ari wanted to hang over the mantel."

Ari laughed. "You know I was teasing."

An awkward silence ensued. Carly had never felt so ill-at-ease around her sister. She sensed Norah was struggling with something—if only she knew what it was.

"Hey, that's a great tree you picked out," Nate said brightly. "Did you go to one of those places where you cut it yourself?"

"Nah," Ari said. "Zach—Gina's boyfriend—and I took the easy way out. We went to the tree lot in town."

"Speaking of Gina, how is she doing?" Norah asked softly. "We heard she was interviewed by the police today."

"She was," Carly said fretfully. "I'm relieved they didn't detain her, but she's worried out of her mind. It seems the prop manager claimed he wasn't sure if she helped him untangle Marley's *ponderous* chain or not."

"Actually, in the story, the ponderous chain is Scrooge's," Nate clarified. "When Marley's ghost first appears to Scrooge, he tells him that Scrooge's own chain was as full and heavy as Marley's was seven Christmas Eves ago." In a booming voice, Nate recited Marley's lines: "You have labored on it since. It is a ponderous chain!"

Slack-jawed, Ari sat back and stared. "Wow, maybe you should play Marley."

"That's if the play even goes forward," Nate said doubtfully. "If the police don't arrest the killer soon, the whole thing might tank. For the opera house, it would be a fiscal disaster, not to mention a blot on our reputation."

Carly hadn't thought of that. She'd been focused primarily on Gina's dilemma.

"Have you talked to the police today?" she asked Nate.

Nate's eyes flickered, and he rested a hand on Havarti's furry neck. "I have indeed. In fact, this afternoon I gave two of the state police detectives a tour of the opera house."

"Did they give you any idea of who their suspects are?"

Nate's laugh was harsh. "They asked a lot of questions about a lot of people, including Gina. But if they suspected anyone in particular, they weren't in a sharing mood."

In Carly's dealings with the police, she'd had the same experience.

"Nate," she said, "Norah mentioned that you knew Hannah Collier from your middle school days."

He crossed his legs at the ankles. Havarti snuggled into the crook of his arm. "That's exactly right. Hannah was my middle school music teacher when my family lived in New York. It was she who introduced me to opera. She heard me singing one day, and . . . well, the rest is history. So, when she approached me over the summer about leasing the opera house for several performances of *A Christmas Carol,* I was instantly on board. She lucked out, too. At the time we were in negotiations with a ballet company to perform *The Nutcracker,* but they canceled the gig."

"I didn't realize so much goes on behind the scenes," Ari commented.

Nate gave a wry smile. "It can be a cutthroat business, for sure. Jealousy, backstabbing, even bad acting—it's all part of the biz, to use a phrase. We try to make every performance look as seamless as possible, but there are occasional glitches."

Like an actor being murdered in his dressing room?

Carly waited a few beats and then said, "Don Frasco, the local reporter, took a bunch of pics with his phone yesterday while everyone was waiting for the play to resume. He shared them with me this afternoon."

"Really?" Nate sounded curious. "Anything interesting?"

Carly slid her cell off the table beside her, located the photos, and handed the phone over to Nate.

He scrolled through them slowly, his expression blank. Then his eyes narrowed, and his face tightened as he enlarged the screen. "Whoa. Here's one with me in the background. I don't look too happy, do I?" His nostrils flared. "Lennon had just left the stage and was heading, I assumed, for his dressing room. I grabbed him by the arm and told him to get his act together or he'd be out on his ear. Only I didn't say ear."

"Let me see." Norah snatched it from his grasp. "Oh my God, that *is* you, arguing with that horrible Prescott Lennon."

Carly's insides, already achy from overeating, sank like a pile of rocks. She gave her sister a look that said, *Are you kidding me?*

Norah suddenly realized the insensitivity of her comment. "I-I'm sorry. That was terrible of me, wasn't it?" She shrank against the sofa and buried her face in a throw pillow.

Nate set down the phone and gave Havarti a gentle nudge. The dog jumped off the sofa, and Nate reached for Norah. He wrapped his long arms around her and pulled her to his chest. With that the dam burst, and Norah broke into sobs.

Ari ran into the kitchen. He returned moments later with a glass of ice water and a box of tissues. He set them on the side table next to Norah.

When Norah's tears finally abated, she took several sips of water. In a wobbly voice she said, "I am so sorry. I spoiled this whole evening, didn't I?" She swabbed her eyes with a handful of tissues.

Carly squeezed onto the arm of the sofa next to her sister and rubbed her back. "Sweetie, you didn't spoil anything," she soothed. "We're all stressed to the max over this. You just reacted, that's all. Sometimes it's good to let everything fly." She tried to sound jocular, but Norah shook her head.

"Listen, guys, I think it's time we went home," Nate said softly. "It's getting late, and we all need a good night's rest."

Ari rose from his chair and retrieved their things. "Thank you both for the fantastic meal, and for your company," he said. "You were our first dinner guests in our new digs."

After thanking Ari and Carly for their hospitality, Nate and Norah left. Carly breathed out a sigh—whether from relief or frustration, she wasn't sure. Maybe both.

"What do you think is up with Norah?" Ari asked, snuggling on the sofa with Carly. Havarti straddled their laps, making it clear they were in for the long haul.

"I'm not sure." She told Ari about Norah mistaking the stoneware dishes for their mom's china. "That's so not like her. She knows the difference."

"Do you think she's feeling a little jealous because we're settled in our beautiful new home?" Ari suggested.

"I hate thinking that, but I was starting to get that feeling. Although her compliment about the cozy living room was genuine."

"Not to change the subject," Ari said, "but I never realized opera houses didn't just have operas. I guess in order to survive, they have to branch out."

Carly laughed. "That's one way to put it. A while back, Norah told me that when the Carpenter family first built the opera house, they worried that if it didn't attract enough patrons, it would end up folding. Balsam Dell isn't exactly a thriving metropolis."

"So it was a risky venture," Ari said. "Didn't I read somewhere that they spent tens of millions—buying the land, getting the permits, designing and building the place?"

"They did. Apparently, they had enough investors to make the project work. Architecturally, it was a major undertaking. The intent was to maintain the profile of the old farmhouse while designing a state-of-the-art opera house behind it."

"In my opinion," Ari said, "they succeeded. That building is a marvel."

Carly yawned and ruffled Havarti's fur. "I'm beat."

"Yeah, me too."

"Then bedtime it is."

"There's nothing to clean up in the kitchen," Ari said, wriggling out from under Havarti's warm form. "The dishwasher's on. I'll take Havarti outside for one last bathroom break."

While Ari attached Havarti's leash, Carly went into the kitchen and replenished the dog's water bowl. Her head felt fuzzy, floaty. From too much wine? Or had Norah's uncharacteristic behavior sent her thoughts spiraling into a whirlpool of worry?

There'd been so much more Carly had wanted to ask Nate. He'd definitely reacted at the image of himself arguing with—screaming at?—Prescott Lennon in the photo. If Don Frasco showed it to the police, would Nate be questioned about it?

Even if the police did see it, Carly couldn't see them interpreting that as evidence. At best, it was circumstantial, as they say on TV crime shows.

She swallowed two ibuprofen and then got ready for bed. She hadn't told Ari she'd accepted an invitation to join the Colliers for tea at the inn the following day.

It was a discussion, she decided, best saved for morning.

CHAPTER 7

THE DINNER WITH NATE AND NORAH THE EVENING BEFORE HAD LEFT CARLY with a hangover. Not the kind produced by alcohol, the kind resulting from a combination of sleeplessness and stress. The icy wind that followed her to the back door of the restaurant only added to the blahs weighing on her mind.

She slammed the door hard, shutting out the cold. Inside the restaurant, she cranked up the heat, flicked on the lights, and got the coffee maker started. She stashed her outerwear in the kitchen closet, pulled her cell out of her tote, and shoved the tote into the closet with her other belongings.

In the dining room, she poured herself a mug of steaming coffee and scrolled through her phone. She was surprised to see a text from Norah at this hour—her sister was *not* an early riser. Carly tapped it open.

You didn't even open our gift.

That was it. No smiley emoji to show she was only teasing. No mention of their get-together the evening before.

"Well, of all the things to whine about," Carly muttered to herself. Yes, they'd forgotten about the gift bag under the tree. With everything else going on, was it any wonder?

Carly was tempted to send off a not-so-polite retort. Instead, she texted back a bunch of holiday emojis. She tapped the arrow before she could add a snarky footnote.

The lock in the front door turned and Nina stepped inside. Since they never knew who would arrive first in the morning, she and Valerie had their own keys.

"Good morning!" Nina said with a big smile. "I swear, that walk from the parking lot gets colder every day!" She draped her things over the rack at the front of the restaurant, topping them with a pair of fuzzy plaid earmuffs. Carly poured her a mug of coffee.

Carly felt bad that her employees had to park across the street in the town parking lot. The rear of her building had room for only two cars. The one beside Carly's was for the tenant who lived above the eatery, which these days happened to be Gina.

"You do look frozen. Have your coffee," Carly urged.

They sat on adjacent stools, and Nina added a packet of brown sugar to her coffee. Around her neck was a handmade necklace. It consisted of a string of red beads from which several colorful charms dangled.

"How did your evening go? Did you have a good time?" Nina took a tiny sip from her mug.

"It was great, thanks. Nate and Norah brought delicious gourmet food. My stomach was aching by the time they left." It wasn't entirely the truth, but she didn't need to burden Nina with her family issues.

"It's so nice to have family close by," Nina said, sounding wistful. "I'm really happy for you, Carly." She drained her mug in three long gulps. "Hey, for the holidays, I've been thinking about experimenting with a grilled cheese made with fruitcake. What do you think?"

"Fruitcake." Carly wrinkled her nose. "Isn't that what everyone dreads at Christmastime?"

"Some people do, but others love it. We could pair it with Brie, which is perfect with fruit. If I try making it, will you taste it?"

Carly smiled at Nina's enthusiasm. "Of course I will. I'll be placing a special bread order later today, so why don't you add it to the list? But check with Sara Hardy first to see if they can bake one."

Sara Hardy was one half of the Colm and Sara Hardy team, the husband-and-wife bakers who owned Hardy Breads. They milled the flour for their artisan breads in their own stone mill. Since Carly was one of their best customers, they were always willing to make a specialty bread at her request.

They both opted to skip having a breakfast biscuit. Carly was still feeling the aftereffects of the meal from the night before, while Nina claimed she was saving the calories for later.

"Wait a minute, this is Tuesday," Nina remembered. "What about Gina?"

Gina had a standing date every Tuesday morning to join them in having one of the cheesy biscuits.

"Shows you where my head is," Carly said with a sigh. "I forgot my own bestie."

She texted Gina, who begged off because of so much work at the card shop. Carly wondered if that was only an excuse. Was Gina embarrassed by her status as a person of interest in Lennon's murder?

"I'll do the bathroom today," Nina said after she finished her coffee. "You have enough on your mind."

Carly smiled at her employee. "That's no reason you have to take my turn."

She still marveled at her luck the day Nina first walked into the restaurant. Nina had a home business in which she baked cookies so buttery and eye-catching that they were irresistible. Armed with a sample container of her stunningly decorated creations, she'd hoped to make the eatery one of her customers.

As fate would have it, Grant had left for an emergency that afternoon. Only Carly and Valerie were left to feed a horde of young kids and their camp counselors, all of whom were dripping wet from a sudden, wind-driven rainstorm. Surveying the happy chaos, Nina insisted on helping Carly take orders and serve. She'd virtually saved the day, or at least the afternoon.

The rest, as Carly liked to say, was history.

Carly was sprucing up the booths and Nina was scrubbing the bathroom when Valerie came in. She wasn't alone. Her husband, Chief Fred Holloway, came in with her.

"Hey, everyone," Valerie greeted. "I brought a guest today." She gazed up at the chief with adoring eyes, her smile a mile wide.

Carly loved seeing the two together. Since their early summer engagement and autumn wedding at the Balsam Dell Inn, Chief Holloway had morphed into a softer, gentler version of his former self. Now, with another murder to deal with, she wondered if his sharper edges might show signs of reappearing.

"Chief, this is a surprise," Carly said, though it really wasn't. She suspected he'd come in to offer information—and to issue the usual warnings about not getting involved in the investigation.

Valerie poured him a cup of coffee and one for herself. "Let's all sit," she said.

Carly knew what that meant. The chief wanted to have a chat with them.

They slid into a booth. Holloway sipped his coffee and flashed a brief smile at Nina and Carly.

"I want to share a few things about what happened on Sunday," he began. "Carly, you were a witness to some of it, but not to the actual crime scene—although I suspect Gina described to you what she saw in that dressing room."

"She did," Carly confirmed, feeling a slight twinge in her stomach. The sight of the chain wrapped around the actor's neck was no doubt etched in Gina's mind.

The chief continued in a solemn voice. "The cause of death hasn't yet been determined. It might take another few days, possibly longer."

"But . . . wasn't he, you know, strangled with the chain?" Carly asked, baffled.

Holloway shook his head. "The chain was apparently for effect. Certainly not tight enough to cause asphyxiation. And before I say anything further, I want to emphasize that this is strictly among us. I'd appreciate it not being shared with Suzanne. The fewer people who know, the better chance we have of unmasking the culprit."

"What about Gina? And Ari?" Carly quickly added.

"Gina has been briefed. One of the state police investigators paid her a visit at her shop this morning. I will make an exception for Ari. I know he can be trusted to keep this confidential."

Carly felt dumbstruck. If the chain hadn't caused Lennon's death, then what did? She rubbed at the goose bumps crawling up her arms.

The chief finished off his coffee, pushed aside his mug, then folded his hands on the table. He spoke evenly, but with a grim overtone. "Carly, we've done this dance before. I know Gina's a person of interest, but there are others, as well. I urge you to leave this alone and refrain from asking questions. I don't have to remind you of the risks. However," he added, "should you inadvertently stumble upon information that might help the police, I'd appreciate you sharing it with me immediately."

That was an interesting twist to his usual spiel. Was he saying that he almost expected her to ask questions?

Nina looped her arm through Carly's and squeezed. "I don't want anything to happen to you. Please listen to the chief."

"I promise, I will listen," Carly said softly. "Right now, my focus is on planning for my first Christmas in our new home."

"And don't forget, you also have a summer wedding to plan," Valerie said with mock sternness, tapping her finger on the table.

Carly laughed. "Not a chance of me forgetting that," she said, a thrill racing through her at the thought of marrying Ari. "Especially with my mom reminding me about it at least twelve times a day."

She and Ari had decided on Saturday, July 12, as their wedding date. A nondenominational ceremony, followed by a celebratory dinner, was to be held at the Balsam Dell Inn. Their honeymoon destination was yet to be determined.

Holloway tapped both hands sharply on the table. "Good. Then we have an understanding. Thank you for the coffee." He turned to Valerie and kissed her on the cheek. "See you later, sweetie." His voice was like warm honey.

Valerie walked him to the door, where they engaged in a brief hug. Nina cleared the mugs from the booth, and they began getting ready for the day.

Carly headed into the kitchen to get the food prep started. She wanted so badly to put the murder out of her mind. Unfortunately, it was stuck there, like a sliver under her skin.

She intended to keep her promise to the chief. She really did. But what if the police decided Gina was the prime suspect? What if they arrested her for murder?

Carly remembered that she needed to let Valerie and Nina know about her date with the Colliers for afternoon tea at the inn. Luckily, when she dropped the news on them, they took it in stride.

"Have fun, and eat lots of goodies," Valerie told her with a grin. "We'll hold down the fort!"

"And take pics," Nina added. "I want to see what a real English tea looks like."

• • •

The eatery remained busy through the lunch crunch. Suzanne was loving the tips—people seemed to be more generous at this time of year. Carly felt a pinch of guilt about not telling her about the questions surrounding the deceased actor's cause of death. But the chief had his reasons for discretion, and Carly had to respect them.

It was close to one o'clock when a dapper-looking gentleman came into the eatery. He looked straight out of *GQ,* if there was a version for elderly gents.

Garbed in an impeccably tailored wool coat, he sported a tartan scarf that was wrapped around his neck and tucked beneath the coat's lapels.

Carly was sliding a container of salad into the fridge under the counter when she spotted him. After glancing around for a moment, the man removed his gloves. Suzanne was taking orders, and Nina was picking up sandwiches for a party of four. Valerie was busy at the grill flipping grilled cheese.

Grabbing a menu, Carly strode up to him with a smile. "Good afternoon, sir. Would you like a booth? We have a few free ones toward the back."

The man removed his flatcap hat, revealing wisps of white hair that barely covered his balding pate. His gentle smile revealed graying teeth, but his blue eyes twinkled with cheer. "Oh, I don't think you need to waste an entire booth on one old man," he said with a mild chuckle. "I'm happy to take a counter seat."

Carly winked at him. "I'm going to give you a booth anyway. Follow me."

Once the man was situated, Carly brought him a cup of coffee. There was a curious air about him, putting her in mind of a country gentleman from days of old. She thought she'd seen him before, but where? Was he part of the entourage that was in town to produce *A Christmas Carol*?

And then she remembered. She'd seen his face only in profile, but she was sure she was right.

After spending a few moments studying the menu, he ordered a Sweddar Weather—a combined Swiss and cheddar grilled cheese—and a cup of tomato soup.

Carly took his menu from him. To satisfy her curiosity, she bent slightly toward him and murmured, "Ebenezer?"

His smile burst wide, and he tittered with obvious delight. "Oh, my, you're a sharp one. Yes, I'm the old miser, in the flesh. You're not going to blow my cover, are you?" Barry Grimble said in a stage whisper.

"Not at all," she said quietly. "I am still hoping to see you in the performance. I'm Carly, by the way. I was in the audience on Sunday."

The man's smile faded, and he nodded gravely. "Ah, yes. That did not end well, did it? I was so grateful to land the role of Scrooge. When I got the call, I was . . . well, elated to say the least. I hadn't worked in a long time. I would hate for this all to be for nothing."

"Well, I'm pleased you chose our restaurant to have your lunch. I'll put your order in right away."

She scurried off to give Valerie the man's order. *Oh, the questions I could ask,* she thought. Not that they could talk privately. But she sensed a loneliness in the elderly man that made her think he wouldn't be averse to dishing about himself. And maybe about others?

When his order was ready, she delivered it to his table. His coffee mug was empty.

Barry wiggled his bony fingers over the sandwich. "My dear, this looks positively marvelous. It's simply *oozing* with my two favorite cheeses." The touch of drama in his voice made Carly wonder if he was doing a bit of acting. Either way, she liked the old gent.

"Would you like more coffee?" she asked him.

"Oh, I would, but I'm not sure my"—he whispered in a low voice—"bladder would appreciate it."

Carly wanted to point out that they had a restroom, but he'd already violated the TMI rule. She left him to eat his meal in peace, remembering that she had to be at the Balsam Dell Inn by three. There was still plenty of time, but she wanted to freshen up before she left.

After Barry finished his lunch, he pulled out a cell phone from his coat pocket. He tapped it a few times and then paid his bill with cash, adding an enormous tip. Suzanne would be ecstatic when she saw it.

As he was sliding out of his booth, Carly said softly, "I hope you'll get the call that the play will continue. I've looked forward to it for a long time."

"As have I," he said, adjusting his scarf. "The casting director, Hannah Collier, was such a darling for offering me the role. Even if the play flops, I'll always be grateful to her."

"I've met Hannah," Carly told him. "She seems like a lovely woman. Her husband, too. I thought they made a charming couple."

"They do, don't they?" Barry placed his cap on his head and blinked, emotion swirling in his blue eyes. "I only hope this latest . . . *event* won't mar her happiness."

Event? It was a strange way to refer to Lennon's murder. Carly wished they could chat further, but Barry seemed anxious to leave.

Out of the corner of her eye, Carly saw a sleek black limo pull up in front of the restaurant and double-park.

"My ride is here," Barry said with a smile. "Thank you again, Carly, for such a delicious meal. I hope to get back here again before we all have to leave town."

After wishing him well, Carly watched him exit the restaurant. Through the front window, she saw the limo driver hurry to open the passenger-side door for Barry. He held the elder man's arm, ensuring that he didn't slip as he climbed into the car.

Questions churned in Carly's mind, so many that she needed a mental checklist to keep track of them.

Barry Grimble's timing couldn't have been better. She was now more eager than ever to join the Colliers for afternoon tea.

CHAPTER 8

CARLY FELT HER LIPS CURVE INTO A SMILE AS SHE SWUNG INTO THE ENTRANCE of the Balsam Dell Inn.

On the front lawn, the inn's massive fir tree boasted oversized red bulbs and bright colored lights. The white pillars at the porticoed entrance were wrapped in thick garlands of balsam, pine cones, and berries. On the front door, and on each of the windows, huge wreaths glowing with tiny white lights and giant red bows gave the façade a warm, magical feel.

After surrendering her car to the valet, she stepped inside the inn. Another tree in the red-carpeted lobby was decorated with doves made from white velvet. Strands of dark red berries encircled the tree, and a delicate birdhouse rested at the top. Carly knew that the inn changed its theme every Christmas season. This year it was doves—the universal symbol of peace.

Carly checked her coat at the door. A tuxedoed waiter escorted her into the dining room reserved for the afternoon tea. She'd given her name, explaining that she was a guest of the Colliers.

Hannah and Douglas were seated in a cozy corner of the dining room. Carly was glad she'd changed into her black dress slacks and her favorite forest green blouse. Both Colliers were dressed to the nines—Hannah in an elegant sheath of midnight blue, Douglas in a navy wool suit, a crisp white shirt, a tasteful holiday tie.

"Carly, so delighted you could join us." Douglas rose and gave her a light hug, while Hannah took Carly's hand briefly into her own.

"Thank you. I feel honored to be invited," Carly said, meaning every word.

The white linen tablecloth was set with china teacups and saucers, salad plates, and sterling silver utensils. A shallow bowl of sugar cubes and another with lemon wedges sat off to one side. The linen napkins were folded to resemble doves.

"We've chosen the Earl Grey tea," Hannah said, "but if you prefer something different, we can change it."

"Earl Grey is fine," Carly said.

Within a few minutes, a china teapot was delivered to the table and set down on a pewter trivet. Another server came along with a three-tiered stand. On it were miniature scones, cups of clotted cream, and two different types of jam.

"Shall I pour now?" the first server asked with a practiced smile.

"Yes, please," Hannah instructed.

"We'll wait for the second course," Douglas said, obviously familiar with the drill.

"Yes, sir."

After tea was poured, both servers slipped away. Carly squeezed a wedge of lemon into her tea and added a touch of cream.

She suddenly felt self-conscious, having afternoon tea in the elegant old inn with people she barely knew. At Hannah's urging, she plucked a cranberry scone from the tiered tray. She slathered it with clotted cream and added a touch of apple jam.

Douglas and Hannah followed suit, Hannah opting only for a smidgeon of raspberry jam.

For a while they made small talk—the Vermont weather and the service at the inn, for starters.

"Carly," Hannah asked, "have you known Gina long?" She took a delicate sip of her tea.

"Yes, actually, since grade school. We've been friends for most of our lives."

Carly didn't mention the falling-out they'd had after high school graduation. It was resolved now, but for well over a decade they didn't speak to one another. She finished her scone and contemplated her next choice.

"How nice for both of you," Hannah said. "Carly, I . . . want you to know I never believed for a moment Gina was guilty of harming Prescott."

"You mentioned that before, and I'm grateful," Carly acknowledged. "Gina wouldn't harm a fly if it landed in her soup. She'd probably scoop it out and try to save it." She gave a lame smile that made Douglas chuckle.

"Well, I haven't met the young woman personally," Douglas said, adding more sugar to his tea, "but Hannah is an excellent judge of character. If she knows Gina is innocent, then I do too."

Carly chose another scone, an almond one. She broke it in half, savoring the heavenly aroma. "Thank you. I appreciate that. Um, Hannah, forgive me if this sounds intrusive, but do you think the prop manager could've been involved in Mr. Lennon's death?"

Hannah looked surprised at the question. "Curt Blessings? Why would you ask that?"

"Gina mentioned that when he spoke to the police, he said he didn't recall if Gina had helped him straighten out the chain or not. That makes it sound like she only touched the chain when she—"

"Killed him?" Hannah's face paled. "Yes, I see your point. To my knowledge, Curt had no reason to want to harm Prescott. One day last week, in fact, I saw them sneaking outside together to have a cigarette. There's no smoking allowed in the building."

Carly didn't want to press the issue for fear of Hannah shutting down. Also, she was doing exactly what the chief had warned her against—asking questions.

"I'll tell you who's a piece of work," Hannah said, a touch of vinegar in her tone. "Honey Lennon. Ever since they found her husband's body, she's been wailing about the loss of her beloved Prez. When he was alive, she barely spent

45

five minutes with him, and when she did it was only to snipe at him. In fact, over the past week, she spent most of her time with that woman who does the makeup for some of the actors. Now she wants to whisk his remains back to California so she can give him a proper burial." She gave a theatrical wave of her hand.

"Is that where he's from? California?"

"Not originally, no, but he moved there at some point. Back in the day, he was quite good-looking, before his bad habits caught up with him. The wages of sin," she added tartly.

Carly recalled seeing early photos of Prescott Lennon. With his dark wavy hair, squarish jaw, and large brown eyes, he was once considered quite the heartthrob. Recent photos of him revealed fleshy jowls, watery eyes, and a rough, ruddy complexion.

"Were they married long?" Carly inquired.

"No. Three or four years." Hannah added another dab of jam to her scone. "The man has—had—at least twenty years on Honey, you know. Her real name is *Honoria*. She started out in Hollywood as a hairstylist to the stars. Somehow, she weaseled her way into a bit part in some low-budget movie. Rumor has it she met Prescott at a party. Sparks flew, and Prescott ditched wife number three for Honey."

"So, she's his fourth wife?" Carly said, aghast at the revelation.

Hannah nodded. "She was hoping, through Prescott, to land a bigger movie role. She didn't realize you had to have talent."

Wow. Hannah was really spilling the tea, if all of it was true. Beneath her sophisticated veneer was a razor-sharp set of claws.

A server came up discreetly and stood between Douglas and Hannah. "Would you like me to bring the tea sandwiches now? And may I pour more tea for you?"

Only one scone remained on the first tray. Douglas snatched it up and said, "Yes to both, please. Your timing is perfect."

The empty tray was exchanged for a larger, two-tiered affair brimming with delicate sandwiches. In a dulcet tone, the server described the offerings: Asiago bread triangles with thin-sliced cucumber and herbed cream cheese, smoked salmon and Greek yogurt on toasted wheat rounds, egg salad finger sandwiches sprinkled with house paprika, and sliced cheddar scones with chopped cinnamon apples and spiced butter.

He refreshed their teacups and slipped away.

"I don't know where to begin," Carly said. The mini scones with clotted cream had sated her hunger, but she didn't want to pass up another treat. She'd never had a cucumber sandwich, so she set one on her plate.

Douglas snagged two of each of the sandwiches and piled them on his plate. Hannah gave him a stern look.

His face reddened. "Carly, please forgive me if I resemble a glutton. I was raised in a large family, and it was every kid for himself." He took only a tiny nibble of his egg salad finger roll, as if to placate his wife.

"Oh, I totally understand. My mom used to make brownies for my sister and me. Norah would take a dozen of them up to her room before I even got one. She had a secret hiding place where she stashed them, but I always found them."

Douglas smiled at the story, then took a slow sip from his teacup.

"I, too, was raised in a large family," Hannah put in. "Though mine was what you'd call a blended family. My mother had three children, including me, from her first marriage. After my father died, she remarried a man with two children. They then had another child—a boy." She plucked a smoked salmon round from the tray and set it on her plate. "We weren't wealthy, but we had everything we needed," she said dreamily. "I sometimes miss those carefree days."

Carly sensed an undercurrent of sadness in Hannah's tone. After an awkward pause, she tasted her sandwich. She'd expected it to be bland, but the cream cheese blend was a perfect complement to the crisp cucumber slices.

"Hannah, why do you think the Lennons argued so much?" Carly wanted to remind her where she'd left off the conversation.

"My opinion? Because they couldn't stand each other. Once the novelty of marrying a so-called star wore off, Honey realized she was stuck with a toad." Her lips curved into a smug smile.

The mental image made Carly want to burst into giggles. To stifle the urge, she piped in quickly with a different topic. "I had an unexpected visitor to my restaurant today. Barry Grimble came in for lunch. He seemed like a pleasant man." She looked at Hannah. "He praised you for your kindness, and for offering him the role of Scrooge. He said he was ecstatic when you contacted him about it."

"That's sweet of him to say. If anyone deserved the role, it was him. He was a perfect fit for the old miser." She laughed delicately. "Doesn't he look straight out of Dickens?"

Carly only smiled.

"Good old Barry," Douglas said with a shake of his head. "I met him quite a while ago in New York. If the man ever caught a break, it was only from someone throwing a raw egg at him." When he saw Carly's expression, he touched her hand. "I joke, my dear. I was only pointing out that the man is a magnet for bad luck."

"Sadly, Douglas is right," Hannah said with a sigh. She took another salmon round from the tray. "After his first wife left him, he fell into a deep depression. He claimed she was the sun that lighted his world. Without her he couldn't function. It was a long time ago, and I didn't know him back then. But the

47

tabloids certainly did. They had a veritable field day with his troubles." Her lips twisted with scorn.

"That's so sad," Carly said. "But at some point, he must've gotten past it."

"He married again, eventually," Hannah went on. "It didn't work out, nor did the next wife. During the tryouts for the play, he told me he'd resigned himself to being alone. He has two corgis that he dotes on."

"Does he live in Vermont?" Carly asked her, sliding a cheddar scone off the tray.

"No, he lives in Lenox, Mass. He rents an apartment from an elderly woman in one of those stately old homes. She lets him have the dogs, so he's content there."

"What about you, Hannah?" Carly said casually. "Have you always worked in theater?"

At that, Hannah flashed a genuine smile. "Not always, but it was my first love. After a year of college as an education major, I dropped out and moved into a tiny studio apartment in Manhattan. I got a job at one of the lesser theaters, doing every bit of grunt work they could throw at me. One day I learned they were going to be doing a run of *The Glass Menagerie*. Oh, how I wanted the chance to play Laura Wingfield." She clasped her hands over her chest.

"Did you try out?" Carly drained the tea in her cup.

"I did. They gave the part to a well-known Hollywood actress. Needless to say, I was crushed."

Douglas reached over and patted his wife's hand. "Remember, dear, it's water over the dam. We all know how people like that land those roles, don't we?" he added meaningfully.

"Of course, darling. You're right." Gazing into his eyes with adoration, Hannah covered his hand with her own. Carly couldn't help noticing the sizeable pear-shaped diamond on her ring finger that sent wide bands of light dancing over the ceiling.

"So, tell me, how did you two meet?"

Hannah gave a tinkling laugh. "Douglas and I were both living in New York—two towns away from one another. A few years ago, I joined a club that takes its members by bus once a month to a popular Broadway play." She looked at her husband, as if prompting him to continue.

"Lucky me," Douglas said, beaming at his wife, "I joined the same club. I was divorced, Hannah was single. We knew from the moment our eyes met that we'd each found our soulmate. We were married ten months later."

"What a beautiful story," Carly said. "Love at first sight. Douglas, do you also work in theater?"

He sat back with a chuckle and straightened his napkin. "I'm afraid not. Much as I love theater, I have zero talent. No, I'm a financial advisor. I work primarily with a large law firm that handles trust accounts."

Which no doubt explained the Colliers' lifestyle, Carly thought.

"Hannah, Nate told my fiancé and me that you know each other from his middle school days."

She nodded. "When the world of drama bitterly disappointed me, I went back to school and finished getting my teaching degree. After that, I spent several years teaching music to uninterested middle schoolers. It wasn't very rewarding. During my years of teaching, I had only a handful of students who appreciated *real* music. But the one who stood out was Nate Carpenter."

"So that's how you met Nate?"

"Yes, and he was a model student, so dedicated and talented. When I first heard him sing, I felt as if I'd been transported to the Metropolitan Opera. I lent him my collection of opera CDs, and the rest is history." Her lashes fluttered dreamily. "I like to think it was I who helped him find his true calling."

Carly smiled politely, then finished the last bite of her cheddar scone. "Are any of the other actors staying here at the inn?"

"No," Douglas piped in. "The actors receive housing allowances for the duration of the performances, although a few live in the area. The ones who don't booked rooms at the big hotel over near the highway. But as for Grimble, I overheard him say he's been staying at a B and B here in town. Since the play is currently in limbo, he plans to head home today."

"You *overheard* all that?" Hannah sounded mildly perturbed. "When did this happen?"

Douglas cleared his throat. "Oh, um, this morning, dear, while you were having your beauty sleep." He winked at her. "I needed something at the drugstore, so I went out before breakfast. I saw Grimble there. He was talking to that makeup girl—you know, the one with all the tattoos. They didn't see me, so I didn't bother to say hello."

With a shake of her head, Hannah picked up her teacup. "I'll never understand these young girls today, wanting to deface their bodies like that." She took a sip of her tea.

Carly was tempted to reveal that she'd recently gotten a tiny grilled cheese sandwich tattooed above her left ankle. Ari thought it was adorable, but it took her mom a week to get over it. Once she did, she had to admit it was cute.

The third course arrived—a tray of sweets and pastries that would rival those of any Paris patisserie. Out of sheer politeness, Carly forced down a pink macaron.

"Hannah," she asked, "do you think the play will go on as scheduled?"

With a perplexed look, Hannah said, "Honestly, I'm not sure. Prescott had an understudy, a talented young man. Not quite old enough to be Marley, but makeup can fix that. I would like it to go on as scheduled."

"The understudy, are you referring to Malachy?" Carly dabbed her lips with her linen napkin.

Hannah looked surprised. "Yes, why? Do you know him?"

"No, Gina mentioned him to me, that's all. She said he's a good actor."

Carly thought of at least a dozen more questions she wanted to ask, but the Colliers had been gracious hosts, and she didn't want to cross a line. Not to mention that her stomach felt like a balloon ready to burst.

Before they left, the server came by with three exquisitely wrapped gold boxes and gave one to each of them. Through the clear cellophane window, Carly saw that her box contained three petit fours, each one frosted in a different pastel shade with a tiny white dove on top.

She thanked the Colliers for their hospitality, and they each gave her a warm hug. Hannah promised to update her with any news of when, or if, the performances would resume.

Outside, the air had gotten even nippier. Carly tucked her knitted coat collar around her neck. The valet was prompt with her car, and she tipped him generously. Once inside her Corolla, she turned up the heater.

Now the question was, how would she ever eat her mom's turkey pot pie after the feast she'd just enjoyed?

CHAPTER 9

By THE TIME CARLY GOT HOME, ARI HAD STRUNG THE LIGHTS ON THE TREE. He gave her a kiss, then hung her coat in the closet while she picked up Havarti and squeezed him in a hug.

"They look wonderful. You placed them perfectly," she said, setting Havarti down. She looped her arm through Ari's and he pulled her close. "I'm glad we decided on the colored lights instead of the blue ones. It's so much more festive."

"I totally agree. Since the lights are kind of a pain to put up, I thought I'd string them before you got home. When your mom and Gary get here, we can do the fun part—trimming the tree."

"You found the box with my decorations?" Carly asked.

He laughed. "I did, after lifting about twenty other boxes. Luckily, they were labeled so I didn't have to guess what was inside."

A sudden pang gripped Carly. Most of her tree decorations were the ones she and Daniel had put up every year. His accidental death a few years before had been a crushing blow. They'd been living in northern Vermont at the time, a few hours' ride from Balsam Dell. Her grief eventually became manageable, and she moved back to her hometown. When the opportunity arose to take over the lease of a failing ice cream parlor, she opened the business she'd long dreamed of—a grilled cheese eatery. Best of all, her mom and Gary had decided that their "Florida experiment" was over. They returned to the cooler climes of Vermont, and Carly couldn't have been happier.

"On second thought," she said, a catch in her voice, "maybe we should just use the new ones we bought. That way they're ours and ours alone, right?" She pasted on a smile, but Ari saw right through her.

"Honey, you told me you had some old favorites," he said softly. "Whichever ones they are, I think they belong on our tree. For now, I have some cider mulling on the stove. Can I tempt you?"

She laughed and swiped at her eyes. "I wondered what the spicy aroma was. And yes, you can *always* tempt me."

They'd no sooner snuggled up on the patterned sofa, glasses of warm cider in hand, than Carly's mom and stepdad arrived.

"We're here!" Rhonda chimed, stepping inside the foyer. She kicked off her boots, revealing bright green socks emblazoned with Santa's reindeer. Clad in a candy-cane striped sweater and black leggings, she was a poster girl for the holidays. "Oh my gosh, this room looks so beautiful!" She squashed Carly in a bear hug.

Her husband, Gary, his rimless eyeglasses fogging up, looked ready to drop the oversized cardboard box he was clutching for dear life. Ari quickly relieved him of the burden and carried the box into the kitchen. He returned with two more glasses of cider.

After Carly took their coats, Rhonda and Gary each dropped into a cushioned chair. Between them was the antique piecrust table that the former owner, Joyce, had gifted to Carly and Ari. Carly treasured it more for its sentimental value than for its actual monetary worth.

"You've done a marvelous job with this house," Gary said, wiping his eyeglasses with a tissue. Havarti trotted over to him, and Gary lifted the dog into his lap. He laughed when the dog licked him square on the lips.

"Thanks," Ari said. "Our contractor was the best. Always on time, and never cut corners. We lucked out, big-time."

"We're just relieved it was finished before Christmas," Carly noted. "Once the holidays are over"—she winked at Ari—"we have a wedding to plan. Oh! Speaking of which, I had afternoon tea at the inn this afternoon. I'm *sooo* glad we decided to have our wedding there."

Rhonda's mouth gaped open. "You didn't tell me about afternoon tea. Come on, we need details."

Carly explained how she'd been invited by the Colliers to join them for tea at the inn. "It was in gratitude for my eatery's support of the production," she hurried to explain. "My ad is in the back of the playbill."

"As are many others," her mom noted with a hint of suspicion. "I know you all too well, daughter of mine. I hope you're not trying to probe into that actor's death. Because if you are—"

"Mom, don't worry, okay? I'm not going to *probe* anything. Besides, the chief already warned me about asking questions." She felt her cheeks growing warm, and not just from the heat pouring out of the registers.

Carly gave them all a sanitized version of her convo with the Colliers. Mostly she described the elegance of the inn's décor and the unforgettable delights served with afternoon tea. She emphasized that Hannah had voluntarily dissed Honey Lennon—no "prodding" needed there. And yes, Carly herself had mentioned Barry Grimble, but only to compliment the kindly old gent.

Rhonda looked slightly mollified, but Carly knew her mom well. She wasn't totally convinced Carly was telling the entire truth.

"Well, I'd better get those turkey pot pies in the oven," Rhonda announced, draining her cider glass. "Carly, you come in and help me. We'll let the men enjoy some male bonding time together."

Carly followed her mom into the kitchen, where four miniature pot pies, each in their own crock, sat in a square metal pan. She turned on the oven. "Three fifty?"

"Three seventy-five," Rhonda corrected. "Once the oven's preheated, set the timer for twenty minutes. The crust should be browned by then. We'll zap the gravy before we serve everything and warm the rolls in foil."

Carly patted her abdomen surreptitiously. *Please make room for more food,* she silently begged.

A few minutes later, Rhonda slid the pot pies onto the middle rack and slammed the door shut. "Do we need to set the table?"

"Nope, it's all set." Carly crossed her arms and frowned at her mother. "Mom, are you mad at me because I had tea with the Colliers?"

Rhonda pursed her lips. She reached for her daughter's arm and tugged her over to the kitchen table. "Sit," she instructed, and they both sat down. "No, I'm not mad—and this isn't about the murder, if that's what you're thinking. Your sister left here last night in quite a state. When I talked to her this morning, she was beside herself. Can you tell me what happened?"

"Mom, I'm as baffled as you are," Carly said. "It started when she asked me why I was using *your* china at dinner. She assumed you'd given me the dishes you'd promised her."

"I gave you the stoneware, not the china." Rhonda puffed out an exasperated breath. "Did you point out her mistake?"

"Yes, and she acknowledged it. I thought she was over it. But then later, in the living room, I was showing her and Nate the pictures Don Frasco took at the opera house on Sunday, where everyone was milling around the lobby waiting for the performance to resume. There's one of Nate in the background, arguing with . . . the actor who died."

"Ah, that explains it." Rhonda shook her head. "Your sister said you practically accused Nate of killing that man."

"Seriously?" Carly threw up her hands. "That is not what happened. I'm sorry Norah is so upset about all this, but I most certainly did not accuse Nate of *anything,* let alone . . . you know, murder."

Rhonda's eyes teared up. "I know. I was sure that wasn't what happened. Norah hasn't been herself lately, and I don't know what's wrong."

Carly thought back to the previous night's conversations. When Nate said he'd love to have a dog, Norah had shot him a dark look.

"I don't like thinking this," Rhonda said, "but I wonder if Norah is feeling jealous, what with her younger sister having a lovely new home and an upcoming wedding."

The same thought had crossed Carly's mind, but she'd instantly dismissed it. Norah was always so bubbly, so sure of herself. Envy wasn't one of her traits.

Carly reached over and squeezed her mother's hand. "Would you like me to talk to her?"

Rhonda sagged. "Lord, yes, I would love that. Thank you, sweetheart."

That decided, Carly and her mom called the men to dinner. The turkey pot pies—loaded with chunks of turkey, veggies, and a light gravy—made for a complete meal. Carly groaned at the thought of the pumpkin pie, a dessert she normally loved, sitting in the fridge. Plus, they still had some of the yule log left over from dessert the night before.

"Why don't I clean up the dishes while the rest of you start on the tree," Carly offered. She felt like a stuffed turkey herself, especially after eating most of her pot pie.

"Not a chance," Rhonda insisted, rising from her chair. "Between you and me, we'll make short work of it. Our menfolk"—she bent to give Gary a peck on the cheek—"can start setting out the decorations. We'll all have pie after we decorate."

The men went into the living room, while Carly and her mom performed cleanup duty. Ten minutes later, Rhonda delivered a tray of pie slices and coffee mugs to the living room.

Carly stopped short at the sight of Gary and Ari untangling a silver foil garland they'd pulled from one of the boxes. A nauseating vision filled her mind—a metal chain of cash boxes wrapped around Jacob Marley's neck.

"Wait, don't unravel that," she said, removing the garland from their grasp. "It's old, and we bought new ones, remember?" she addressed Ari.

He looked at her strangely. "You don't want this? It was in your box of favorites."

"I know, but the one we bought with the fake popcorn and berries is much nicer." She smiled and said, "We need to start our own traditions, right?"

Ari nodded and said, "Whatever you want, honey. I agree, this one is kind of ragged." He rolled it into a ball and shoved it into one of the boxes.

As if he knew decorating the tree was a job for humans, Havarti rested on the sofa and watched everyone add the trimmings. Each time an ornament was attached to a branch, his tail thumped the cushion in approval. One of the bulbs was imprinted with the dog's name and face, a gift from Norah the previous Christmas. She'd been so tickled to find a vendor at the mall who made and personalized them by hand.

Carly's heart twisted at the memory. The thought of Norah being upset with her made her feel like a terrible sister. She had to set things right.

From the box of Carly's old decorations, they chose only a half dozen or so, mostly silver and gold bulbs. The rest were from the whimsical selection she and Ari had found at a holiday-themed shop.

Rhonda stole away for a moment to retrieve something from the pocket of her faux fur. She returned with a roundish item covered in bubble wrap.

"This is for you and Ari, for your first tree. Be careful taking off the wrap."

Carly carefully opened the wrapping, and her eyes widened. "It's . . . a blue Delft tree ornament," she breathed, touching it lightly. "Oh, look at the windmill. Where on earth did you find this?"

"Do you like it? I bought it at my favorite consignment shop. It's about thirty years old, or so I'm told. I hope—"

"Mom, this is unbelievable," Carly squealed, handing it to Ari. She squeezed her mom and then hugged Gary.

"I know you've been wanting to collect blue Delft," Rhonda said, "so I hope this will get you started."

Ari gave Carly the ornament, his dark brown eyes gleaming. She reached up and slid the attached ribbon over a branch close to the top. "There, now our little canine detective won't be tempted to check it out."

They all laughed, and then indulged in dessert and coffee. Stuffed as she was, Carly managed to swallow every last crumb of her pie.

Gazing around at the people she loved most, her emotions swelled. A tradition had been started, she realized—one she vowed to continue every holiday season.

But next year, the tree trimming would include Norah. And Nate, if they were still together.

• • •

After her mom and Gary left, Carly stretched out on the sofa with Havarti. *Our first tree,* she thought, smiling at the decorated balsam with its red, blue, and green lights. Next year at this time, she and Ari would be married. The idea sent a warm thrill through her.

Ari had insisted on clearing the dessert dishes and was finishing up in the kitchen. He returned holding two snifters of brandy. "The man at the liquor store told me brandy's good for your immune system."

Carly smiled and sat up so he could join her. "Then let this be our last drink of the evening. I'm ready to drop any second."

"Yeah, me too."

They clinked glasses and each took a sip. Carly felt a surge of heat rush down her throat. "Mmm, I'm already feeling relaxed. I'm going to sleep like an ox tonight."

Ari set down his snifter and jumped up. "We never opened Norah and Nate's gift bag last night. Shall we do it now?"

"Good grief, yes." Carly set down her snifter.

Ari came over with the bag and Carly removed the tissue paper. Inside was another tree ornament—this one crafted to look exactly like a grilled cheese sandwich.

"Oh, Ari, look at the tag. It's handmade from molten glass poured into a mold."

Ari held the ornament to the light. It shimmered like gold. "Really beautiful, isn't it? Now I feel bad we didn't open this last night."

Carly swung her legs off the sofa. "Let's hang it, and I'll text a picture to Norah."

Ari hung the ornament on an upper branch, close to where the lighted angel perched at the top. Bathed in the ambient light, the ornament sparkled.

We love it! Carly texted to Norah, along with the pic. She'd added a few kissy face emojis before sending it off.

Seconds later, Norah responded. *About time you opened it! We're happy you love it.*

Carly let out a sigh of relief. Norah seemed to be over her snit.

Thursday was Carly's day off this week. She'd arranged it with her team so she could have a day of holiday shopping. Valerie, Suzanne, and Nina were each going to do the same.

She texted Norah back. *Lunch Thursday? My treat.*

Norah replied, *I'm in. How about Fussy Nana's?*

Carly confirmed the restaurant and agreed to meet her sister at noon. She blew out a long breath.

Sibling crisis averted. At least for the moment.

CHAPTER 10

"BISCUIT TODAY?" NINA REMOVED TWO LIGHTLY BROWNED BISCUIT HALVES from the grill and set them on the cutting board.

Carly slid onto a stool and dropped her tote beside her. "Not a chance," she said, shrugging out of her coat. "I ate enough yesterday to feed everyone in Vermont for a month."

"I'm sure you're exaggerating," Nina said playfully. She flipped her grilled biscuit halves onto a plate and added a thick slice of cheddar to one half. Then she topped it all with the other biscuit half and pressed it lightly before slicing it in two. "Sure you don't want to split this with me?"

Carly waved a hand. "I'm positive. I think today's going to be a salad day."

Nina took a bite of her biscuit and chewed slowly. "Man, I could eat these three times a day," she said after she swallowed. "Have you heard any more from Don? Is he investigating the murder?"

That question came out of nowhere, Carly thought. "Um, not since Monday. Why?"

"Just wondered," Nina said with a shrug. "You guys seem like good friends. I'm surprised he doesn't come in more often."

"He doesn't do cheese, remember?"

"Oh, yes, I remember now." Nina giggled. "Funny guy, isn't he?" She bit off another hunk of her biscuit.

Carly wasn't fooled. The two cherry red dots sprouting on Nina's cheeks told the real story.

She was crushing on Don.

Although Carly and Don had worked together on a few murders, Carly knew little about his social life. Mostly she knew that he lived alone in an apartment above his landlady's garage. He worked mostly from home—unless he was out chasing a story, which was rare. The articles in his free paper were typically about local activities and recreational events. It was the ads from town businesses that kept him afloat.

Carly finished her coffee and went into the kitchen to begin food prep. Valerie came in a few minutes after eight thirty, and Suzanne breezed in ten minutes before her regular start time of eleven. Carly didn't keep track of their hours—if any of them needed time off, or came in late, she knew they made it up in work ethic. Nothing was ever left undone, and customers were always treated like longtime friends. The fact that they always pitched in to help each other was a sign that Carly had been blessed with a dream team.

The outside temperature was rising under a bright winter sun—thirty-nine degrees and climbing. *Balmy,* Carly thought with a chuckle. It was the kind of day that attracted customers in droves, folks who were tired of hunkering inside to keep warm and were eager for some fresh air.

The two customers she didn't expect were Honey Lennon and her sidekick, the woman with the tattooed arms. But there they were, waiting to be seated.

"I'll get these two," Carly quietly told Suzanne. She grabbed two menus and hurried over to the pair. "Hello, welcome to our eatery. May I show you to a booth?"

Unsmiling, Honey nodded. "Yeah. That'd be great."

Carly seated them across from the restroom—the only available booth at that moment. Handing them menus, she couldn't help noticing Honey's expertly applied makeup. It was a bit glammed up for daytime, but she wore it well. Her companion's makeup was more subtle, light shades of rose and gray that accentuated her raven-black hair and deep green eyes.

Both women shrugged their coats off their shoulders and perused the menu.

"Can I get you something to drink while you decide?" Carly asked them.

Honey stared up at Carly, and her gaze hardened. "I've seen you before. Weren't you with that Gina woman the day my hubby was murdered?"

The customer in the booth behind Honey shifted in her seat but didn't turn around.

"I'm Carly, and yes, I was at the opera house on Sunday," she murmured. "I'm so very sorry for your loss, Mrs. Lennon. I'm sure it was a terrible shock."

"Ya think?" Honey's eyes narrowed. "And if you knew who I was, why didn't you say something?"

"I was respecting your privacy," Carly replied in a quiet tone.

Honey had no answer for that. She pushed her menu at Carly. "I'll have a coffee with cream and a plain grilled cheese with tomato soup. Extra chips on the side."

"Is cheddar okay?"

"Yeah, whatever. What're you having, Ashley?"

Carly saw Suzanne slide a look in their direction, a scowl on her face.

The other woman, Ashley, handed Carly her menu, revealing an intricate pattern of vines tattooed on the back of her hand. "It all looks so good. I'll have a Party Havarti, but no soup. I'm allergic to tomatoes. Do you have any hot chocolate?"

"We sure do, and ours is delicious. Whipped cream?"

"Perfect," she said. "Thank you."

At least one of them is polite, Carly thought, striding off with their orders. Honey had been snarky, but at least she hadn't accused Gina of murder. *Yet.*

"That's an interesting design on your hand," Carly said to Ashley when she returned with their beverages. "Are they vines of some sort?"

"They're actually willow tree branches." Ashley pulled up her sleeves a few inches and displayed more of the inkwork. "I have them on both arms. They go all the way to my shoulders."

"The artwork is amazing," Carly said. "I have a tiny grilled cheese on my left ankle. I got it a few months ago."

"That's so cute," Ashley said with a genuine smile.

"I'm sorry, I never introduced myself," Ashley said. "I'm Ashley Blanchard, one of the cosmeticians hired to do makeup for some of the actors. Not the head cosmetician, but at least I got my foot in the door. Working with actors is kind of a dream job for me."

Honey glowered at her friend and then looked up at Carly. "Maybe you could check on our orders instead of gabbing?"

"Of course. They should be ready any time."

As rude as Honey was, Carly cut her some slack. She'd lost her husband in a terrible way. She had every right to be angry.

When Carly returned with their orders, Ashley was speaking in low tones and squeezing Honey's hand. From the snippets she caught, Carly guessed that Ashley was scolding her friend for lashing out.

She set down their platters. "Please let me know if you need anything else."

Behind the counter, a tub of dirty dishes was piled high. Carly grabbed the tub and hip-checked the swinging door into the kitchen. Suzanne trailed behind her.

"What's that chick's problem?" Suzanne barked, hands on both hips. "I couldn't believe the way she talked to you. I almost told her to take a long walk off a short pier."

Carly explained who the customer was.

"She could still act like a decent human," Suzanne muttered with a shake of her head. She removed a sealed container from the commercial fridge and pushed through the swinging door.

When Carly returned to the dining room, Honey and Ashley were finishing up their lunch. Honey dabbed her eyes with a tissue.

"Your lunches are on the house," Carly said, addressing Honey. "And again, I'm sorry for your loss. Is there anything I can do?"

Honey sniffled loudly. "Yeah, you can tell the cops to release my husband's body so I can take him back to California and give him a proper burial. Isn't one of your people married to a town cop?"

Carly wasn't sure where Honey had gotten her information, but she had no intention of revealing who Valerie's husband was. "It's the state police who are conducting the investigation," she explained. "You'll need to contact them."

Honey shoved a fresh tissue under her nose. "It was so horrible when they made me identify his body. They said it had to be official, that I was his only family member. I totally lost it when I saw that poor, crooked little pinky of his. He couldn't help it—it was something he was born with, but I always teased him about it. And now—" Her shoulders shuddered, and she broke into sobs. A few customers looked over, but then discreetly looked away.

Ashley shoved her arms into her coat. "Carly, thank you for your kindness. Honey needs to get back to the hotel and rest. Get your coat on, sweetie," she said to her friend.

When both women rose, Ashley glanced at Carly's hand. "That ring is gorgeous. Are you engaged?"

"Thank you. Yes, I'm getting married next summer."

"Congratulations!" Ashley gave her a tiny hug, ignoring the nasty look Honey bestowed on her.

Carly thanked them both and pushed out a breath of relief after they left the restaurant. If she'd had the opportunity to ask a few more questions, she felt sure Ashley could've given her some useful intel about Honey. Were she and Honey longtime friends? Or had they bonded during the rehearsals for the play?

Maybe it was time to chat with Gina again. She might know if there'd been any breaks in the case.

For starters, did the police know yet what killed the actor? Were there any other fingerprints on the chain? Her head was so full of questions, she could barely keep track of them.

She went into the kitchen and pulled out her cell, then texted Gina: *Have time for a chat after work?*

Gina's reply was instantaneous: *Zach and I want you and Ari to join us for pizza and peppermint ice cream tonight at my place. Can you make it?*

Carly almost laughed. More fatty food?

She'd check with Ari, but she was sure he'd be on board. She gave her friend a tentative "yes" but promised to confirm in a few.

• • •

When it was near closing time, Carly began wiping down tables. She was fluffing up the faux poinsettias in one of the vintage soup cans when Don came up behind her.

"Hey."

Carly jumped at the voice and whirled around. "Hey, yourself. Don't sneak up like that. You scared me."

"I said 'hey.' What more do you want?" He flopped into the booth she'd just cleaned.

"Sorry. I'm kind of jumpy today." She dropped down opposite him. "How's the paper coming this week?"

"I turned it in to the printer a few hours ago. The police are being so closemouthed about the murder, I didn't have much to report."

Carly nodded distractedly. "Something tells me this investigation is going to take a long time."

"Yeah, I agree. So many people were at that performance. Narrowing down suspects is going to be a beast of a task."

Don was right. Aside from the invited guests and the actors, there were people behind the scenes whose jobs were to make everything run smoothly—technicians, wardrobe people, makeup artists—a nearly endless list.

Carly noticed Nina going over to the refrigerated case and removing a bottle.

With a coy smile, Nina came over and set it down on the table in front of Don. "Hey, how's it going? You forgot your root beer."

"Oh, um, hi. Thanks. I can't stay long, so I'll take it to go." His freckles deepened with color as Nina went back behind the counter.

Don leaned toward Carly. "Listen, I did a little digging into Prescott Lennon's background. Found out some interesting stuff."

"Do share," Carly urged, leaning her elbows on the table.

Don pulled out his cell and tapped it a few times. "For starters, did you know he was born in Vermont?"

"I did not," Carly said. "Where, exactly?"

Don scrolled upward on his cell. "Middlebury. Says he lived there until he was in his teens, when his parents moved to New York. He played some sports but was more interested in theater . . . blah blah." More scrolling. "Returned to his hometown in his twenties to appear in summer stock. Disappeared for a while, then moved to Massachusetts, where he was slated to perform in the ill-fated production of *Sins of the Rich*. He—"

"Wait. Why was it ill-fated?" Carly interrupted.

Don shook his head. "Doesn't say. I'm going to do some more digging and see if I can find out what that was about. Anyway, after that he moved to LA, where he tried out for a number of movie roles, with no luck. I'm paraphrasing here." He scrolled up again. "Oh, he did get a part in a TV ad for some antacid I never heard of. That was back in two thousand nineteen."

"Sounds like a checkered career, at best," Carly noted. "What about family?"

"Um, let's see. Parents both deceased, one sister, doesn't say where she lives. Spouses—seems he was on number four," Don said dryly.

Hannah had said the same thing, that Honey was the actor's fourth wife.

It all begged the question, why did Hannah give Lennon the role of Marley in the production of *A Christmas Carol*? Had she met him before? Did she share a past with him? Or had she felt sorry enough for him to offer him the role out of the goodness of her heart?

"Not much else, other than piddly stuff. I'll send you the link to this bio, if you want it."

"Please." Carly wanted to do some serious googling herself. The last few days had been so busy she'd had little time to do much other than work and entertain. And attend a tea party—she'd gotten some good intel from that. But it had also left her with more questions.

Don sent her the text, tucked his root beer bottle into his jacket pocket, and slid out of the booth with a promise to do more digging.

"Have a great evening," Nina warbled as he pushed open the door.

"Um, yeah, you too."

With a wave of his hand, he was gone.

CHAPTER 11

"I CAN'T BELIEVE I ATE TWO HUGE SLICES," CARLY MOANED. "AFTER THE LAST two nights, I swore I wouldn't eat again for a month."

Ari laughed. "Yeah, but at least you ate a salad for lunch. I had fish and chips."

Zach cleared the table of pizza boxes and paper plates, then smiled at everyone. "You all saved room for peppermint ice cream, I hope."

"We did!" Carly, Ari, and Gina said in near unison.

KitCat issued a loud meow, as if to say, "Don't forget me!"

Carly lifted the little cat into her lap. "No ice cream for you, but you can have kitty treats. I'll try to slip you a few extras," she said in a stage whisper. "But don't tell your mom."

Minutes later, they were all hunkered in the living room, which was an extension of the kitchen, with bowls of ice cream in hand. In front of the large window that faced the street, Gina's evergreen twinkled with strands of colored lights. At the top was a star, the one Gina had rescued from the junk pile when her dad was cleaning out the attic.

KitCat nestled beside Carly on the sofa, nibbling on her fishy treats. Once the treats were gone, the cat ambled over to her fluffy bed and curled up for a catnap.

"So, when is your surprise guest arriving?" Carly swallowed a spoonful of ice cream. "It's getting kind of late."

"Soon," Gina said. "He couldn't leave work till seven thirty. He should be here any time."

Gina had sprung the news on her as soon as she and Ari had arrived. "I invited someone over who might be able to give us some deets on what happened Sunday. Not for pizza, only for ice cream."

Now Carly's mental antennae were springing up like weeds. She couldn't imagine who the mysterious visitor could be.

A few minutes later, someone knocked lightly on the door. Zach jumped up to greet the visitor, and a young man came in. Carly's eyes widened. The surprise visitor was Malachy Foster.

Malachy pulled off his beanie, and his tight black curls sprang to life. He shoved the hat in his jacket pocket, then joined the others in the living room. Zach brought him a huge bowl of ice cream.

"Aw, thanks, man. Ice cream's my major weakness. Hey, everyone," he greeted the group.

"We meet again," Carly said, not sure how much she should trust him.

"Yeah, and I really owe you for letting me warm up in your car the other day. You did me a solid. I was freezing my a— I mean, my tail end off waiting for my brother to find the place." He shoveled a large spoonful of ice cream into his mouth.

"Malachy texted me this morning," Gina explained. "He witnessed something on the day of . . . Lennon's death, and he wanted to share it with me. He can explain it better, so I asked him here so he can tell all of us what he saw."

Malachy's brow creased. He'd already polished off half his ice cream. "I was in the audience that day, but at the back where no one could see me. Like I told Carly the other day, I'm the understudy for the Marley part." He smiled nervously. "I know what you're thinking, that I'm too young to be Jacob Marley. But put enough makeup on me and you'd be amazed at the transformation."

Exactly what Hannah had said. It's all about the makeup.

"A few hours before the dress rehearsal started, I'd just come out of the bathroom at the end of one of the hallways. That place is so vast I kept getting lost. So many corridors." He gave a slight laugh. "Anyway, I saw someone scuttling toward the so-called star dressing rooms. It didn't strike me as odd, until I thought about it the next day." He looked thoughtful, then swallowed a spoonful of ice cream.

"Malachy, tell them who you saw," Gina said with a touch of impatience.

"It was Mrs. Fezziwig, or rather, the actor who played her. She was wearing a flowery yellow dress that looked way too big for her, and she had on a gray wig. I thought maybe she was running out to have a smoke—there's no smoking allowed in the building. The thing is, once you go out through any of the side or rear exits, you can't get back inside. They lock automatically."

KitCat, who'd been curled up in her fluffy bed, chose that moment to check out the visitor. She sidled over to Malachy and gazed up at him.

"Hey, kitty, where did you come from?" He grinned, set down his empty ice cream bowl, and lifted her into his lap. Purring loudly, she rubbed her face against his chest. "Aw, you're a sweetie, aren't you?" he cooed, rubbing between her ears.

"That's unreal," Gina remarked. "She's not usually that friendly until she gets to know someone."

With that, KitCat curled up in his lap and made herself at home.

"So, did you see her go outside?" Carly asked him.

"No, I lost track of her because I was heading the other way. But I didn't hear a door close, so I'm guessing she went down one of the side corridors. It wasn't till the next day that I found out Jess—that was Mrs. Fezziwig—claimed her yellow dress had disappeared from the costume room."

"How did you find out?"

Malachy stroked KitCat's fur. "Some of us have been texting each other. Jess told one of the other actors that her Mrs. Fezziwig getup went missing from the costume room before the performance. She figured someone was trying to sabotage her. At the last minute, they had to fit her for an alternate costume."

Zach looked confused. "But who would sabotage her?"

"There was a rumor that she'd captured Lennon's eye, if you get my drift. And in case you're wondering, Jess doesn't look anything like old Mrs. Fezziwig." He gave a wry smile.

Gina raised her hand. "I can testify to that."

"Anyway, Lennon supposedly tried to get her to *visit* his dressing room, but she blatantly refused. Several times," he emphasized.

This new information made Carly's head whirl with fresh suspicions. If Honey thought her hubby was hitting on Jess, she might have decided he needed to pay for his wandering eye. Or maybe Jess herself felt threatened enough to end his unwanted advances. Either scenario was extreme, but still within the realm of possibility.

"You think Mrs. Fezziwig might be the person who . . . ?"

He shrugged. "Or someone dressed like Mrs. Fezziwig. The thing is, with me being Lennon's understudy, I'm worried the cops might think *I* had a motive to, you know, get rid of him."

"But they questioned you, right?" Ari, who'd remained silent, finally spoke up. "Did you tell them what you saw?"

"Yes and yes," he responded. "I told them everything I told you. But I have a bad feeling the cops aren't through with me. They asked if I had any plans to leave town."

"They asked me the same thing," Gina said dismally.

Malachy glanced toward the front window. "Hey, guys, thanks for listening, but I gotta bounce. I'm a third-year drama major at the college, and I have early classes tomorrow. Plus, I borrowed my brother's car." He kissed KitCat on the nose and gently set her on the carpet, then rose from his chair.

"Thank you for sharing all that," Gina said, getting up to see him to the door. "The more informed we are, the better."

He nodded. "It felt good to get that off my chest. In case the worst happens and I get tacked onto the suspect list, at least you'll know my side of it."

You're probably already on the suspect list, Carly thought soberly.

After Malachy left, a thought struck Carly.

No one who treated a cat so lovingly could possibly be a murderer.

CHAPTER 12

On Thursday morning, after Ari kissed her goodbye and left for work, Carly spent an hour or so cleaning the downstairs. When the kitchen was spotless, including the tile floor, she vacuumed the living room. The tree had shed a few needles and she wanted to make quick work of those.

The upstairs, which had been Carly's original apartment, was now being used mostly for storage. Eventually it would be a guest bedroom, with its own kitchen and bath. But she'd save that for another day. Today she had other, more important tasks on her mind.

Carly sat down at the kitchen table and booted up her laptop. She opened a blank document where she could list her prime suspects. That way, she could google the names and add notes to the document as she went along.

First, the list.

Malachy had given them valuable insight into some of the animosities brewing behind the scenes. She topped her list with Honey Lennon and Jess (Mrs. Fezziwig).

Barry Grimble, aka Ebenezer Scrooge, was next. She didn't know if he'd had any past with Lennon, but that's what she hoped to find out.

Then there were the Colliers—Hannah and Douglas. Neither one had a motive that she could glean, but Hannah must've been furious when Lennon stalked off the stage on Sunday. Had she stormed into his dressing room and done the deed? Or had her husband done it for her?

One big stumbling block—Carly still didn't know the cause of Lennon's death.

Early that morning, she'd texted Chief Holloway. He agreed to meet her, but not until later in the day. Since today was her day off, she invited him for coffee and snacks around four, or whenever he could get there. At least in her own home they could talk privately, without interruption or fear of being overheard. Unless Havarti was working as a double agent, that is—in which case she'd be forced to give him a big smooch and extra doggie treats.

Ashley Blanchard was a mystery. She'd seemed glued to Honey's side, yet their personalities were so contrary to each other's. At least that was the impression they'd given. How long had they been friends? That was also a mystery. Carly added her to the list.

Then there was Curt Blessings, the prop master. Hannah claimed he'd been on good terms with Lennon, at least as far as she knew. But he'd hedged when questioned by the police, claiming he couldn't remember if Gina had touched the chain or not. Gina said he'd violated the rules by allowing her into the prop room, so he'd probably been covering his tracks. But if he'd lied about that, what else did he lie about?

Malachy was her final suspect, but she hesitated to add him. Observing how gentle he was with KitCat at Gina's apartment, she couldn't envision him killing anyone, or even hurting someone. Yet, as the understudy to Lennon, he did have a valid motive for wanting the actor out of the picture. She plunked his name at the very bottom of the list.

On to googling.

Carly didn't find much on Honey Lennon. She was listed on Lennon's bio page as wife number four but had no social media pages of her own, which shocked Carly. For someone who wanted desperately to be an actor, why didn't she put herself out there? Was she hiding something?

She moved on to Jess—whose full name she found on the website for the opera house. Jessica Terwilliger was thirty-one, with several credits to her acting career, mostly in local theaters. An attractive brunette with a heart-shaped face and huge brown eyes, she'd long dreamed of making it to Broadway. But she also loved her day job working for a local nonprofit, so she planned to stay in Vermont for the time being. Her social media pages were full of family pics and roles she'd played in different performances. It seemed unlikely she'd stoop to killing someone, but that didn't mean she didn't. Being hit on repeatedly by a predator like Prescott Lennon might have pushed her over the edge.

Next up was Barry Grimble. Carly was surprised to learn that he was only seventy-one. He'd given the impression of being a much older man. The actor had quite a history, none of it negative as far as Carly could see. His first wife, Fiona Farley Grimble, divorced him in 1991 after three years of marriage. Grimble went on to marry again, and then again. Both pairings had ended in divorce. It made Carly wonder if Grimble had a fatal flaw. Or was he simply impossible to live with? Was he the kindly old gent he'd appeared to be, or was that a façade—something a gifted actor could easily pull off? He'd been in several well-known movies, but never in a leading role. He'd always played bit parts. He was the actor whose face always looked familiar but whose name no one ever remembered.

Googling Ashley Blanchard was a cake walk. The young woman was on Facebook, Instagram, Threads, and a few sites Carly wasn't familiar with. She gave makeup demonstrations on TikTok, where she had a huge following.

As for work, Ashley had a rental space in a popular Pownal spa, where she sold makeup and gave both demonstrations and makeovers. Her specialty was doing makeup for bridal parties, for which she charged a hefty fee. If she'd had a motive, it wasn't an obvious one. So how did she and Honey know each other? Had they been friends before *A Christmas Carol* came to town? Or did they meet when Ashley was hired to do makeup for some of the actors?

Her brain heading into overdrive, Carly dropped her head into her hands and groaned.

The chief was right. This was a job for the authorities. The police would narrow down the suspects and solve the murder. That's the way the system worked.

Stop it. You helped them before, and they need your help now. The chief almost said as much, didn't he?

She got up and made herself a cup of steaming tea, a break from her usual coffee. Maybe the spicy orange blend would jump-start her senses, force her to look at things from a different angle.

Carly knew what the real problem was—she usually did this with Gina. When they'd worked together on prior murders, their minds always synchronized. While tossing ideas back and forth, they'd stumbled over more than one devastating secret.

But Gina had her own troubles, not the least of which was being a person of interest in Lennon's death. This time, Carly was on her own.

"Curt Blessings," she said aloud to Havarti.

The dog, snoozing at her feet, took that to mean: *treat time!* Carly laughed and slipped him a few liver and cheese snacks. He licked his lips, then settled down for another nap.

Blessings had an interesting background. Another Vermonter, he was fifty-seven years old. He'd worked most of his career handling props for various theaters, either in his home state or in Massachusetts. Carly's pulse spiked when she tripped over a newspaper clipping from 2012, describing his arrest and conviction for growing and selling marijuana. He'd gotten off with a suspended sentence. Vermont had since legalized the use of cannabis, with certain conditions. But at the time, Blessings had broken the law.

Hannah, as director, had auditioned and chosen the actors. Did she check them out first? Ask for résumés? Or had she known them from her years of experience in theater? Although Carly had attended numerous plays, the inner workings were a mystery to her.

She started to google Malachy when she noticed the time. "Shoot! I'm meeting Norah at noon, and I haven't even showered yet."

She saved the Word document and closed her laptop. If there was time before the chief arrived later, she'd continue checking out the other names on her list.

By eleven forty, she was showered and dressed. She had just enough time to meet Norah at Fussy Nana's at noon.

• • •

The new café in Balsam Dell had once been a two-family home. Purchased by a local family, it had been refurbished and repainted in shades of green and white. Known for its homemade Italian specialties, it had rocketed to popularity within a few short months.

Norah was waiting inside the restaurant when Carly arrived. Already seated, she smiled and waved when Carly approached her table.

Carly hung her tote over the back of her chair and draped her coat over it. "This place is adorable. I'm glad you suggested it."

"I knew you'd love it. Nate and I were here a few weeks ago and the food was superb."

A white vase containing two red roses rested in the table's center. Murals of scenes in Italy adorned every wall. The aroma of spicy tomato sauce and sauteed garlic wafted throughout the dining room.

A demitasse cup of espresso rested in front of Norah. "Hope you don't mind. I was dying for an espresso."

"Of course I don't mind."

Despite the lines beneath her green eyes, Norah looked lovely.

"Your hair is gorgeous," Carly said. "I love the new highlights."

"Thanks. I had it done yesterday. This time I went a tad darker, toned down the blond." She fluffed the back of her head with her hand.

Carly glanced around and grinned. "It's about time Balsam Dell had an Italian restaurant that wasn't a pizza parlor."

"Give me a break," Norah teased. "You love pizza."

"I do, but I love Italian food more."

Relieved to hear her sister sounding more like her old self, Carly ordered a macchiato, an espresso with a touch of steamed milk. A young server delivered a basket of fresh baked bread to the table, along with seasoned oil for dipping.

Norah ordered the lobster ravioli, while Carly chose the homemade lasagna.

"Thanks again for that ornament, Norah," Carly said after the server went off with the orders. "Ari and I really love it. It's even more special because it's for our first tree." She helped herself to a slice of warm bread.

"I'm happy to hear that."

"Bread?" Carly pushed the basket toward her sister.

Norah shook her head, and her green eyes welled with unshed tears. "The other night . . . I wasn't mad at you, you know. It's just—lately my emotions have been all over the place."

"I know that," Carly said gently. "I only wish I knew what was bothering you."

Norah pulled in a breath. She ran a manicured finger over the rim of her demitasse cup. "Before I met Nate, my business was thriving. I was earning great commissions, even with the competition from all the online job posting sites."

Norah worked as an executive search recruiter. She specialized in matching qualified job seekers with high-level positions in legal firms and technology companies.

"But you're still working, right?" Carly asked.

"I am, but not as much as I did before. When Nate and I were away on the opera tour over the summer, some of my regular clients were frustrated when they couldn't reach me right away. Meanwhile, I was touring all those wonderful cities with Nate, watching him perform with big-name opera stars during the evening. I mean, I was really on a high, you know?"

Carly smiled. "It does sound fantastic."

"Yeah, it was but—" Norah pressed her napkin to her eyes. "After a while, it got kind of old. Sure, we went to museums and plays and ate in five-star restaurants. But after a while, I just wanted to be working again. I wanted to feel productive." Norah blew out a sigh. "I-I think going on that trip did some harm to my business. A few of my steady clients seemed to have dropped off the face of the earth."

"Norah, I'm so sorry," Carly said, her heart aching for her sister. "Have you talked to Nate about it?"

Their server came by with their meals and set them on the table. Carly's lasagna looked delicious, but her appetite had tanked.

Norah poked at a ravioli square with her fork. "I have, and he's very sympathetic. I just, I don't want him to think that I blame him, because I don't. It was *my* choice to travel with Nate, *my* choice to . . . fall in love with him," she said raggedly. "I help him at his office, too. He's brilliant and creative but he's not a detail person. That's where I fill in the gaps. He's gotten to where he depends on me."

Carly wished she could offer a solution to her sister's dilemma. After years of dating pretty boys and fly-by-nights, Norah had finally found her one true love. It seemed she hadn't been prepared to face the compromises that went along with every good relationship.

"Norah, what is it you miss most?" Carly asked quietly. "And don't give me a quick answer. Think about it first." She took a bite of her lasagna.

Norah tasted a tiny corner of her ravioli, then set down her fork. "I don't have to think about it. I miss being *me*, Carly. I miss the Norah who'd stay in her jammies till noon on Sundays with a pile of magazines and a pint of cookie dough ice cream. I miss the Norah who'd let her gas tank get close to E without enduring a lecture about the risks of being stranded on a dark road." Her eyes flared. "I miss the Norah who didn't need a reminder to save her work before closing out a document!" She slugged back a long gulp of her lemon-flavored seltzer.

Carly sat back, dumbstruck. How long had Norah been feeling this way?

Norah covered her cheeks with her hands and shook her head. "I am so, so sorry for that rant," she said in a shaky voice. "I didn't mean it the way it sounded."

"You don't need to be sorry." Carly reached over and squeezed her sister's hand. "You've been holding that in for a while, haven't you?"

Norah nodded, her eyes misting.

"Well, I'm glad you shared it with me. That's what sisters are for. Now, what are we going to do about it?"

"We?" Norah smiled, then she grew serious. "I know I need to have an honest heart-to-heart with Nate. It's so hard because he's so kind and caring and loving. It's just . . . sometimes, I feel I'm being smothered because he hovers over me so much. He's like an emotional helicopter. I know there are worse things, but sometimes it drives me crazy!"

"He's a major worrywart," Carly said.

"Yeah, raised to the tenth power," Norah grumbled. She stabbed her fork into a ravioli square and shoved the entire thing into her mouth. "Mmmm . . . this is scrumptious," she mumbled over a mouthful of food.

"Don't talk with your mouth full," Carly scolded, then broke into a grin.

Norah burst into giggles and swallowed. "Okay, *Mom*."

They enjoyed the rest of their meal chatting about plans for the holidays and what gifts they were buying for whom. After Carly paid the check along with a generous tip, she leaned toward Norah and said, "There's one person you didn't mention in your gift-giving."

Norah frowned. "Who did I forget?"

"You," Carly said softly. "I'm not telling you to be selfish, only to indulge in some self-love. Take time to enjoy all the little things you've been missing. Except for the gas tank thing—you really do need to fill it before it gets down to E."

Norah laughed. "You're a good sister, you know that?" She began sliding her coat over her shoulders.

"I learned from the best. But I do have two favors to ask. First, will you please have a talk with Mom? She is super concerned about you."

"Mom? You mean the original helicopter?" Norah rolled her eyes.

"Yes, but that's sort of her job as a mom," Carly defended.

"Okay, I guess I have been kind of droopy. I'll call her later. What's the other favor?"

"Would you mind if I asked Nate to give me a tour of the opera house? If he's not too busy, that is."

"Are you kidding? I know for a fact he'd be thrilled that you asked. If you text him now, you'll catch him in his office." Norah slid her leather gloves on, her lips pursed. "I assume this is about the murder."

"Kind of," Carly confessed. "I just want to get a feel for where everyone was in relation to everyone else that day. And don't worry—I'm meeting the chief at my house later today to share everything I think might help the police."

"I know I can't stop you," Norah said with a sigh. "Just watch your back and carry that pepper spray in your pocket."

"Will do," Carly assured her.

"As for me, I'm going to pay a surprise visit to a client I haven't heard from in a while. I want her to know I'm back and better than ever."

They hugged and went to their separate cars. Carly texted Nate, who said he'd see her in twenty minutes.

CHAPTER 13

IN THE LOBBY OF THE FLINTHEAD OPERA HOUSE, NATE GREETED CARLY with a hug.

"Come on in my office and tell me what you'd like to see," he said warmly. "This place is pretty vast."

He escorted her to the end of a long corridor that led from the foyer—the same corridor the first responders had rushed down that awful day when Gina had screamed for help. When they reached the end, they turned left and walked another thirty feet or so. Nate opened the door to his office and waved her inside.

The office was stylish but simple, with clean, uncluttered lines. Nate's plain oak desk was graced with a wide-screen laptop and separate keyboard, along with a wire basket of neatly stacked papers. In one corner was a printer. Carly smiled at the photo of him and Norah that rested on one corner of the desk. Behind the desk was a large window, beyond which was a snow-covered field. She imagined cows grazing in the pasture, back in the days when the land had been a dairy farm.

Carly sat down opposite Nate at his desk. He folded his hands and studied her with his amber eyes. "I assume you're trying to figure out what happened on Sunday."

She smiled. "You saw right through me. The thing is, this building is so spread out and, to be honest, more than a little confusing. When I was with Gina and the officers who were questioning her, I got lost trying to get back to the lobby."

Nate chuckled. "Understandable. I mean, I could navigate this entire building blindfolded, but to a newcomer it's definitely a maze. Come on, let's take a tour. Although you can't see it from the façade, the building is designed in a half-circle pattern."

He led Carly in the direction from which they'd come, pausing in front of a door marked *3* with a gold star at the top. "This was Lennon's dressing room. The police removed the crime scene tape, but they asked me not to move anything yet, in case the techs need to come back. We're free to go inside, but only if you want to."

Carly winced. "I do, but it feels morbid knowing he died in there."

Nate touched her shoulder. "I hear you." He opened the door and they stepped into the dressing room. Carly moved her gaze over the contents, trying to take in as many details as possible.

A smallish couch stretched along one wall. Next to that was a sturdy table that held both a mini-fridge and a microwave. A vanity dresser with a lighted mirror rested against the opposite wall. In a far corner was a three-sided, full-length mirror. Carly remembered Gina telling the police that she'd spotted Lennon's boot sticking out from behind the mirror. Beyond the mirror was a bathroom, the door to which was open.

"He had his own bathroom?" Carly asked.

"All the star dressing rooms have their own sink and commode," Nate explained, using air quotes around the word *star*.

"Ah," Carly said. "May I take a closer look at the vanity?"

Nate nodded. "Absolutely. But no photos, please."

"Of course." She admired him for his deference to Lennon's memory.

The vanity table was strewn with makeup, combs, bottles, and other miscellaneous items. Nothing stood out, but she wondered why the police hadn't removed the items as potential evidence.

"I'm surprised the crime techs didn't remove all this stuff," Carly noted.

"Yeah, I was too. But again, they reserved the right to come back if they needed to. I talked to one of the troopers that day. He said the techs were laser focused on the drinking cups that were all over the room. There was also a portable clothing rack in here, but they removed that as well."

"What was so special about the drinking cups?" Carly asked him.

Nate crossed his arms over his chest. "Good question. Lennon never threw them away—just left them all over the room for the cleaning people to pick up." He shook his head in disgust. "He was forever sending his wife to the snack bar for soda, he liked those highly caffeinated ones. If the snack bar was closed, she'd have to drive out to a fast-food joint or a gas station. She wasn't the most genial person, but I felt sorry for her, the way he ordered her around."

"They had their own car?"

"A rental. He'd asked for a private limo but was promptly set straight. Even the main actor provided his own transportation."

"What if she wasn't around when Lennon wanted his energy drinks?" Carly asked him.

"Then he'd scream for Hannah or our head maintenance person, Jeff Dandrow. I hate to say it, but Lennon had the manners of a warthog. I never saw an actor so entitled."

Which was probably why he didn't make it in Hollywood—or anywhere else, Carly surmised. He must've been a nightmare to work with.

"Can I ask you something, Nate? And it's fine if you don't want to answer."

Nate held out his hands. "I'll answer anything I can. The sooner the police nail this killer, the sooner we can all go back to normal."

"I'm wondering if you ever saw Lennon try to get, well, a little too friendly with any of the women actors." She felt her cheeks burning at the question.

"Not personally, but I heard through the rumor mill that he'd set his sights on a certain young woman. For privacy's sake, I'm not willing to share her name."

"That's okay. I was just wondering."

"You sound like a police investigator, which you practically are," he joked. "Ever think of changing careers?"

She smiled. "Not a chance. I only wish this little town would stop having murders."

"Amen to that." He shoved his hands into the pockets of his neatly pressed trousers. "Norah worries about you. She says you cavort with murderers."

Carly groaned. "Not intentionally. You know that."

"I know. I was only teasing. By the way, did you ladies have a good lunch today?"

"We had a great lunch. I definitely want to go back to Fussy Nana's with Ari as soon as we get a free evening."

Nate threw out his arms. "Hey, we should all go together some night!"

"Now that's a great idea. Let's pick a date, soon."

He gave her a thumbs-up and led her back into the hallway. Then he stilled for a moment, his eyebrows drawn together. "Carly, is . . . is Norah okay?"

Tricky question. She was sure Norah had shared her feelings in confidence, yet she didn't want to pretend with Nate.

"She is, but I had the feeling she's trying to get her business back on track," Carly said carefully. "She mentioned that her clientele has dropped off a bit."

He rubbed his fingers over his eyes. "Yeah, I know. I hate seeing her struggle. She has such talent and drive, and she's terrific at her job. She helps me so much around here."

"You don't have an assistant?" Carly asked.

"I do, but he's part-time and nowhere near as efficient as Norah." He broke off, as if a light had dawned. "I think maybe I've been depending on her too much. Don't get me wrong. She's never complained. Did you know she watches every one of my performances, even if she's seen the same one three times?"

Carly shook her head. "No, I didn't." She was learning things about her own sister she'd never known before.

"You know what?" Nate said. "You've ignited a fire under me. I'm going to insist she take a break from helping me—and from watching me perform."

Carly smiled to herself. "You're a good guy, Nate, you know that?"

He laughed. "Come on, let me show you the inner workings of this place."

Retracing their steps, they turned the corner back to the main hallway. At the door marked *Costumes*, Nate slid a set of keys out of his pocket and unlocked it.

Carly gasped at the sight of rack after rack of colorful, intricate costumes. "This is amazing. Where do they all come from?"

"Most are rentals. Once they get here, we adjust them as needed to fit the individual actors."

Carly strolled toward a rack lined with ample-sized flowered dresses. Was this where Mrs. Fezziwig's outfit had come from? In Jessica Terwilliger's photos, she'd looked fairly slender. How had she ever worn one of these?

Nate noticed her studying the dresses. He went over and lifted the hem of the first dress on the rack. Cloth pockets the size of saddles were stitched into the lining. "See these inner pockets? If the character is plump, for example, our costume expert can use them to add padding. And the elastic waist is designed to be very flexible."

"So, with adjustments, a thin woman can transform into a pudgy Mrs. Fezziwig, right?"

"Exactly."

Carly's gaze drifted to the far wall. Along a series of shelves, wigs of every shape and color were lined up. She strolled over to take a gander at them. "This is incredible, Nate. I'm really getting an education here."

He grinned. "It's pretty amazing, isn't it?"

After spending a few more minutes in the costume room, Nate led her down a stairway to the lower level. He flicked on a series of switches, and the massive room filled with light.

"This is where most of the magic happens," he explained as he continued walking. "At this point we're standing below the stage."

Carly felt like a kid visiting a big city for the first time. Stage props covered a huge area. She recognized Scrooge's curtained, four-poster bed.

"How does all this stuff get onto the stage?"

Nate grinned like a cat who'd plundered a fish market. "See all these trap doors?" He pointed at the ceiling. "This is how most of the scenery gets lifted to the stage. There are trap doors above the stage, as well, for the same purpose. These days it's all automated, though some of the old theaters still do it mechanically with pulleys and ropes."

"I'm awed by all this," Carly said, then thought of something. "Nate, when Marley's ghost first appeared onstage at the dress rehearsal, it looked like he was floating over a sea of fog before he got down to stage level. How did they do that?"

Again, Nate smiled. He was in his element. "The fog comes from a machine hidden at the side of the stage. Not only did it create the ghostly effect, it obscured the trap door that raised Marley through the floor. Once the door was lowered and Marley's feet reached stage level, the fog dissipated." He spread his hands and his eyes widened. "Like magic."

"Honestly, it is magic to me." Carly had no idea so much technology was involved in putting on a performance.

"See that door back there?" Nate pointed at a door behind them. "That leads to the orchestra pit. That's where the musicians enter."

Back on the main floor, Nate led her into the theater itself. He explained the lighting, the seating, and how it was all used to give the audience a captivating experience. While it was fascinating stuff, Carly wasn't seeing anything that could help pinpoint the killer.

"Nate, I noticed a lot of exit doors along the corridors. Are they used regularly or are they only emergency exits?"

"The latter, pretty much. If you leave the building through one of those doors, you can't get back inside without going to the front of the building. Unless you have a key, but only a few of us do." Nate gave her a sly look. "I can almost see the wheels turning in that insightful brain of yours."

"I was just wondering if someone could have sneaked *inside* through one of those doors the day Lennon was murdered."

"Nope. Not unless it was someone with a key. My opinion?" he said somberly. "Whoever killed Lennon was already in the building."

Carly mulled that. She suspected Nate was right. No one knew the opera house as well as he did.

"Nate, would you humor me while I go outside through one of those doors? The one closest to Lennon's dressing room?"

"Uh, sure, if you want to. Good thing you left your coat on."

Once again, they went down the corridor. Nate opened the exit door that was nearly opposite Lennon's dressing room. A gust of frigid air smacked Carly in the face.

"Wow, the wind has really picked up," she said, pulling her quilted collar closer.

Nate was already shivering in his pullover sweater. "What is it you're hoping to find?"

"I'm not sure," Carly said. "Is it possible the killer left the building this way, or through one of the other doors?"

"Well, like I said, they lock automatically after they close. Let me show you."

They stepped outside and he allowed the door to close, then tried to get back inside. The door didn't budge. When he pulled his key ring from his pocket and located the correct key, the door opened easily.

"Could someone jam something in the door so that it can't close all the way?"

Nate laughed. "For security reasons we discourage it, but it happens all the time. It's usually when someone sneaks out for a smoke or some fresh air."

Carly gazed around at the expanse of snow-covered ground. The scene was breathtaking, so tranquil and undisturbed. At the far edge of the field, the land was thickly forested. To the right, she could just see a corner of the parking lot.

Looking around, she noticed multiple sets of footprints in the now frozen snow, some of which led in the direction of the parking lot.

"Nate, whose footprints are all these?" Carly asked.

"Mostly the police investigators, but media trucks started pulling up as soon as the news hit the airwaves that day. Some of those folks started tromping around the building, hoping to grab someone for a statement. The police shooed them away and cordoned off the area with yellow tape, but by then it was too late." He looked pained. "There was such chaos that day, it was nearly impossible to control the lookie-loos."

Which meant that if the killer came in or out of the building through an exit door, his or her footprints would have gotten trampled by scads of others, Carly thought.

Nate rubbed his arms briskly. "Man, I already feel like an icicle. Shall we head back inside?"

"Of course," Carly said, feeling bad for making him freeze.

She was glancing around one last time when she spotted something—a tiny red object in the snow at the edge of the building. Whatever it was, it was at least fifteen or twenty feet away.

"Nate, I'll be back in two seconds. Wait for me inside!"

Before he could ask why, Carly trekked over to the object, her boots making crackling sounds as they pierced the icy surface. She was grateful the snow was only about three inches deep, and also that she'd worn her heavier boots.

When she reached the object, she bent low for a better look. It resembled a cap to a medicine bottle—a very small bottle at that. She picked it up gingerly, then slid it into her coat pocket. It was probably nothing. But what if it was important and the crime scene techs had missed it?

"What were you doing?" Nate asked when they were back inside the building.

Carly showed him what she'd found. "I'm sure it's probably nothing, but I want to show it to the chief. Do you have an envelope I can put this in?"

"Sure do. Let's go back to my office."

On their way back to Nate's office, a thirtyish man with broad shoulders and tousled blond hair ambled toward them from the opposite direction.

Nate grinned. "Hey, Jeff. How's it going today?"

"As shipshape as it can be, boss."

"Carly, this is Jeff, the head of our maintenance staff. He keeps this place running like a well-oiled machine."

"Aw, don't exaggerate." Jeff's blue eyes shone above his sculpted cheekbones.

"And Jeff, this is Norah's sister, Carly. She owns that fantastic grilled cheese restaurant in town."

"Are you kidding? I love that place! Great to meet you, Carly." Jeff shook her hand vigorously. "Hey, Nate, I left a message on your desk. It came into the main number. Something about that costume that went missing."

Missing costume? That got Carly's attention. Malachy had mentioned at Gina's the night before that Jess—Mrs. Fezziwig—claimed her costume had disappeared from the costume room some time before the dress rehearsal.

"Thanks, Jeff. I'll take care of it."

"Nice to meet you, Carly!" Jeff called out as he scurried off toward the lobby.

Nate plopped onto his chair and invited Carly to sit. "Poor guy. Last week, after one of the early rehearsals, he offered to get takeout for everyone. Lennon ordered penne Alfredo, or so he claimed. Jeff brought him penne marinara, and Lennon went nuclear on him. Threw the pasta against the wall, made a godawful mess. Jeff, of course, had to clean it up, although everyone scrambled to help him. Jeff apologized profusely, but Lennon continued calling him terrible names. I mean, really bad ones."

Carly was horrified. "Were you there when that happened?"

"No, I heard about it later. If I'd been there, I'd have tossed Lennon out of the building."

Carly shook her head. "He really was an unpleasant man, wasn't he?"

"One of the worst I've ever worked with," Nate said darkly. "Hey, would you like some coffee? The snack bar is closed, but I can make some in our little kitchen."

"No, thanks, I've got to run," Carly said. "Not to be nosy—"

"But you will." Nate gave a teasing laugh.

"Okay, I will," Carly admitted. "What was that about a missing costume?"

Nate picked up Jeff's message and frowned at it. "The actor who plays Mrs. Fezziwig claims her costume went missing from the costume room some time before the dress rehearsal on Sunday. I'm sure it's just misplaced. Someone probably stuck it on the wrong rack. I'll search for it later." He tossed the message aside.

"Is the costume room usually locked?" Carly asked.

"Yes, but on days we're having performances we leave it unlocked so people can go in and out at will." Nate sighed. "Anyway, she needs to take this up with Hannah. I'll give her a call."

"Speaking of Hannah," Carly said with a grin, "she told me that you were her favorite student in middle school."

"She did?" Nate laughed. "When did she tell you that?"

"I had afternoon tea at the inn a few days ago with her and her husband. They wanted to thank me for being a sponsor."

"Really?" Nate tented his hands and sat back in his chair, a thoughtful expression on his face.

"Is that surprising?" Carly asked, alarmed by his reaction.

"Oh, no, not at all. She's a very gracious woman. I just . . . I hate thinking this, but I might've put too much faith in Hannah because of our history from my school days." His face fell. "The thing is, I can't help wondering—oh boy, this sounds crazy—but I can't help thinking that if she hadn't introduced me to opera all those years ago, maybe I wouldn't be where I am today. I feel indebted to her."

Carly sat back and looked at him, then shook her head. "Nate, I don't believe that for a minute. Teachers are wonderful influencers and mentors, but you would have discovered your passion either way."

He smiled self-consciously. "You think so?"

"I know so."

"Thanks for that. I was disappointed in some of Hannah's casting choices, though." He lowered his voice. "Well, one casting choice—Prescott Lennon. I still can't imagine why she chose him."

"Did you ask her?"

"No. In retrospect, I should've nipped the whole thing in the bud. Heaven knows I'd witnessed enough of Lennon's bad behavior to insist that Hannah kick him out of the cast. But if I ask her about it now, she'll feel even worse than she already does. I'm sure she's blaming herself for the dress rehearsal going south in such a horrible way."

"Yes, I'm sure she is," Carly agreed, though she hadn't gotten a strong sense of that from Hannah.

Nate ran a hand through his thick hair. "This could've been such a great week, Carly. *A Christmas Carol* was getting a lot of press, and people were excited about it. Don't get me wrong—I'm sad that a man died a needless death. But if he hadn't been here at all, he'd still be alive. And we'd all be looking forward to Saturday's opening performance."

Carly's heart went out to him. In an act of kindness and loyalty to his former teacher, he'd compromised the reputation of his opera house.

"I hear you, Nate, and I'm so sorry. I didn't think to ask this before, but does this building have surveillance cameras?"

"It sure does. Our system is wireless, so it's pretty high-tech. The cameras cover the lobby, the opera house itself, and the main corridors leading from the lobby. They're not in the branch corridors, and for obvious reasons they're not in the dressing rooms." He gave up a quirky smile.

"Thanks. I wondered about that. Did the police ask to review the images from Sunday?"

He nodded wearily. "Yup. They've gone over them with a fine-tooth comb. There were so many people going up and down the halls that day, it was hard to find the smoking gun, so to speak."

Unless the police were keeping it under wraps, Carly thought.

"Listen, I've taken up enough of your time, Nate." She rose from her chair and buttoned her coat. "Can you give me that envelope?"

"Oh, of course." He pulled open a desk drawer, removed a small white envelope, and handed it to her.

"Thanks." She dropped the bottle cap into the envelope and tucked it into her tote. "And thanks for the tour. It was fun, and informative."

"I was happy to do it. I'm pretty darn proud of this place, you know. If we ever had to shut down—"

"That won't happen, so don't even think that way."

He walked her out to the lobby and gave her another hug. She promised to get in touch with Norah to choose a date for both couples to have dinner at Fussy Nana's.

Carly hurried out to her car. The wind was even more bracing now, stinging her face and ears.

But the visit had revealed some interesting tidbits. Now she was even more anxious to have that conversation with the chief.

CHAPTER 14

CHIEF HOLLOWAY ARRIVED A FEW MINUTES PAST FOUR. HAVARTI GREETED him by running around his ankles and bouncing off his knees. The chief bent down and rubbed the dog between the ears, earning his hand a thorough lick.

Carly took his jacket and hat and invited him into the living room. She'd plugged in the tree lights as soon as she'd gotten home, giving the room a warm glow.

Excusing herself, she went into the kitchen. She returned with two coffee mugs and a slice of her mom's leftover pie.

"Rhonda's pumpkin pie?" Holloway's smile was genuine. "I'll take that any day." He swallowed a few bites and looked over at the lighted tree. "That's a beautiful tree. Val and I will be doing ours this weekend. Our first tree as husband and wife." His eyes sparkled at the prospect. "As for this place, you and Ari have done a great job."

"Thank you. We really love our new digs. We have a ways to go upstairs, but the downstairs is in pretty decent shape."

After Holloway swallowed his last bite of pie, he cleared his throat. "I assume you invited me here because you have questions."

"I do," Carly said. "But I also have some info I'd like to share."

He smiled. "Ladies first."

Carly launched into her spiel, beginning with her chat with Hannah and Douglas Collier, and ending with what she'd learned from her tour of the opera house.

Holloway took another sip of his coffee, then set down his mug. "Okay, so, let's break this down. First, Hannah Collier. She claims Lennon and his wife had a contentious relationship, which we already knew. That alone doesn't make Honey Lennon a murderer."

"But—"

"Let me finish. Then there's the drama student, Malachy Foster, who was the understudy to Lennon. Now *he* had motive." Holloway wagged a finger. "He might've killed Lennon so he could be the new Jacob Marley."

Carly pinched her lips together. She wanted to defend Malachy but had nothing to base his innocence on—except for his kindness to Gina's cat.

"As for Curt Blessings," Holloway continued, "he may or may not have lied when he said he didn't remember if Gina handled the chain. It's possible he simply forgot."

Carly had to refrain from rolling her eyes at the ceiling. Did the police seriously believe that?

"Then there's Jessica Terwilliger. Yes, Carly, we're aware of her problem with Lennon. The police do know how to conduct interviews. As for the costume going missing, that's new information—and thank you for supplying it. I'm wondering why Ms. Terwilliger didn't mention it when we questioned her."

Carly gave a half shrug. "She probably didn't think it was important."

Or maybe, if she believed Lennon had stolen it, it might have encouraged her to kill the man who'd harassed her all week.

"As for Jeff Dandrow and the infamous spaghetti incident—"

"Penne," Carly corrected. "It was penne, not spaghetti."

"Okay, penne," Holloway said with a tight smile. "The police know about that, too. Several witnesses already reported it."

"So, is he a suspect, too?" she pressed.

Holloway paused. "He's on the list, but for reasons I can't disclose, he's not a serious suspect."

Carly felt like a balloon someone had punctured with a pin.

Observing her expression, the chief said, "The missing costume could be important. I wish we'd known about it sooner. I'll follow up with Nate on that."

Over the past year, the chief and Nate had developed a friendship of sorts. Whoever imagined Holloway loved opera?

"We're also looking into Barry Grimble," Holloway said, "but we believe it's a dead end."

Holloway laughed when Havarti trotted over and licked his hand. He lifted the dog into his lap and rubbed his furry head. "I remember the day Carly rescued you," he cooed to the dog. "We drove you over to Doctor Anne, didn't we?"

Carly remembered that day well. The little dog, scruffy and homeless then, had been poking around near the dumpster behind her eatery. Thinking the little guy might be lost, she went outside to check it out. In doing so, she stumbled upon the lifeless body of Lyle Bagley—Gina's ex-husband.

The police had instantly descended on the area, but not before the dog had scurried into the restaurant through the back door. After the dust settled and Lyle's body was removed, Chief Holloway had been kind enough to drive her and the dog to his daughter's veterinary hospital. They'd hoped that Doctor Anne could help locate the owner.

Days later, after Lyle's killer had been caught, it was clear that the little Morkie didn't belong to anyone. Doctor Anne persuaded Carly to adopt him, something for which Carly was forever grateful.

And while she enjoyed watching the chief get all cuddly with Havarti, she still had questions. "May I continue?" she piped up.

"Go right ahead."

She began by giving him the envelope with the tiny bottle cap, explaining where she'd found it. "It might be nothing, but it might be something."

Holloway peeked inside the envelope. His eyes sparked with interest. "Did you handle this at all?"

"Only to put it in my pocket, and then in the envelope."

The chief tucked it into his shirt pocket. "I'll be sure this gets sent to the lab right away. As you said, it might be nothing."

Carly was getting frustrated. She'd given Holloway a ton of information but hadn't gotten anything in return. She folded her hands in her lap. "Chief, have the police figured out what killed Prescott Lennon? It's already been four days."

After a long silence, Holloway replied, "They have. They found traces of a particular substance in one of his drink cups. More than that, I can't disclose. And that," he cautioned, "stays strictly between you and me."

She nodded. "So, you're saying he was poisoned?"

"That's right."

"But you can't tell me what the poison was?"

"I cannot." He leaned forward for emphasis. "Carly, this is critical. If the killer gets wind that we've identified the poison, they'll destroy the evidence."

"I understand," she said, but she wanted to scream. She remembered something else. "Chief, this might not be related to Lennon's death, but I heard that one of the toilets at the opera house got clogged on Saturday. They had to call a plumber. A police car showed up as the plumber was leaving."

Holloway's jaw twitched. "Where did you hear that?"

Bingo. Something finally lit a fire under him.

"From the horse's mouth, sort of," she said airily. Under Holloway's steady glare, she relented. "Okay, Don Frasco told me. The plumber told him." She explained about Don having a burst water pipe.

"It never ceases to amaze me," the chief said with a clenched jaw, "how fast information gets around in this town."

"Do you know what was in the bag that was flushed?" Carly prodded.

The chief shook his head and chuckled. "You are unbelievable, you know that?" He set a wriggling Havarti on the floor. The dog sped off toward the kitchen.

"It was a black plastic bag with two prescription bottles inside. Whoever flushed them didn't count on the containers not making it down the pipes."

"Prescription bottles?" Carly said. "With labels?"

He nodded. "Medications. For one Prescott Lennon. It seems someone didn't want him to have his daily meds."

Carly had suspected drugs, but not prescribed drugs. Had someone—the killer—thought they could eliminate Lennon by getting rid of his meds? It didn't sound very efficient, if that was the case. And why flush the bottles?

"May I ask what the prescriptions were for?" she asked.

"Heart and anxiety meds. That's all I can say. Carly, I have about fifty thousand things to take care of at the station before I can go home. Thank you for the coffee and pie, but I really have to bail on you." He rose from his chair.

"I understand, but what about Gina? Is she still a suspect?"

His brow furrowed. "I'm afraid so. For whatever reason, Lennon took a strong dislike to Gina. Several people witnessed their verbal clashes. But the other thing, the main thing, is that her fingerprints are on that chain. Blessings still refuses to admit that she helped him untangle it. We simply can't rule her out."

Carly's heart sank. With all the people who'd despised Lennon, how fair was it to keep Gina, who barely knew him, on the list?

She followed the chief to the door and gave him his jacket and hat. "Thanks for coming over, Chief."

His hand on the doorknob, he stared straight into Carly's eyes. "From our conversation, Carly, it's obvious you've been asking questions."

She felt heat creep into her cheeks. "A few, but mostly of people who came to me. I didn't seek them out."

Holloway heaved a guttural sigh. "I'm not going to lecture you this time, but just be extra careful. And if anything feels even slightly off, call me immediately. Don't wait until . . . well, I don't think I have to elaborate."

A shard of pride surged through Carly. In his own way, the chief was acknowledging the critical role she'd played in putting a few bad guys behind bars.

She gave him an amused smile. "That, Chief, I can promise."

• • •

After the chief left, Carly decided on a veggie frittata for dinner. She'd downloaded the recipe a few weeks earlier after searching for healthy, casserole-style meals. It called for diced sweet potatoes, chopped red onion and green pepper, and coarsely shredded kale. She wasn't a fan of kale, but the other ingredients would probably overpower it. Plus, Ari loved eggs, and six were needed for the recipe.

She gathered all the supplies, then set them down next to her cutting board and her stainless-steel chopper. First, she wanted to check in with Nina to see how their day went at the restaurant.

She tapped Nina's number on her cell. "Hey, it's me. Just checking in to see how you're all doing."

Nina laughed. "Everything here is hunky-dory, boss. We served enough grilled cheese today to feed an entire army. So how was your shopping day?"

"Um, it was good. I didn't get to do much shopping, but I had a wonderful lunch with Norah at that new Italian café."

"What do you mean you didn't do much shopping?" Valerie squawked.

"I'll explain tomo— Hey, Nina, was that Val? Did you put me on speaker?" Carly said with mock outrage.

"I did. Listen, before you hang up, you had a visit today from that woman who was here yesterday, the one with the gorgeous tats."

"Ashley Blanchard?"

"Yep. I'll text you her business card. She wants you to give her a call."

"Okay, thanks. I'll look into it."

"Oh, and Don was here, too. He said he had more intel for you." Nina giggled. "Isn't it cute the way he talks like a spy?"

"Adorable," Carly quipped.

More tittering in the background. "Um, Carly," Valerie said, "you're going to get a surprise tomorrow. A *good* surprise," she hastened to add.

"A surprise? What is it?" Carly demanded.

"Seriously, Carly, you think we're going to spoil it by telling you?" That from Nina.

Carly sighed into the phone. "No, I guess I'll have to wait. If you guys are okay to close up, I'll see you tomorrow."

She heard the pair laughing as she disconnected. Seconds later, Carly's cell pinged with the image of Ashley's business card. "Ashley Blanchard, cosmetician and makeup consultant," she read aloud. "Wedding parties a specialty." The card was edged in a fancy design similar to the willow pattern Ashley sported on her arms. Curious as to why Ashley had stopped in to see her, she set the card aside for later. Dinner first, then she'd make the call.

By the time Ari got home, she was ready to put the frittata together. Havarti scampered at his heels as he strode into the kitchen.

"Whoa, what's all this?" Ari asked after giving her a hug.

Carly smiled. "It's going to be a veggie frittata. I found the recipe online."

"Excellent. Let me wash up and I'll pour us each a glass of wine." He kissed her cheek and went off to the bathroom, returning a few minutes later.

Havarti was munching on his kibble when Ari filled two wineglasses with their favorite Chardonnay. "Sit for a minute, honey. Tell me how your day went."

They sat together at the kitchen table. Carly related the details of her lunch with Norah and her tour of the opera house. She ended with the chief's visit, and what she'd learned about Lennon's cause of death.

Ari took a sip of his wine. "You've had quite the day. Why were you so interested in the layout of the opera house? Because of what happened on Sunday?"

"Exactly. Ari, I know everyone thinks I ask too many questions. But Gina is still a suspect, and from what the chief said, a strong one. It's crazy. We all know Gina wouldn't kill anyone!"

He nodded thoughtfully, worry lines pleating his brow. "Did anything jump out at you during your tour?"

"Actually, a few things. Nate's head maintenance guy, Jeff Dandrow, had an altercation with Lennon only a few days before he was . . . murdered. And it was over something dumb, a take-out order Jeff apparently got wrong."

"Hmmm," was all he said.

"Plus, I asked Nate if I could look around outside. We went out the door closest to Lennon's dressing room. Next to the building, I found a tiny cap from a medicine bottle. I've already given it to the chief. And get this," she went on, "the chief said the cause of death was poisoning, but he wasn't allowed to tell me what the poison was. They're worried that if the killer gets wind of it, he, or she, will destroy the evidence."

Ari rubbed his forehead. "There's so much to this, Carly. Look, I know you want to help Gina, and I do, too. But I'm getting concerned about who you talk to. Especially since a lot of the suspects are actors—people who *pretend* for a living. They can lie and be totally believable."

"I know, you're right," she said with a groan. She finished by telling him about the missing costume.

"That might have nothing to do with Lennon's death," he pointed out.

"Again, I know that. But sometimes things that don't seem important really are."

Ari smiled at her and squeezed her hand. "Come on, let's eat. What can I do to help?"

. . .

After they'd eaten the frittata and decided to skip dessert, Ari and Carly went into the living room to relax. They kept the lights low and lit the candles, giving the tree an even more magical glow. Havarti hopped up between them, spreading his furry form across both their laps.

"That recipe's a keeper," Ari commented on the frittata. "Let's have it more often."

"We will." Carly rested her head on his shoulder and closed her eyes, feeling suddenly sleepy. Her brain had been running on information overload for so long, it felt good to give her mind a rest.

It didn't last long. The thoughts she'd assumed were resting had worked their way into her conscious mind.

"Ari, I just remembered, I have to make a quick call. Be right back, okay?" She kissed his cheek, then took her cell phone into the kitchen.

Ashley Blanchard sounded delighted to hear from her. "I know you're a busy woman," she said, "so I'll cut to the chase. You probably saw on my card that I'm a cosmetician, and that I specialize in wedding parties."

"I did," Carly confirmed.

"Well, I rent a small space at a spa in Pownal. Since you said you were getting married, I'd like to offer you a courtesy makeover. Facial, makeup application—the whole enchilada. If you're happy with it, maybe you and your attendants will use me for your wedding? I can offer a great price."

Wow. Carly hadn't expected that. She wasn't sure she needed help with the minimal amount of makeup she usually wore. But Ashley sounded so sincere, it was hard to refuse. It also might be a good way for Carly to pick her brain—especially if Honey Lennon wasn't around to glower at her friend every time she opened her mouth.

"Ashley, that sounds great. I'm just not sure when I can squeeze it in."

"I figured that, but I have a slot open tomorrow at six p.m. Will that work?"

Carly thought for a moment. She'd have to leave work a bit early, but she was sure Nina and Valerie wouldn't mind. Especially if she told them it was wedding-related.

"I think that'll work," Carly told her. "But I'll confirm with you in the morning. I want to check with my team first."

Ashley laughed. "You must be great to work for. The salon is easy to find, but I'll text you the directions anyway. Lots of parking next to the building."

With tentative plans made, Carly disconnected the call.

The last thought that tugged at her mind before falling asleep was, *What the heck is the surprise?*

CHAPTER 15

FRIDAY STARTED OUT SUNNY AND BRIGHT, WITH A WIND CHILL OF MINUS five degrees. Carly hurried to unlock the back door of the eatery, her fingers already morphing into Popsicles. She was startled to find both the lights and the heat on. The dining room was toasty warm, and an enticing scent tickled her senses.

She halted in her tracks and glanced around. What was going on? Who'd gotten to work so early? Loosening her scarf, she moved quietly toward the counter. She'd almost reached the front of the restaurant when she spied the dreadlocks. Then a head popped up from behind the counter, a grin spreading across his handsome face.

"Grant!" Carly screamed. She dropped her tote on the floor and raced around the counter. He lifted her in a massive hug and swung her around.

"Talk about a sight for sore eyes," he said. "Man, it's great to see you."

When she caught her breath, she said, "Grant, what are you doing here? Don't you have classes?"

"I do, but this week they're all online so I'm spending time with my folks. That's what I love about my school, the schedule is so flexible."

Giggles erupted from the kitchen. In the next instant, Valerie and Nina burst through the swinging door and joined them in a group hug.

"Isn't this the best surprise *ever*?" Nina cried.

"It's a fabulous surprise." Carly sniffed the air. "Is that bacon I smell?"

Grant laughed. "Of course. What else? I made the biscuits early this morning. They're from a recipe I experimented with in one of my classes. Val is keeping them warm in the oven."

"I'll get them," Valerie said, flouncing back to the kitchen. She returned with a basket of fluffy biscuits covered with a cloth napkin.

Carly's eyes widened when Grant lifted the napkin. Dotted with specks of bacon and bits of orange cheddar, the biscuits gave off an aroma that made her taste buds tango.

"You'll also see bits of scallion in them," Grant said. He poured coffee and gave each of them a warm biscuit on a plate. "And for the pièce de résistance"— he held up a small bowl—"my homemade maple butter. Come on, let's sit down and dive into these babies."

They all scurried into a booth. Nina eyed her biscuit for a long moment before slicing it in half. She gave Carly an odd look.

And then Carly remembered. Nina didn't eat meat.

The bits of bacon were small, but still, they were meat. Carly sent her a silent message—*it's okay to refuse.*

Nina smiled at Carly and nodded, then spooned maple butter over each half. She ate the biscuit slowly, not with her usual enthusiasm.

Carly, meanwhile, slathered a layer of maple butter on her biscuit and took her first bite. The combo of sweet and tangy was heavenly. "Grant, this is so good."

Valerie concurred. Within five minutes, everyone except Nina had devoured their biscuit.

Grant shot a worried look at Nina. "Nina, is yours okay?"

"It's fine," she said. "It's a delicious recipe. It's just . . . well, I don't eat meat."

Grant looked contrite. "Nina, I am so sorry. I should have remembered that. I could easily have left out the bacon."

"It's okay. Not to worry." She smiled and drank another slug of her coffee.

While they enjoyed more coffee, Grant shared stories from culinary school. He looked so happy it made Carly's heart soar.

"I mean, culinary school rocks and everything," he said, "but I miss you guys so much. Carly, if it's okay, I'd like to stay here all day and help out. If anyone wants a few hours off or wants to leave early, I'll be here to cover. I plan on staying till closing."

Tears stung the backs of Carly's eyes. She took a deep breath, hoping no one would notice. She knew it was selfish, but she wished Grant could stay forever. Hiring him had been one of the best decisions of her life. He'd helped make her eatery the thriving place it was. He was also a caring friend.

Valerie, seated beside him, squeezed him in a hug. "Can I take a few hours off for shopping? I'm going nuts trying to figure out what to get Fred for Christmas."

"You don't even need to ask, and take your time." After a pause Carly said, "Um, is it okay with everyone if I leave at five thirty?"

Nina slugged back a mouthful of coffee. "Sure. What's up?"

"I made an appointment for a facial and a makeup demo. If I like the results, I might have it done on my wedding day."

The women squealed, and Grant gave her a thumbs-up. "I can't wait for your wedding," he said, stretching his arms over his head. "Let me know what I can do to help. I'm only a text message away."

"I know." Carly smiled at the group. "What would I do without all of you?"

After they'd finished eating and put everything away, the daily routine began. Valerie and Grant agreed to take turns on the grill. Grant also wanted to wait tables for a few hours so he could greet customers he hadn't seen in a while.

Carly had just finished cleaning the bathroom when Don Frasco came in. Grant was organizing things behind the counter in preparation for a busy day. His dark eyes beamed when he saw Don. They did the fist bump thing—Don wasn't much of a hugger.

"Hey, you're early," Carly said. "Let me put this stuff away and we can talk."

Don snagged himself a root beer and slid into a booth, then set his cell phone on the table. He pulled the latest edition of the *Balsam Dell Weekly* out from inside his jacket and dropped it on the table. "I brought this in case you didn't see it yesterday."

Carly refilled her coffee mug and joined him. "Thanks. I haven't seen it." She lifted the paper and skimmed the first page. The headline read *Murder Mystery at Opera House Leaves Police Stymied.*

"Quite the headline," Carly observed. "The article isn't very long."

"Yeah, I told you. No one would talk to me. So anyway, I dug deeper into Prescott Lennon," Don said in a low voice. "The man's had quite the life." He twisted off the cap of his root beer bottle, then tapped at his cell. "Remember when I said he was on his fourth wife when he died? Well, guess who wife number two was?"

"I don't want to guess. Tell me."

He sat back with a sly smile. "Fiona Farley, formerly known as—"

Carly slapped her hands on the table. "Fiona Farley Grimble! Barry Grimble's first wife."

"You got it." Don took a long pull on his root beer. "After she divorced Grimble, she took back her original name."

This was news, Carly thought. Did the police know it? Surely they'd done a thorough investigation of Lennon's background.

"Now, that doesn't mean Grimble is guilty," Don pointed out. "But it does give him potential motive."

Carly recalled what Hannah had told her during their tea date. After Grimble's first wife left him, his life had fallen apart. He remarried twice, but neither union stuck. Could he have carried a decades-long grudge against Lennon?

"I found out something even more curious," Don said, waggling his auburn eyebrows. "Remember that so-called ill-fated play, *Sins of the Rich?*"

"The one Lennon was supposed to star in before it was abruptly shut down?"

"Yup. Get this." Don scrolled up on his phone. "I found an old clip from a community newsletter from nineteen ninety-nine. The theater was in Arlonville, Mass—kind of a small, family-owned place but popular with locals. Lennon was slated to appear in the play. It was written by a John Winslow, another unknown. For whatever reason, Lennon was replaced by another actor shortly before the play opened."

"Maybe he got sick?"

"Doesn't say. The way this is written, it suggests he might have been forced out."

"Interesting." Carly took a sip from her mug. "Who was the other actor?"

"I haven't been able to find out. I'll tell you, Carly, the whole thing sounds fishy. Almost like there was some sort of cover-up, you know? That's why I want to get to this Winslow guy. He might be the only one who could tell us what happened."

"Have you googled him yet?"

He grinned. "It took a few phone calls, but I think I located the playwright. John Winslow is sort of a common name, but if it's the same guy, he owns a framing shop over the border in North Adams."

"That's not far." Carly tapped a finger to her lips. "Did you try calling him?"

"I called once, and they said he wasn't available. That's on my agenda for today. Yesterday I had to get the paper out and then I had a dentist appointment." He cupped his cheek and grimaced. "I swear, that guy's a butcher. I need to find a new dentist."

"If you need a recommendation, I can give you one," Carly offered.

"Yeah, maybe sometime next century. Anyway, I've got places to go, people to see." He slid out of the booth just as Grant came over and handed him a paper bag.

"Bacon and tomato sandwich for later," Grant said with a wide smile.

"Aw, thanks, man!" They did another fist bump.

"I'll let you know if I find out anything new," Don promised, waving at Carly. "Later!"

Before Carly had a chance to get up, Grant slid into the booth opposite her. "Were you and Don discussing the murder?" he asked quietly.

"We were, and I don't want you to worry, Grant," she added quickly. "I'm keeping the chief informed of anything I find out. Nothing's going to happen to me."

Grant studied her for a long moment. "I'll be at my folks' house for the next nine days, so if you need anything, I'm here for you, okay? And I mean that. I'm not just saying it."

"I know you do." Carly smiled. "Are you really happy at school, Grant?"

His brown eyes lit up. "Honestly, Carly, I am happier than I've ever been. Culinary school is everything I expected, and more. Ellie and I see each other on weekends. Life is truly awesome."

Carly had met Ellie only once, but she'd liked her immediately. She was warm and intelligent, and Grant had seemed smitten by her.

"Good. That's what I wanted to hear. Now, let's get to work."

She was sliding out of the booth when an article at the bottom of the *Balsam Dell Weekly*'s front page caught her eye. "Food banks profit from local woman's efforts."

Carly's breath caught. Below the caption was the photo of a young woman, smiling as she stuffed two boxes of cereal into a brown grocery bag. The tagline read: *Jess Terwilliger packs a week's supply of staples for a family experiencing hunger.*

The article went on to describe Jess's efforts on behalf of a nonprofit organization that helped stock food banks in several localities in southern Vermont. "People have been so giving this season," Jess was quoted as saying, "but we're still in need of nonperishable canned and boxed goods, along with gift cards to local markets. This year, we're also asking for restaurant gift cards, so those in need can treat themselves to a hot meal without the stress of having to prepare it." It went on to give the address where donations could be dropped off or mailed. Carly smiled when she saw that it was based in Balsam Dell. Best of all, it opened at eight a.m.

She stuffed the paper into her tote and went into the kitchen. Grant was starting on a fresh batch of tomato soup, and Nina was slicing a log of sharp cheddar. Valerie had bacon sizzling on the griddle.

"Hey, guys, do you mind if I take a quick ride?" She explained that she wanted to deliver gift cards to the nonprofit mentioned in the article.

"That's a super idea!" Valerie said.

"And a generous one," Grant added.

"Excellent. Okay, hold down the fort. I won't be long!"

Armed with five gift cards, Carly jumped into her Corolla. The donation center was located at the end of an aging, dull gray strip mall near the highway. From the outside it didn't look large enough to hold scads of donated food. Inside, however, a massive room was lined with neatly stacked shelves, each aisle labeled as to types of nonperishables.

The room was chilly, but Carly hoped she could wrap up her visit quickly. Glancing around, she spotted Jessica Terwilliger right away. She was removing food jars from a wheeled dolly and placing them on a shelf.

"Hey, good morning!" Jessica said, coming over to greet her. Her brunette hair was pulled back into a short ponytail, and she wore a red holiday sweatshirt over navy leggings. "I'm Jess. What can I do for you?"

Carly explained who she was and the purpose of her visit.

"Oh, my, that is so kind of you!" Jess accepted the envelope from Carly and peeked inside. She tapped her chest. "This is unbelievable. Thank you so much! I only hope other restaurants will follow in your generous footsteps."

The spiel was a little overdone, but Jess's gratitude sounded genuine. Now Carly had to figure out how best to pose her questions about Sunday's disastrous performance.

"I'm happy to do it," Carly said. "I'm glad I spotted the article in the paper. Um, Jess, I'm actually a close friend of Gina Tomasso. She's one of the carolers in *A Christmas Carol*."

Jess's perky smile collapsed. "Gina. She's a sweetheart, isn't she? Poor thing, finding Lennon's body the way she did. After the horrid things he said to her, it's a wonder she didn't give it a swift kick!" Immediately, she lowered her head and covered her eyes. "I'm sorry. That was so uncharitable of me, wasn't it?"

"No worries. I understand. I already knew he said some harsh things to Gina. Did he ever talk to you that way?"

Jess narrowed her eyes. "He did, but in a different way. A suggestive way, if you get my meaning." She shuddered. "Always inviting me into his dressing room with that leer in his eyes. Ugh. The guy gave me the creeps every time he walked past me. Which he made a point of doing—often."

"Jess, I'm sorry he did that to you," Carly said. "Did you do anything about it?"

She huffed out a breath. "I finally reported it to the director, and she said she'd speak to him. I never found out if she did, because . . . well, by then it was too late. But something weird happened that same day, and I'm sure it was Lennon's doing. My costume disappeared from the costume room. I know it was there Saturday afternoon, but by late Sunday morning it was missing."

"You think Lennon stole it?"

"I'm sure he did. Who else would do that? Problem was, we couldn't find it anywhere. It was darling, too," she said, a dreamy look in her eyes. "Bright yellow with flowers all over it. Long story short, I was forced to choose another dress and ask the seamstress to make last-minute adjustments. It wasn't nearly as bold as the yellow one."

Right then, a young man came down from another aisle and strode up to Jess. "Hey, Jess, I put away all those tomato sauce cans. If you want—" He stopped abruptly and stared at Carly, then his lips broke into a smile. "You're Carly, right? I met you yesterday. At the opera house."

Carly felt her heart thud.

The man was Jeff Dandrow, the head maintenance person at the Flinthead Opera House.

CHAPTER 16

ON HER WAY BACK TO THE RESTAURANT, CARLY COULDN'T STOP THINKING about Jess Terwilliger and Jeff Dandrow. She'd been so surprised to see him that any questions she might've had died on her tongue.

It probably meant nothing. They'd told Carly they were friends, but from the glow on their faces she suspected it went beyond that. Jeff explained that he volunteered a few hours each morning to help Jess stock the shelves with donated food. It made perfect sense, especially if they were dating, but the coincidence still bugged her.

She had to stop overthinking it. True, both had been verbally mistreated by the deceased actor. But that didn't mean they'd worked together to poison him. Or that one took it upon himself, or herself, to avenge them both.

Back at the restaurant, Nina was wiping down the tables in the dining room and freshening the faux poinsettias in the tomato soup cans. Suzanne had come in early. She'd been tipped off about Grant's visit and was eager to see him.

The sight of her "team" working together so effortlessly gave Carly's heart a major lift. At a few minutes before eleven, Nina turned the *Closed* sign to *Open*, and their busy day began.

It was after two when Don Frasco stopped in again. One side of his face was swollen, and he looked miserable. He slid into a rear booth opposite Carly.

"You didn't grab a root beer. What gives?" Carly said.

"My mouth is killing me. Root beer will only make it worse."

"I thought you went to the dentist!"

His freckled cheeks flushed. "Call me a wuss, but I walked out in the middle of a root canal."

Carly threw up her arms. "That means you weren't getting enough Novocain. I'm going to text you my dentist's name and you're going to make an appointment with her immediately. Tell her it's an emergency and that I recommended her."

"Okay, okay. I'll do it after I leave. I came in to tell you that I finally talked to that playwright who wrote *Sins of the Rich.*"

"John Winslow?" Carly's pulse jumped.

"Yup. Turns out he owns that framing shop in North Adams, Winslow Framing. Not very creative for a playwright. I had to leave about fifteen messages before he finally took my call. Unfortunately, it was short and not so sweet. He refused to discuss what happened the day *Sins of the Rich* was shut down for good. After which he instructed me not to bother him again or he'd file charges against me for harassment."

"Yikes. Whatever happened must've been pretty bad if the playwright himself won't talk about it. Especially after all this time."

"Yeah." His expression bleak, Don tapped the table. "Text me that name and I'll make the call."

"My cell's in the kitchen. You'll have it in a minute. One last thing. Did you interview Jess Terwilliger for the article about her nonprofit asking for donations?"

"Nope. The outfit she works for sent it in as a press release. I needed some filler, and it fit perfectly on the front page."

Carly thanked him, and they both slid out of the booth. After wishing him good luck, she texted him her dentist's name and phone number.

She only hoped he wouldn't chicken out before making the call.

• • •

When Carly told Ari about her appointment with Ashley Blanchard, he was fine with grabbing a burger from a local diner. He sounded pleased that she was doing something wedding-related instead of worrying about Gina.

The directions were easy. The spa in Pownal was located on a main road, in a historic home that had been renovated several years earlier. Carly was happy to see a glut of cars in the parking lot. That meant it was a popular place, with plenty of people in the building.

Though she'd learned the hard way that a charming smile and pleasing personality could disguise the heart of a killer, she wasn't worried about Ashley. She seemed to be the only person who cared about Honey Lennon.

Ashley's rental space was a small but cozy room graced by papered walls and soothing aromas that put Carly instantly at ease. Along one wall was a counter laden with creams and brushes and makeup containers of all sorts. On the opposite wall was a painted gold comedy/tragedy mask, the symbol of opposite themes in drama.

"I'm so glad you made the appointment," Ashley said with a bright smile. "Have you ever had a facial?"

"I haven't," Carly admitted.

Ashley laughed. "Yay, a first-timer. I promise, you're going to love it."

Carly rested her head back in the salon chair, and Ashley wrapped a scented towel around her hair. For the next half hour, Carly's face was treated to a gentle massage with luxurious creams and potions that felt like heaven on earth. Unfortunately, she had to remain quiet, but Ashley turned out to be a talker.

"I grew up in Waitsfield," Ashley said, placing protective pads over Carly's eyes. "Single mom, unknown dad. Mom wouldn't tell me his name. My mom's name was Willow and she was beautiful. She loved the theater and always wanted to be an actress. I guess that's why I'm drawn to it myself. Except that

I'm a terrible actress." Ashley gave a tinkling laugh as she applied dots of cream to Carly's forehead. "Her claim to fame was a walk-on role in *Hedda Gabler*—summer stock, nineteen ninety-two. After that, she found herself pregnant with me." Ashley's voice grew faint. "She never acted again. She had to work two jobs to keep us afloat."

Oh my gosh, Carly thought, her face covered in velvety goo. She was desperate to insert questions into Ashley's stream of chatter, but she had to remain still.

When the facial was completed, Ashley removed the pads from Carly's eyes and swiped her face with cotton balls. She finished by blotting her face with a warm towel. "There, how does that feel?"

Carly touched her cheek. It felt softer than butter. "Wonderful. I feel so refreshed."

"Great!" Ashley said. "On to my favorite part, the makeup."

Ashley wheeled over a rolling tray filled with bottles and tubes and set it next to Carly's chair. "I've selected the colors I think work best for you. Let's give it a try, shall we?" She wiggled her fingers eagerly.

Ashley started by applying a thin layer of foundation to Carly's forehead, chin, and cheeks. "Wow, this blends beautifully with your skin, which is lovely by the way."

"You mentioned that your mom's name was Willow," Carly said as Ashley closed the bottle and set it aside. "Is that why your arms and hands have those willow branches?"

Ashley plucked a large brush from the tray. "That's exactly why. It's in honor of my mom. I lost her three years ago."

Carly felt terrible. "Ashley, I'm so sorry. I didn't mean to bring up sad memories."

"No, that's fine." Ashley touched Carly's shoulder. "I've made peace with her death." She ran the brush lightly over Carly's face.

Carly had hoped to watch what Ashley was doing, but her chair was tilted back too far to see the mirror. "So, you never knew your dad?"

"That's correct. It doesn't bother me, though. You can't miss what you never had, right?"

"I suppose," Carly replied, though she wasn't sure she agreed. She'd lost her own dad when she was seven, and though she had only vague memories of him, she sometimes missed his calming presence. "How did you and Honey meet? Have you been friends a long time?"

"Oh, no. We only met about three weeks ago, when the actors arrived in town. I'd emailed my résumé to the director, figuring she'd just delete it. When she called and wanted me to come over for an interview, I nearly fell on the floor!"

Carly wondered if it was typical for the director to choose the makeup people too.

"So, anyway," Ashley went on, more animated now, "I met Honey the day after she and her husband got into town. We were both at the snack bar at the opera house, and she commented on my makeup. From there . . . well, we just clicked. I feel like I've known her forever." Ashley opened a container of loose powder and swished the brush over it.

"How is she handling her husband's death?" Carly asked.

"Close your eyes," Ashley instructed, then swept the brush lightly over Carly's brow and chin. "She's doing better. Not as weepy as she was before. She sure wants out of this town, though," Ashley said flatly. "She said if she'd wanted to go to the North Pole, she'd have hopped on Santa's sleigh."

"She hates the cold?"

"And small towns."

There was something else Carly was curious about. "The day you were having lunch at my restaurant, Honey mentioned her husband's crooked pinky. What was that about?"

Ashley paused, then, "Oh. I remember now. Her husband had a condition called clinodactyly. It's when a pinky finger is crooked because a bone isn't shaped right, or something like that. I think his dad had the same thing."

That rolled right off her tongue, Carly thought. How did she remember the word?

"In fact, one day after a rehearsal I heard another actor make a wisecrack about it. And not a casual one either—a very crude one. It disgusted me," Ashley spat out.

Carly started to respond when Ashley bent so close to examine her handiwork that their noses were practically touching. "Oh, Carly, these colors are perfect on you, especially with those beautiful green eyes. I can't wait to do your wedding party—if you choose me, that is."

Reluctant to commit to that, Carly said, "Did you have much interaction with Prescott Lennon?"

Ashley hesitated, then said, "Practically none. He wasn't Mr. Personality, that's for sure. And he wasn't very nice to his wife. I have no tolerance for men like that."

"I don't either," Carly agreed. "When was the last time you saw him?"

"I— Wait, why do you want to know that?"

"No particular reason," Carly said, aiming for nonchalance. "I only wondered if you saw Gina Tomasso that day. The police still have her on their suspect list. She and I are best friends and I'm super worried about her."

"Now that I think about it, I don't even remember seeing him that day. Honey wanted me to go out for pizza with her. She said she was sick to death of sitting through those boring rehearsals. But I was in charge of makeup for the Cratchits, so I couldn't leave the opera house."

Carly wanted to press her more, but she sensed Ashley had reached her limit. Any more questions might arouse suspicion.

By the time Carly's makeup job was complete, it was nearing seven o'clock. A huge grin on her face, Ashley raised the chair and gave her a small hand mirror. "What do you think?"

Carly stared at her image. The makeup Ashley had applied was subtle but flattering. Carly's green eyes were enhanced by soft shades of gray and mauve. "Ashley, you did an amazing job." She flashed a genuine smile. "My fiancé might not recognize me when I get home."

Ashley laughed, clearly tickled. "Thank you. Before you go, I'm going to give you samples of everything I used so you can practice at home."

While Ashley packed samples in small containers, Carly fluffed her flattened hair in the large mirror. As she did so, she noticed a photo collage on the wall adjacent to it. Pictures of Ashley in all stages of life were arranged in the cutouts. In one photo, Ashley looked to be about seven years old. She was grinning as she held up a huge makeup brush to a young woman's overly rouged cheeks. Her mom's maybe?

Ashley caught her studying the collage and giggled. "I've always loved makeup. Can you tell?"

"You followed your passion from early on. I think that's great. Now, what do I owe you?"

"Absolutely nothing! I told you, it's my treat. Just . . . please keep me in mind as your wedding day approaches. You don't need to come here—I go to the wedding venue." She gave Carly the kit containing samples of the makeup she'd used, along with a business card.

Carly thanked her and left. She was home by twenty to eight, much to the joy of a little Morkie, who leaped into the air like a jack-in-the-box the moment she entered the house.

"There's my sweetie," she sang, stooping to hug Havarti.

The tree was lit. Scented candles flickered on the mantel.

Ari came in and stopped short when he saw Carly. "Whoa! You look beautiful. I mean, not that you don't normally, but—"

Carly laughed and waved a hand at him. "I get it. I get it."

He kissed her hair, careful not to smudge her made-up face. "That woman did a great job."

"I think so, too." She lowered her tote to the hallway table. "Honestly? I had visions of leaving there looking like a circus clown, but she really did a professional job." She rubbed her hands together. "And now I need something warm for supper."

Ari made her a bowl of oatmeal with dried cranberries and sliced almonds. They sat together in the kitchen, sharing the events of their day, the highlight of Carly's being the return of Grant.

Something had stuck in her head, though, a tiny detail that flitted through her mind but didn't stay long enough for her to latch on to it. It probably wasn't important. Maybe it would come to her after a solid night's sleep.

CHAPTER 17

AT QUARTER PAST SIX SATURDAY MORNING, CARLY'S PHONE PINGED WITH a text from Gina. *Call me!* was all it said.

Uh-oh. Gina rarely texted that early unless it was urgent.

Carly called her instantly. "Hey, what's up?"

"That was quick. Well, there's good news and bad news. For starters, Hannah called an emergency meeting at the opera house late yesterday for all the actors and musicians and technicians. The powers that be, and that includes Nate, want the performances to go on as scheduled."

Carly was stunned. "But that would mean tonight and tomorrow, right?"

"Exactly, plus next Saturday evening and next Sunday's matinee. According to Hannah, Nate's been fielding angry calls from ticket holders all week. If the performances don't go on as scheduled, people will start demanding their money back. And that will be a disaster, both fiscally and professionally."

Carly and Ari had bought tickets to attend the final performance with her mom and Gary, the matinee on December fifteenth.

Slipping her fleece robe on, Carly headed into the kitchen and poured herself a mug of coffee. Ari had gotten up early and was out walking Havarti, but he'd made coffee first, bless him. "So, what's the bottom line?"

Gina laughed. "The show must go on. Malachy is totally ready to take over as Jacob Marley, so everyone agreed to perform this evening."

"Including you?"

"Um, no. I'm the only one who declined. They don't need me. I'm only a caroler."

"Oh, Gina—"

"Don't worry. I'm fine with it. I refuse to set foot in that building again until Lennon's killer is arrested. But there's another glitch."

"Uh-oh." A bad feeling washed over Carly.

"The prop guy, Curt Blessings? He didn't show up for the meeting. When Hannah couldn't reach him, she sent her husband to check on him. He'd been staying with an aunt temporarily because she lives right outside of town." Gina sighed. "Douglas Collier found Blessings lying next to his car in the driveway, unconscious and freezing. Someone had shot him in the shoulder. If they were trying to kill him, they did a poor job of it, thank heaven. He was rushed to the hospital, but his condition is being kept under wraps. The police aren't allowing any visitors, not even his poor aunt."

"It's really scary that someone shot him right in his aunt's driveway." Carly dumped milk into her coffee. "The aunt never heard anything?"

"Nope. Claimed she was inside all day and never looked out the window. She did hear a pop sound, but she thought it was from a car."

"I hope he'll be okay. So, who's going to replace him?"

"Nate's own technicians are. They're pros and they know every scene in that play. I'm not sure why they didn't use them in the first place. It's just . . . so sad that it ended up this way."

"Awful," Carly said, feeling a dull lump in her stomach. "Darn! It's Saturday. I have to get ready for work. Let me know if you hear any news about Blessings."

"You got it."

A half hour later, showered and dressed, Carly warmed up her car and headed to the restaurant. Ari's plans for the day included Christmas shopping and unpacking some of the boxes in the upstairs part of the house.

Carly was first to arrive at the eatery. She turned up the heat and put on a pot of coffee, then stuffed her belongings in the kitchen closet.

"Good morning!" a voice warbled from the dining room.

Carly went through the swinging door and saw Nina pouring herself a mug of coffee. Today she was clad in a lime green top that brushed her slender hips over a pair of cherry red leggings. Plastic elves the length of teaspoons dangled from her ears.

"Here you go, boss." She poured a mug of coffee for Carly. "How was your appointment last night with the makeup woman?"

Carly slid onto a stool and smiled, sliding her cell out of her pocket. "I'll show you."

Ari had taken pics of Carly with her own phone so she could show her team the results of her salon visit.

"Oh, you look dazzling!" Nina gushed, scrolling through the photos.

"Thanks. The facial was the best part, so luxurious. I'd like to do that more often."

Valerie came in just then and Carly handed her the phone. "My salon night," she said.

"Well, look at you," Valerie teased. "All made up and ready to get married."

"Not quite." Carly took the phone from her. "I have a long way to go, and lots to do before that can happen."

Nina twisted her fingers anxiously. "Um, Carly, if it's okay with you, I'd like to offer customers the grilled cheese I designed? Grant helped me with proportions, and we both thought it was a winner."

"Is this the one with the fruitcake?"

"Yup. Sara at Hardy Breads told me they've gotten lots of requests for fruitcakes this season. She created her own recipe, and I tasted a slice. It is beyond delicious, even if you don't like fruitcake. Instead of using large chunks of fruits and nuts, she chopped them small so they didn't overwhelm. For someone like me who has texture issues, it makes all the difference."

Carly shrugged. "Sure. I don't see a problem with offering it. Be prepared to explain what's in the fruitcake, though. Some customers are crazy picky and will want to know every ingredient."

"I'm ready for that," Nina said with a grin. "Instead of biscuits this morning, I thought we could all sample a small bite of my fruitcake grilled cheese, if you guys are up for it. I'm calling it Scrooge's Redemption, but the name is totally up to you, Carly."

Carly grinned. "That's a great name. And I definitely want to taste it."

Nina scurried behind the counter. She'd already put two sandwiches together, all they needed was to be buttered and grilled.

Minutes later, she removed the sandwiches from the grill and sliced them into quarters. She set them out on a plate so everyone could help themselves.

"You used Brie!" Valerie said before she even swallowed. "Scrooge's Redemption indeed—this is scrumptious."

"We tested it with cheddar," Nina explained, "but it didn't work with the fruitcake. The creamy, melty Brie was the best choice."

Carly swallowed her first bite, and her eyes popped open with surprise. "Oh, yum. This is amazing, and I'm not a fan of fruitcake."

Nina looked ecstatic. "Really? Oh, you guys just made my day." She squeezed her hands together and bounced on her toes.

"Show me how you made them," Valerie said after draining her mug. "I want to be sure mine'll come out as good as yours."

With that, their day began.

• • •

By two o'clock, the eatery had barely had a break in business. Shoppers, laden with bags and accompanied by little ones, had invaded the eatery in droves.

"I should have ordered more fruitcake," Nina groaned, flipping over a Scrooge's Redemption on the grill. "I'm all out now."

"That's okay," Carly said. "Your new sandwich was a hit, so I'll order more first thing on Monday."

Suzanne, who'd arrived fifteen minutes early that morning, shuttled over to the counter. "Whew! Business is rocking today. How's that coffee coming?"

"Ready in thirty seconds," Nina promised.

"I'm low on tomatoes," Valerie called out as Carly set down a mug under the spout of the hot chocolate dispenser.

"Give me one minute." Carly squirted a mound of whipped cream over the hot chocolate and topped it with red and green sprinkles. She delivered it to a little boy in a yellow snowsuit, then hurried into the kitchen.

She'd already sliced a mountain of tomatoes that morning, so all she needed was to take them out of the fridge. As she dashed back to the dining room with the container, her cell phone rang in her pocket. She plunked the tomatoes on the counter next to Valerie and grabbed her phone. The caller was Hannah Collier.

She went into the kitchen to take the call. "Hannah?"

"Yes, Carly. I'm so glad I reached you." She sounded breathless. "Have you heard about Curt Blessings?"

"Yes, Gina told me this morning. I was so sorry to hear that."

"I-I've been trying to find out his condition, but the hospital's been ordered not to give out any information."

"I'm sure that's for his own protection," Carly soothed.

"Yes, but . . . Carly, you're friends with the police, right? I wonder if you could find out how Curt is doing."

Carly hesitated. "Well, I do know the chief of police. But if they're refusing to release any news of Curt's condition, I'm sure he won't tell me anything. He does everything by the book."

"I was afraid you'd say that." Hannah's voice cracked. "I'm . . . I'm sick with worry over him. First Prez, and now this. I feel as if our play has been cursed!"

"It's not cursed," Carly assured her. "Maybe we'll know more by the end of the day. I'm afraid I do have to get back to work, but if I hear anything I'll be sure to call you."

"Thank you," Hannah said, almost choking on the words. "I just thought . . . well, never mind."

Hannah disconnected without another word.

• • •

By three, business had thinned out. Only a handful of customers lingered in the booths. A few regulars sat at the counter nursing coffees.

Peering out her eatery's front window, Carly smiled at all the shoppers hurrying along the sidewalks. Bundled against the cold, they hoisted colorful bags, sipped from paper cups, and clutched little ones' mittened hands all at the same time. The streetlamps had morphed into giant candy canes, and every shop boasted a wreath on its door. Window displays featured reindeer, jolly elves, and gaily wrapped packages, hoping to entice shoppers to stop in and browse—or better yet, to buy.

Across the street was Balsam Dell's town green, where, during the summer months, local vendors set up booths and tables, selling everything from hand-crafted dog collars and backpacks to popcorn and cotton candy. Now blanketed with snow, the green had been transformed into a miniature North Pole. While Santa bounced kids on his lap and perused their wish lists, elves served coffee and hot chocolate to the adults. Vendors—garbed in puffy jackets, beanies, and gloves with cutout fingers—peddled everything from personalized ornaments and gift baskets to specialty toys.

"At least the sun is bright today," Valerie noted, coming up beside Carly. "Otherwise, they'd all freeze out there!"

"I think they're dressed pretty warmly," Carly said. "Why don't you go over for a while? Maybe buy a special ornament for your tree?"

Valerie snapped her fingers and pointed at Carly. "Now that's a great idea. This is our first Christmas as a married couple!"

Carly headed into the kitchen, her thoughts drifting to Hannah. The poor woman had sounded so distressed over Curt Blessings's condition. Carly felt bad for cutting the phone call short, but the eatery had been jammed with customers.

Taking a short break, Carly sat at the small table near the window and booted up her tablet.

Where to begin?

An idea had begun to take shape in her mind. Twenty-five years ago, Prescott Lennon had been cast to appear in a play written by John Winslow, a relative unknown. After Lennon was cut from the cast and replaced with another actor, the play was abruptly shut down. So far, that's all the information she had. News articles about the event were nearly impossible to find. Winslow had refused to talk to Don, even threatened him with harassment charges if he didn't stop calling him.

So what didn't he want to talk about? What was he afraid of? Was he guilty of something?

Carly googled Winslow Framing, and a website popped up instantly. The site was tasteful, with complementing colors and samples of their work. They also sold artwork and other doodads, but framing appeared to be their specialty. Their contact info was listed at the bottom of the page.

Carly started to tap the phone number into her cell, then caught herself. Even if she called on a pretext, the moment she mentioned *Sins of the Rich*, Winslow would probably hang up.

She had a better idea. She went to the page that listed the store's hours. As she'd hoped, they were open on Sunday, from ten to five.

Ari would be watching football with Zach. That would take up the entire afternoon. And Carly had thought of the perfect excuse for visiting the frame shop.

Back in June, after she and Ari had officially announced their engagement, they'd had photos taken by a professional photographer. So far, she hadn't shown them to anyone. She was waiting for her wedding announcement to go into the paper so she could surprise her family and friends.

The photos, she had to admit, were quite flattering. If she were to have one professionally framed, it would solve the problem of what to get her mom for Christmas. The photographer had included several eight-by-tens in the envelope he'd given them.

Don had already worn out his welcome with too many calls to John Winslow. Maybe she could persuade Gina to tag along with her to the framing shop. Unless Gina had changed her mind about participating in the play, which was entirely possible.

Carly tapped her number on her cell.

"Hey, what's up, lady?"

"Do you have plans for tomorrow?"

"Yeah, finishing up invitations for a fancy-schmancy New Year's Eve party. I'm almost done, just putting on the final touches. I'm working with glittery gold paint and it's all over my fingers."

Carly explained her mission.

"Count me in! You shouldn't be going there alone, anyway," she scolded. "Zach and Ari will have their eyeballs glued to the TV all afternoon. Maybe you and I can grab a bite somewhere before we head to North Adams."

"What about the guys?"

"Let them eat cake!" Gina gave out a loud horse laugh. "Actually, I'm serious. Zach is bringing his mom's holiday lemon cake over to your house. Even I have to admit it's the best cake I've ever tasted."

"I like the way you think," Carly said. "How about if I pick you up at eleven thirty?"

"I'll be waiting with bells on."

"No bells, please. They'll distract me while I'm driving."

"Smarty pants."

Their plans made, Carly disconnected.

CHAPTER 18

SATURDAY EVENING WAS USUALLY PIZZA NIGHT. CARLY AND ARI WOULD order from their favorite delivery place, crack open a bottle of wine, and settle in to watch a movie.

"I think I'm pizza'd out this week," Carly said, dropping onto the sofa next to Ari. "Any other ideas for supper?"

He squeezed her shoulder, one eye on the college football game he was watching. "I heard that Canoodle the Noodle has delivery now. Shall we try them again?"

"Ooh, I like that place." She slid her phone out of her pocket and googled the restaurant. After studying the menu, she said, "Can we try the artichoke pasta?"

"Anything your heart desires."

"Your team must be winning." She kissed him on the cheek. "I'll order it now." She glanced around. "Hey, where did our faithful companion disappear to?"

Ari laughed and pointed under the tree. "He's been sleeping there for over an hour."

Carly tiptoed over to the tree. Havarti was snoozing with his chin resting on a wrapped package, his paws on either side as if to guard it against marauders.

The package, Carly knew, contained a box of his favorite liver and cheese treats. After snapping a few pics—maybe for a holiday card?—she headed into the kitchen and called the restaurant. The wait would be nearly an hour, so she fired up her laptop.

One task she'd never completed was the list of suspects she'd started a few days earlier. And now she had another name to add—Jeff Dandrow.

Motive? Jeff had taken a verbal beating from Lennon for getting his take-out order wrong. Then his friend—girlfriend?—had been the victim of Lennon's unwanted advances. But even together, those offenses didn't add up to a reason to kill someone. The act of poisoning required forethought, not to mention choosing a poison that would do the trick.

It might help if she knew what the poison was. But the chief had made it clear that it was not to be divulged.

Googling Jeff Dandrow didn't yield much information. In a prior job, he worked at a fitness club as a front desk associate. Other than that, he didn't seem to have a social media presence. Carly wondered if Nate had checked his references before hiring him.

She moved on to Malachy Foster, and there she hit the jackpot.

Malachy had performed in several plays, mostly at his college and one in summer stock. All minor roles, though he did portray the teenaged newspaper boy in *A Streetcar Named Desire*. One snarky online reviewer posted, "It's easy to land the better roles when you spend every class cozying up to the drama teacher." A disgruntled fellow student with an ax to grind? Or was it a glimpse into a more driven side of Malachy's nature?

Malachy's social media pages were chockablock with photos and video clips from his various performances. The short scene he'd performed in *Streetcar* appeared to be his "claim to fame." Portraying Jacob Marley at the opera house would be a huge stepping stone to bigger and better parts. Did he covet the role desperately enough to poison Lennon?

Carly groaned. When she thought about it, nearly everyone who knew Lennon had a reason to want him out of the picture. A nice man, he was not. Or rather, hadn't been.

The doorbell rang, jarring her out of her thoughts. She heard Ari answer it. Seconds later, he came into the kitchen carrying a large brown bag. "Dinner's here! Man, this smells good."

Carly closed her laptop and quickly set the table. Ari poured the wine. Moments later, they were dining on whole-wheat thin spaghetti with roasted artichoke hearts, and rolls made from wheat flour and Greek yogurt.

"This food is unbelievable," Ari said, stabbing a roasted artichoke heart with his fork. "We have to order from here more often."

Carly laughed. "You're eating so fast I'm surprised you can taste it."

He gave her a sheepish look. "Sorry. It's fourth quarter—"

"Say no more. Take your dish into the living room and watch the rest of the game."

Ari jumped off his chair, grabbed his dish and his wineglass, and gave her a quick kiss. "You're the best."

"I know."

Havarti raced after Ari, so Carly finished her meal and put away the leftovers. Too full to even think about dessert, she went back to her laptop. Up until now, she hadn't really focused on the Colliers.

She started with Douglas.

After scrolling through links of the wrong Douglas Collier, she recognized the one she was looking for from the photo on his website. As he'd claimed, he was a financial services advisor. He worked with law firms and individuals seeking to invest through a trusted source. From the posted reviews, he came highly recommended. The photo had either been touched up or taken about a decade earlier. Was he trying to appeal to a younger clientele by using an older photo?

There was also a link to a newspaper clipping announcing Douglas Collier's marriage to Hannah Fergus. Aha, a maiden name! It was accompanied by a photo of the couple, in which both looked ecstatically happy.

Hannah Fergus Collier was all over the place. She'd been secretary of the theater club she and Douglas had belonged to. She'd chosen the plays, collected the dues, and arranged for the bus rides into the city.

About three years ago, before her marriage to Douglas, Hannah Fergus had formed her own small theater company. Her town's library had its own theater and was pleased to lend it to Hannah on an "as needed" basis. She recruited non-union actors looking for a chance to get noticed by a random critic. She loved the classics—*Death of a Salesman*, *The Mousetrap*, and her favorite, *The Glass Menagerie*.

Sadly, a local critic had aimed his slings and arrows at what he'd termed the "Fergus Follies." One bad review after the other made Hannah's productions seem like fourth-grade-level comedies.

Carly suddenly felt terrible for her. She'd known Hannah for less than a week, yet the woman's gracious demeanor had somehow affected her. Now she really felt guilty for cutting Hannah's call short. But Carly didn't know Curt's condition. Even if she did, she wouldn't share it with anyone. If Curt's attacker found out that he might recover from his injuries, he might try to finish him off.

But why Curt? Why did the attacker want him gone, or at least put out of commission? Carly could think of only one reason.

Curt knew who killed Prescott Lennon.

CHAPTER 19

THE WEATHER COOPERATED ON SUNDAY MORNING. NO PRECIPITATION, although clouds were moving in. Snow was predicted for later in the day, but Carly planned to be home well before that.

"Have you heard any news about last night's performance?" Carly questioned her friend. She and Gina were on their way to North Adams to check out Winslow Framing.

"I heard from one person," Gina said dully. "Malachy sent me a text this morning raving about it. He said his performance was the best he ever gave."

"What about the play itself? Did it go off without any glitches?"

Gina shrugged. "As far as I know, it did."

Carly reached over and squeezed Gina's arm. "Are you sure you're okay with not being a caroler? You could always get there in time for this afternoon's performance instead of going to North Adams with me."

"No, definitely not. That place gives me bad vibes. I'm not sure I'll ever want to go back there."

Carly hoped that wasn't true, but she switched topics. "I never had a chance to tell you about my spa night."

"I hope the story comes with visuals," Gina said with a laugh. "I want pictures, lady."

"They're on my phone. When we stop for lunch, I'll show you."

Carly and Gina waited until they got to North Adams before choosing a place to eat lunch. The city itself sparkled with holiday lights and decorations. A massive lighted tree graced one end of Main Street, near the city's monument.

"Parking isn't easy here, is it?" Gina grumbled. "'Tis the season, I guess."

They'd driven around the public parking lot twice without finding a free slot.

"There!" Gina shrieked, sending Carly's heart into palpitations. "That lady's pulling out. Quick—get it before someone else does."

"I see it. I see it."

Carly swung her Corolla into the parking space just as a red SUV was bearing down on them.

"Nice job." Gina grinned and unhooked her seat belt. She tapped at her phone and pulled up the map she'd saved of downtown North Adams. "If I'm reading this right, the framing shop should be about two blocks from here. But let's eat first."

"I'm for that. I'm starving."

The main street was reminiscent of Balsam Dell's downtown. Shops and businesses in older, well-kept buildings were bedecked with wreaths and bells and elaborate window scenes made from sprayed-on snow. After walking a block or so, they paused in front of a sub shop that offered "monster-sized subs."

"I could go for a sub," Gina suggested, rubbing her gloved hands together.

The sub shop had about six tables. Gina ordered a ham and cheese pocket with the works, and Carly ordered a Greek veggie pocket with feta cheese.

Before diving into her lunch, Carly hung her tote carefully on the back of the empty chair beside her. The envelope with the photos was in there, and she didn't want it to bend. She hoped John Winslow would be in his shop, and not on a lunch break or out for the day.

After they finished their lunch, Carly wiped her hands on a napkin and dug out her phone. She showed Gina the pics from Friday's visit to Ashley's salon.

Gina's dark brown eyes widened as she scrolled through the photos. "Carly, you look fantastic. You *have* to let her do your makeup on your wedding day."

"She wants to do it for my whole wedding party," Carly told her. "She'll come to the inn and do it there."

"Yay! Count me in for sure. You think Norah will go along with it?"

Carly had asked Norah to be her maid-of-honor.

"She might, but she's fussy about her own makeup brands. I'll leave it up to her."

Carly took her cell back from Gina and looked again at the pictures. Darn, she wished she'd taken a photo of Ashley's photo collage. She'd seen it only for a few seconds, but something, *something* about it kept grasping at her subconscious mind.

"Speaking of Norah," Gina said, "I almost forgot to tell you. She stopped in at my shop yesterday looking for holiday cards. Taylor was working the register, and I guess she was getting agitated with all the customers. After Norah paid for her cards, she marched right to the back of the shop to speak to me."

"Uh-oh."

"She caught me up to my eyeballs in those New Year's Eve invites I told you about. The customer needs them by Tuesday. Anyway, in her charming Norah way, she lectured me about leaving that poor young woman alone to handle an overload of customers on a busy Saturday."

Carly winced. "Oh boy." One thing about Norah—she always spoke her mind.

"She said I should have been out front helping Taylor, or at least hired a temp to work on busier days. I explained about finishing the invitations, but she cut me right off."

"So what did you say?"

Gina let out a deep sigh. "She was absolutely right. I've been a terrible boss, Carly. It's no wonder everyone keeps quitting on me."

"You're doing the best you can. And you're putting in crazy hours."

"Maybe, but Norah has a plan. After observing Taylor, she noticed that she's meticulous and careful about her work, she's just not fast enough at it. And she's more of an introvert than a people person."

"Okay. So what's the plan?"

"Turns out Norah has a client, a big land surveying firm that's looking for someone to manage their office. From the job description, she thinks Taylor might be a perfect fit. She's going to arrange for an interview early this week."

"And Taylor's okay with that?"

Gina laughed. "She's over the moon."

"But where does that leave you?"

"If Taylor gets the job, she won't have to start until after Christmas. In the meantime, I'll hire a temp to help out in the shop while Norah finds the right person for me. She already has a few candidates in mind and she's anxious to set up interviews."

Carly was amazed. She'd always taken Norah's skills for granted, but she'd never seen her in action. She now saw a side of her that made her feel prouder than ever, and grateful to have such an amazing sister.

Gina gathered up her purse. "I guess we should go. You all set?"

"Yup. I'm ready."

Bundled against the cold, they set out for Winslow Framing. They found it only a few doors down from the sub shop.

The store was fairly sizeable and awash with light. Works of art were displayed on the walls in creative groupings. Sculptures of all sizes sat on tables. Shoppers browsed and checked out prices, most of which Carly was sure were out of her range. At the back of the store was a large overhead sign that read *Custom Framing*.

"Let's do this." Gina slid her arm through Carly's, and they beelined for the back of the store.

Two customers were ahead of them. A lanky man with a lined face and straight gray hair waited on one customer, while a petite, dark-haired woman with a blinking Santa pinned to her sweater helped the other customer choose a frame.

After ten minutes or so, the lanky man was free. With a weary smile he said, "Help you ladies?"

Carly opened her tote and pulled out the envelope. "Yes, hello. I have a photograph I'd like to have framed. As a Christmas gift for my mom." She removed it from the envelope and set it down.

"Hmmm. Nice picture. You know what you want for a frame?"

"I was hoping you might have suggestions. My mom favors shades of dark red, if that helps."

He turned and removed several L-shaped samples from the rack behind him. After trying different sizes and colors against the photo, Carly chose a cherrywood frame with a thin gold edge. "Will it be ready before Christmas?" she asked.

"I wouldn't be in business if I couldn't meet holiday deadlines," he said, scribbling down the order on a yellow pad.

"Oh, good. Thank you." Carly pulled out her wallet. "By any chance are you John Winslow?"

He lifted his head. "I am. I'm the proprietor."

She felt Gina nudge her. "Mr. Winslow, I can see that you're really busy, but I have a question. Did you write *Sins of the Rich*?"

His eyes turned flinty, and his nostrils flared. "So that's what your game is. Are you that pest who's been calling me?"

The clerk wearing the blinking Santa shot him a nervous look.

"No, but I was at the dress rehearsal last Sunday when Prescott Lennon was murdered. Wasn't he in the cast of your play?"

Winslow flinched. "That was over twenty-five years ago," he hissed through yellowing teeth. "What's Lennon's murder got to do with me?"

"Nothing," she said quickly. "But I was hoping you could shed some light on what happened when your play was shut down."

Winslow glanced behind her, then leveled her with a menacing glare. "Why are you people haunting me? What do you want from me?"

Gina moved up next to Carly, her eyes downcast. "Sir, it's all my fault," she said meekly. "I was the one who found Mr. Lennon's body, and now the police suspect me of, you know, killing him. It probably has nothing to do with your play, but if someone from his past held a grudge against him, whatever you can tell us might be important. I promise, we're not trying to harm anyone. We only want a little information."

He stared at her for a long moment, then blew out a resigned breath. "Let me finish the order and I'll give you five minutes. Not a second more."

Carly gave him her credit card. "Thank you." She felt Gina poke her again, this time in victory.

After the order was completed, Winslow motioned them around the counter. He murmured something to the clerk, then led them into a small office at the back of the store. He closed the door. "Sit," he instructed, waving a hand at two folding chairs. He didn't take a seat himself. Instead, he stood before them with his arms crossed.

Winslow looked at his watch. "We have five minutes. Go."

Carly launched into her spiel, expanding on what Gina had told him and why she was a suspect. "Please," she pleaded, "can you tell us why *Sins of the Rich* was shut down?"

He uncrossed his arms and leaned his backside against his desk, his gaze fixed on the wall. "That play was brilliant. I'd written half a dozen others, but they were trash and I knew it. But *Sins of the Rich*—that was my ticket to the big time. I felt it down to my core." He tapped his chest with his fist.

"I sent the script to the directors at several theaters, but the only one

113

interested was in Arlonville. The family that owned it were icons, ridiculously wealthy. Their heritage went back to the town founders. They were generous when it suited them, and they loved the arts." He squeezed the bridge of his nose with his thumb and forefinger. "They were so proud of their small theater. It was old, but that was its charm. They'd bought it sometime in the nineteen seventies and refurbished it to look exactly as it did in nineteen thirty-eight."

Carly could almost hear the clock ticking, but she remained stock-still.

"I won't bother with details, but Lennon tried out for the lead. He was handsome, energetic, and had a swagger I mistook for talent. Another actor tried out after Lennon, a quiet young man who took acting seriously. In my opinion he was a rising star, but I'd foolishly told Lennon he could have the lead. I had to keep my word." He reached for the water bottle on his desk and took several long gulps.

"Fast-forward to the start of rehearsals. Lennon was a disaster. He couldn't remember five lines in a row, let alone make it through three acts. He'd stumble over words, then blame it on everyone else. I suspect alcohol had something to do with it. I cut him from the lead but offered him a small role where he only had to remember a few lines. He was livid, but he accepted it. I offered the lead to the other actor, who was ecstatic."

Carly wanted to ask him the actor's name but didn't dare interrupt.

"A few rehearsals later, it was all over. My career, that kid's life." His eyes glazed over. "The kid was reciting his opening lines when the stage floor opened up and swallowed him. He fell through the trap door to the room below."

Gina sucked in a breath. "How terrible," she whispered and clutched Carly's hand.

"He might've been okay, but his head connected with some concrete blocks that were stored down there." Winslow's eyes watered and his voice grew ragged. "There were *family* members watching that rehearsal—his mother and sister. I'll never forget their faces . . ." He rubbed his veined hands over his eyes.

Carly and Gina exchanged horrified looks. "But it was an accident, wasn't it?" Carly asked hoarsely.

Winslow's jaw hardened. "No. Someone had cut through the pulleys that operated the trap door. Cleverly, so that it looked like simple wear and tear. And just enough so they'd snap when enough weight was applied."

Gina covered her mouth. She looked as if she wanted to vomit. "Oh . . . my God."

"Mr. Winslow, I-I don't know what to say," Carly murmured. "I didn't realize—"

"You didn't realize. No one ever does, until it's too late." He gave Gina a withering look. "I just relived the worst day of my life, all because I fell for *your* sob story about being a suspect. Let me enlighten you, ladies. Even if I knew, I wouldn't tell you or the police who killed Lennon. Whoever removed him from this earth performed a public service."

Carly swallowed. She felt her hands quaking. "So you think Lennon—"

"I don't think, I know, but I had no way to prove it." His fists clenched. "The police did a half-baked investigation and declared it an accident. I can only guess how much money exchanged hands. It didn't take long for an Olympic-sized pool to be installed at the community center. Or for the police station to get a fancy new workout room. The family that owned the theater were devastated, but they made sure the story was squelched. They closed the theater and let it rot there. The town finally took it for taxes. As for that poor young man's mother, she had to be taken out of the theater that day by ambulance. I can still hear her screams . . ." He covered his mouth with his hand.

Gina burst into tears. Carly slid her arm around her friend's shoulder. She knew better than to ask the actor's name, the one who died falling through the stage. "Mr. Winslow, I'm so, so sorry. It was never our intention to hurt you or anyone, or to dredge up bad memories."

His face was close to purple. "Get out, both of you. I want you out of here now."

Before Carly could object, he stalked over to the door and whipped it open. "If you ever try to contact me again, I'll file for a restraining order. Got it?"

Carly nodded and grabbed Gina's arm.

By the time they pushed through the front door and onto the sidewalk, tears were streaming down Gina's round cheeks. "And now it's starting to snow," she groused. "Could this day get any worse?"

"Come on. We're going home before it snows any harder." Carly looped her arm through Gina's and they hurried to the car.

Fat flakes dotted the windshield of the Corolla. Carly brushed off all the windows while Gina got inside the car and buckled up. If it hadn't begun snowing, Carly was going to suggest a detour to Arlonville. But it was too far, and the roads would be slick. Plus, it would be dark by four thirty. Ari and Zach would go nuts worrying about them.

They probably already were.

She'd no sooner had the thought than her cell rang.

"Honey, I hope you're on your way home," Ari said, sounding concerned. "It's already snowing here, and it's piling up fast."

"No worries. We're leaving North Adams now."

"Please be careful, okay?"

"You know I will. We'll see you guys soon."

Carly drew in a calming breath, then slowly exhaled. She'd been driving on snow-covered roads since she was sixteen years old. She'd never enjoyed it, but she'd learned to navigate slippery surfaces to avoid having an accident. So far, she'd been lucky. But there was always a first time.

It had been a first time for her husband, Daniel, too—the day his truck skidded off an icy bridge and tumbled down an embankment. Exhausted from restoring downed power lines, he'd been delivering wood to a family in dire need during the aftermath of a deadly snowstorm. Carly had begged him to wait until morning, but he'd assured her he'd be fine, that he'd be home within a few hours.

That was the last time she saw him.

Pushing away the memory, she forced herself to focus.

Her headlights on, she flicked on her windshield wipers and eased her gearshift into Drive.

"Well, we learned one thing," Gina remarked as they pulled out of the parking lot.

"And that is?"

"Now you have another name to add to your suspect list. John Winslow."

CHAPTER 20

THE MAIN ROADS HAD BEEN TREATED, BUT THEY WERE STILL SLICK IN SPOTS. Although the plows were out in full force, Carly didn't feel her nerves loosen until they'd crossed the town line into Balsam Dell.

Gina jumped when her cell phone rang in her purse. "It's probably Zach, wondering when we'll be home. Thank heavens we're almost there."

She pulled her cell phone out of her purse, then looked at Carly and frowned. "That's weird. It's Malachy. What does he want?" she said crossly.

"You don't have to answer it," Carly told her.

Gina shook her head and pressed the talk button. "Malachy, what's happening?" Gina listened for a minute or so, then offered him congratulations and disconnected.

"I never realized he was such a braggart." Gina shoved her phone back into her purse. "You'd think he'd just gotten an Oscar, the way he was crowing about his performance."

"I thought you liked Malachy!"

"I did, I mean I do, but now he's acting like one of those spoiled Hollywood brats. It didn't take long, did it?"

"What did he say about the play?"

"He said it was fantastic. The audience went wild at the end. They clapped for a full five minutes."

Carly sensed Gina was feeling disappointed because she'd opted out of both weekend performances. For weeks she'd looked forward to being a caroler in the play. Lennon's murder, while tragic, had robbed her of that joy.

"When we get to my house," Carly announced, "I'm going to make decadent, gooey hot chocolates for all of us."

Gina smiled, and then her eyes watered. "You're such a good friend."

"Ditto."

The moment she swung into her driveway and parked behind Ari's pickup, Carly felt the tension in her muscles relax. She was grateful to be home, safe from the slippery roads. Safe from everything.

Ari and Zach were so happy to see them that they ran to the door the moment they entered the house. "My gosh, we were so worried!" Zach blurted.

Ari hugged Carly hard enough to momentarily halt her breath. Then he brushed snow off their coats and hung them in the closet. "You can't imagine how relieved I am to see you two."

"We didn't go to the Arctic Circle," Carly said dryly, secretly pleased with his over-the-top greeting.

Havarti raced over to greet both women, then begged for Carly to pick him up. She lifted her dog into her arms and winked at Gina. "I'll get those treats I promised and be back in ten."

"Need help?" Gina asked.

"Nope. You sit with the guys. I won't be long."

In the kitchen, Carly filled Havarti's bowl with kibble, then removed a carton of whole milk from the fridge. She gathered sugar, unsweetened cocoa, marshmallows, and a semisweet chocolate bar from her cupboard and set them on the counter. As the milk warmed in her large saucepan, she set the marshmallows on a nonstick cookie sheet and turned the oven on high. While the marshmallows roasted, she added the remaining ingredients to the saucepan and whisked it until the semisweet bar melted. Once the mixture reached a simmer, she ladled equal amounts into four oversized mugs.

The marshmallows were perfect, lightly browned on top. She spooned them up and divided them among the four mugs. She topped them with colorful sprinkles and plunged a red, white, and green candy cane into each mug. They made perfect festive stirrers.

"Masterpieces, if I do say so myself," she said with a self-satisfied giggle.

She set them on a tray with a pile of napkins and carried them into the living room. Gina and Zach were huddled on the sofa. Ari sat in one of the overstuffed chairs.

"These are hot, everyone, so don't burn your lips."

They each helped themselves to a mug.

"Whoa, you weren't kidding when you said decadent." Gina stirred her mixture with her candy cane and took a careful sip. "This is the best hot cocoa I've ever had!"

Zach, sporting a marshmallow mustache, looked as if he'd discovered a new planet. "Okay, like, I'm serious now. This stuff is the nectar of the gods."

"By the way," Carly said drolly, "I saw what's left of the cake in the fridge. I'm amazed there's even a crumb left for Gina and me."

The men looked at each other and burst out laughing. Carly and Gina laughed, too.

From her overstuffed chair, Carly floated her gaze over the living room. The tree lights twinkled in the front window. Ari had switched from the football game to the station that played holiday music. Havarti had returned to his post guarding his wrapped gift.

It was a scene she wanted to store in her mind and keep forever.

Her mug empty, she set it down on the table beside her. She felt her eyelids droop and then finally close.

A loud scraping sound jerked her out of her slumber. She rubbed her eyes and saw Gina scrunched up on the sofa, her head resting on a throw pillow.

Carly rose from her chair and opened the front door. Through the glass storm door, she saw Ari shoveling the driveway, while Zach scraped ice and snow from his car. They both spotted her and waved. She smiled and waved back.

Tomorrow was a workday. They all needed a good night's rest.

Much as she loved her friends, she breathed a sigh of relief after Gina and Zach left. Ten minutes later, Gina texted to say they'd arrived safely at her apartment.

Carly was too tired to describe her stressful day to Ari but promised to fill him in at breakfast.

Sleep came instantaneously that night, but her dreams were dark and frightening. The vision of a man plummeting through a trap door, his eyes wide with horror, awakened her several times.

After a fitful night, morning came as a blessing.

CHAPTER 21

CARLY'S ORIGINAL PLAN FOR MONDAY MORNING HAD BEEN TO LEAVE home extra early and head to Hardy Breads. Although Monday was the eatery's regular bread delivery day, her order usually arrived sometime in the afternoon. She wanted to surprise Nina by having the fruitcake loaves ready for opening at eleven.

She changed her mind when she checked the road conditions online. Although the sun was blindingly bright and the main roads down to bare pavement, the side streets remained treacherous in spots. Much as it made her feel like a wimp, she was still rattled from the trip home from North Adams the day before.

"I wish you had asked me for help," Ari said with a sigh after Carly described her visit to Winslow Framing. "I could've gone there with you." He set two plates of scrambled eggs and wheat toast on the table.

Havarti watched with eager brown eyes, his gaze flicking back and forth between Carly and Ari. Carly reached down and rubbed his furry head.

She smiled at her breakfast. The eggs were fluffy and the toast browned to perfection. "And have you miss football?" she teased him, knowing it was a lame answer.

He pretended to mull the question. "Hmmm, let's see. Would I rather watch football or be there to support my fiancée when she needs me most?" He sprinkled pepper on his eggs and scooped up a forkful.

"Well, how noble of you," she said a bit tartly, then buttered a slice of toast.

Ari swallowed his eggs. "Sorry, that's not how I meant it. Want more coffee?"

"Sure."

He lifted the carafe off the table and topped off their mugs.

"Okay, okay. I get what you're saying," Carly conceded. "But I did tell you where we were going yesterday." She broke off a corner of scrambled egg and slipped it to Havarti.

"Yes, but not *why* you went border hopping when Balsam Dell has two perfectly good framing shops."

Okay, he had her there. But she also wasn't thrilled with his questioning her reasons.

It wasn't a matter of trust. She knew that. He worried about her safety.

Carly had to admit, in the past she'd gotten herself into a few dicey situations asking questions of the wrong people.

"On a more positive note," she said, changing the subject, "downtown North Adams was so beautiful, all decked out for the holidays. It reminded me of our town, only on a larger scale."

He smiled. "See anything there you'd like for Christmas?"

"I might've if it hadn't started snowing. We saw some adorable shops."

Ari swallowed a bite of toast. "Maybe some afternoon we can both play hooky and go shopping there. We'll look for a nice place to have dinner."

"Ooh, I like that plan." She reached over and squeezed his muscled arm.

After feeding Havarti a few more nibbles of egg, she kissed Ari and rinsed her dishes in the sink.

Before she left for the restaurant, she called Sara at Hardy Breads. "Hey, any chance you can add four fruitcakes to my order before the van leaves?"

Sara's smile came through the phone. "You called in the nick of time. I made two dozen loaves yesterday. Colm's loading up the van now."

"Oh, you're a gem." She explained how popular Nina's new sandwich was. "Any chance you can deliver a little earlier today?" she cajoled.

"For you? You bet I can. I'll have Colm put you at the top of his delivery route."

"I owe you big," Carly told Sara with a grateful laugh. "Any grilled cheese you want, on me. Colm, too."

"Don't be silly. You're one of our best customers. But if we ever get away from the bakery, we'll definitely take you up on that offer!"

Nina and Valerie arrived at work almost at the same time. After they all exchanged stories about each other's day off, they went about their daily routine.

"Thank you for ordering more fruitcakes," Nina told Carly, giving her a light hug. Her eyes were bright. Her short blond hair was a new shade, more pumpkin than yellow. "And I made a huge batch of cookies yesterday. I put enough in the freezer to last us through the week."

"That's great. Thanks, Nina."

Carly wished she knew more about Nina's background. She was smart and capable and terrific with people. But in the months Carly had known her, she'd never talked about family or friends. She lived in a small apartment in an older but well-maintained brick building. Carly suspected Nina had suffered some setbacks in life. On a few occasions she'd caught her staring off into space, as if rummaging through old memories.

Hoping for a busy day, Carly worked in the kitchen until opening. Suzanne came in early again, this time bearing gifts.

"I made these yesterday for your trees." She grinned as she pulled out tissue-wrapped gifts from a shopping bag. She gave one to each of them.

They unwrapped their gifts simultaneously. Nina was first to squeal. "Suze, this is gorgeous!" She held up a tree-bulb that was painted gold and topped with a crocheted angel.

Valerie's bulb was sky blue, and Carly's was mint green. The crocheted angels looked too delicate to touch, but Suzanne assured them they were sturdy.

"This is so sweet of you," Carly said. "Thank you, Suzanne. I can't wait to add it to our tree."

Valerie stared at hers, then smiled at Suzanne. "This is way nicer than the one I bought across the street yesterday. You're a sweetheart, you know that?"

"Yeah, don't let it get around." Suzanne hung her coat in the closet and put on a clean apron. "Gave me something to do yesterday while Jake and Josh were out doing *sporty* things." She rolled her eyes. "They rented snowmobiles and rode on a trail. Needless to say, I was not a happy camper."

"Why? You think Josh is too young?" Valerie asked her. She coughed into her upper arm.

"Definitely! I mean, okay, sure, there were other kids there. And they all got safety instructions first. And Jake didn't let him out of his sight." She waved a hand. "Oh, maybe I'm just a crazy old mama bear who worries too much about her kid."

Nina set down her ornament, then went over and took Suzanne's hands in her own. "I'd choose you for my mama bear any day of the week." She hugged her quickly, then left Suzanne staring openmouthed at her as she scurried into the dining room.

Suzanne's cheeks reddened. "Wow. I wasn't expecting that."

Carly wasn't surprised. She'd learned that Nina wore her squishy marshmallow heart on her always colorful sleeve.

• • •

True to her word, Sara had instructed Colm to stop at Carly's before he began his regular deliveries. It was barely nine thirty when his delivery van rumbled into the lot behind the eatery. Carly met him at the back door.

Colm wheeled his dolly inside, his black-rimmed glasses fogging from the sudden warmth. The fruitcakes were on top in a brown paper bag.

"Thanks, Colm. I appreciate your coming by early today."

"No problem." He handed her a clipboard.

Carly signed for the delivery, then handed him a cellophane bag containing two decorated cookies.

"Thanks! I'll eat these in the van. See you next week!" He hustled toward his vehicle.

"One of those is for Sara!" Carly called out.

He waved a dismissive hand at her and hopped into his van.

Carly closed the door against the freezing cold. She suspected Sara didn't stand a chance at getting one of those cookies.

At two minutes before eleven, the eatery opened. Customers trickled in, their noses red from the cold and their appetites hearty.

By the time Carly had a few minutes for a lunch break, she noticed she'd missed a call on her cell phone. The number was from a Massachusetts exchange. Carly played the message.

"Miss Hale, this is Peg Winslow. My husband spoke to you yesterday at our shop in North Adams. Would you please call me? I have some information that might help you." She repeated her name and gave out her phone number.

Carly's heart pounded. Peg Winslow. John Winslow's wife!

Information that might help her.

She sat at the small table in the kitchen, her pulse racing at warp speed. She tapped in Peg Winslow's number.

Peg answered in a voice that was soft and lilting. "Hello? Is this Carly?"

"Yes, Mrs. Winslow. I got your message."

"Thank you for calling me back, and please call me Peg."

"Sure thing. Peg, you said you have some information for me?"

"Yes, but I was hoping to see you in person. Our shop is closed on Mondays, and John will be working all day on orders. I told him I was having lunch with friends and then going shopping. I . . . I googled you and found out you have a restaurant in Balsam Dell. Will you be there all day?"

"I will," Carly said. Good old Google!

"Great. If you don't mind, I can be there in forty-five minutes or so. Does that work with your schedule?"

Heck, yes! Carly almost shouted. "It's perfect."

Carly explained the parking situation in downtown Balsam Dell. After they disconnected, she ate a quick salad and returned to the dining room.

The booths were mostly empty. Three lone diners sat at the counter. She smiled at the one seated closest to the door. His attention was focused on Nina, who stood gabbing behind the counter. From the bits of conversation Carly caught, it sounded as if Nina was regaling him with tales of past baking disasters.

With a wink at Nina, Carly sidled up quietly behind Don. "Well, fancy seeing you here today. How did you make out with your tooth?"

Don swiveled around on his stool, a red flush staining his freckled face. "Geez, talk about sneaking up on a guy." He lowered his voice an octave. "To answer your question, I made out fine. You were right about your dentist. She gave me an emergency appointment on Saturday. Root canal done. Pain gone. Well, almost. But it's a thousand times better than it was."

"I am delighted to hear that."

Don gave Nina a crooked smile. "Hey, I have something I need to tell Carly. I'll be back in a jiff, okay?"

"You'd better be!" Nina's grin was wider than the Walloomsac River.

"How long is a jiff?" Carly teased him as they headed for a rear booth.

"Don't be a wiseacre or I won't tell you about the *very interesting* convo I overheard at the performance yesterday."

Carly's ears perked. "Performance? Did you see *A Christmas Carol*?"

"Don't be so antsy. Let's sit first."

They slid into a booth, Carly's impatience shifting into overdrive. "So, whose convo did you overhear?"

He gave her a smug look, then leaned forward. "Yesterday's performance was sold out, but there was a cluster of seats at the back that'd been earmarked for students. Thanks to Nate—good guy, by the way—I was able to snag one. Free."

Thank you, Nate!

"So again, whose convo did you overhear?"

His eyes glittered. "Three young guys were sitting in front of me. While I waited for the performance to start, I eavesdropped on their chatter. I figured out real quick that they were drama students at Malachy Foster's college. When the curtain closed at intermission, they started dissing him like crazy."

"Dissing how?" Carly asked.

"They called him a showoff, a poser, stuff like that. Then, get this. One of them said, 'Foster does it again! From lowly understudy to the star of the show. Who's he going to bump off next?' Then they all started laughing like a bunch of hyenas."

Carly felt her jaw drop. "Did you ask what they meant by that?"

"I did. Pretending I was Donny the dunce, I tapped the guy on the shoulder and asked—very innocently, mind you—what he meant by that. He said when Foster was trying out for summer stock, the actor who was supposed to be some paperboy in *Streetcar* got violently ill the morning of the performance. Enter Malachy Foster, who knew the lines by heart. He apparently nailed the role and was praised by local critics."

How convenient, Carly thought. Too convenient?

"The actor who got sick, was he okay?"

"Yeah, he was fine," Don said. "Supposedly he'd gotten food poisoning, but they couldn't figure out what triggered it. Quite a coincidence, right?"

"Yeah, for sure." Carly drummed her fingers on the table. "Is that it?"

"What else do you want?" Don asked irritably. He rubbed his fingers over his face and groaned. "I guess it would help to know if the food poisoning was intentional, but we have no way of knowing that."

"The thing is," Carly said slowly, "even if it was intentional, the actor survived. 'Bump off' implies killing someone, doesn't it?"

Don made a face, then said, "Okay, what about this? Maybe Malachy intended to get rid of him permanently but messed up somehow and the guy pulled through."

"But why kill off a fellow actor when you can achieve the same goal by making him too sick to perform? It doesn't make sense."

"Good grief, Carly, we're going in circles. Did you ever consider that Malachy might be a sociopath? You're the one who met him in person. What did you think?"

Carly shook her head. She still had trouble believing Malachy was a killer. She kept picturing how gentle he was with Gina's kitty.

Except that, she had to admit, she'd been fooled before.

"Okay, let's go back to Lennon," Don said, when she didn't respond. "Maybe Malachy only intended to make him sick but somehow it backfired."

Now that she knew about the summer stock incident, Carly had to admit it was a possibility. It would help if she knew what poison had been used. Maybe another call to the chief was in order.

"Did you ask those guys who the actor was who got sick?" Carly prodded him.

"I started to, but then the three of them flew out of their seats and ran for the concession. They didn't get back until the curtain went up. By the time the audience finished their standing ovation, those guys were out of there."

Carly's head was whirling like a top. She rubbed her temples with her fingers, hoping to stave off the headache that was blossoming behind her eyes.

"I have some news, too," she said, keeping her voice low. She gave him a recap of her unpleasant encounter with John Winslow the day before.

Don looked at her with something like awe. "I can't believe the guy actually *talked* to you. He treated me like I was sending him the bubonic plague through the phone."

"Believe me, he was none too pleasant with me and Gina."

"So now we know why the play was shut down," Don mused aloud. "But it doesn't really help, does it?"

It might help if we knew who fell to his death through that trap door, Carly thought.

She glanced at the wall clock. Peg Winslow was due to arrive soon. Should she tell Don she was expecting her? If she did, he'd pester her to let him sit in on their meeting.

No, she decided. Her conversation with Peg had to be private.

"Getting back to Malachy," Carly said, "do you think you can find out who that other actor was who got food poisoning?"

Don shrugged. "I already put a few feelers out, but so far no one's responded. A reporter's work is never done," he said with a long-suffering sigh.

"Cheer up," Carly said with a smile. "As long as the earth is still spinning, it'll never be done."

125

CHAPTER 22

It was nearly three when Peg Winslow came in. Suzanne had already gone home. Nina had taken over the grill for Valerie, who was finishing up a few tasks in the kitchen.

Even without her blinking Santa pin, Carly recognized Peg immediately. Bundled in a black wool coat and plaid scarf, she looked even tinier than the petite woman Carly remembered from the framing shop.

Peg smiled when Carly welcomed her, but her gaze was jittery.

Carly led her to the rear booth, the same one she and Don had vacated earlier. She set down two mugs of coffee.

"Ah, just what I needed," Peg said, unbuttoning her coat. She added sugar to her coffee. "Your décor is charming, by the way. So reminiscent of a kinder, gentler era. If I lived locally, I'd come in here all the time."

"Thank you. It used to be an ice cream parlor, so adapting it to a grilled cheese eatery was a natural transition. Although it did take some work to make it look this way." Carly stirred her coffee. "Tell me, how did you figure out who I was?"

"Oh, heck. That was easy. Your contact info was on your order slip." Peg took a tiny sip from her mug, two worry lines crinkling the bridge of her nose. "John told me about your conversation yesterday. I'm so sorry you had to see him at his worst. He's actually a thoughtful and generous man. What you witnessed was, well, not the real John."

"You don't need to apologize," Carly said. "I felt bad, too—not for me and Gina, but for him. We obviously dredged up some painful memories."

Peg cleared her throat. "I didn't know John back when all that happened. We met about twelve years ago when we both volunteered at the library to assist ESL students—English as a second language. Mostly we joined conversation groups. It was so rewarding. John put his all into it. I'm a teacher by profession, although I work full-time in the store now." She sniffled. "I'm sorry, I don't mean to bore you. Or make excuses for John."

"You're not boring me at all." Carly reached over and gave her hand a quick squeeze.

"Anyway, after we'd been dating a few months, he told me about that terrible day. Carly, he cried his heart out. I was so shaken by the depth of his anguish that I didn't know what to say or do." She blinked. "Soon after that we got married. I've never regretted it. John has his down days, but for the most part we're a happy couple."

Carly smiled. "Then you both chose the right partner. Peg, from what I gathered, your husband believes Prescott Lennon rigged that trap door. Didn't the police question him?"

She shrugged. "Supposedly they did, but nothing came of it. The family that owned the theater was very influential in town. They chose to believe it was an accident, and the authorities deemed it so. The thing is, only a month before rehearsals started, the building inspector cited the owner for minor safety violations. It wasn't clear if the violations were corrected before rehearsals for *Sins of the Rich* began. Or if the violations had anything to do with the trap door."

What a convoluted mess, Carly thought.

"Do you know if the actor's family sued the theater?" Carly asked.

Peg's smile was flat. "I'm not sure about a lawsuit, but John said the young man's family was paid a sizeable wrongful death benefit. I think the owners did it voluntarily to avoid the humiliation of a court battle."

Carly still didn't understand. Why wouldn't the owners want the culprit prosecuted?

"I know what you're thinking," Peg said quietly. "From what John said, the problem was lack of evidence. Sure, Lennon was furious at losing the lead role. Everyone knew that. But there was no evidence to prove he rigged that trap door."

"Circumstantial," Carly murmured. "Not enough to hold up in court."

"Precisely." Peg reached into her purse and extracted a folded sheet of paper. "John told me he destroyed every single reminder of that play. But when we bought our new condo a few years ago, I found this when I was packing up his office." She unfolded the paper and handed it to Carly.

Carly let out a gasp. "This is the playbill from *Sins of the Rich*."

"It's a copy," Peg said. "I kept the original. Not very fancy. John had to use his own funds to have them printed."

The title of the play and the playwright's name were printed in the first section. The actors' names and the characters they portrayed were listed in the middle section. The last section gave credit to the costume designer and the technicians who made it all possible.

"It sure is bare bones, isn't it?" Carly commented, thinking of the glossy, multipage playbill created for *A Christmas Carol*.

Peg nodded. "Everyone thought the play would flop like John's other plays did, so no one wanted to invest in it." Her brown eyes blazed fiercely. "Carly, I read that play. It's superb, and I swear I'm not being biased."

Carly stared at her. "But . . . how did you read it? Didn't you say John destroyed every reminder?"

"He did, but not the original script. I found it hidden in a cardboard envelope in the back of his closet." She blinked back tears. "When push came to shove, I guess he couldn't part with it. He knew it was the best thing he'd ever written."

Carly was so stunned she didn't know what to say. She scanned the actors' names again. Prescott Lennon's was listed as the lead.

"This playbill wasn't the final one, was it?" Carly pointed out Lennon's name.

"Apparently not. I assume John destroyed the others. Either he kept this one intentionally or he somehow missed it."

Carly perused the list of actors. Including Lennon, five were men. Was one of them the actor who took over the lead role, only to be thwarted by his tragic death?

Peg's voice was shaky now. "Being here, telling you what I know, makes me feel disloyal to my husband—something I have never been." She swiped at her eyes with her thumbs.

Carly suddenly felt like a monster. She'd forced John Winslow to relive the tragedy that had changed him forever, all to prove that Gina was innocent of Lennon's murder. The connection between the two deaths was twenty-five years old—and sliver thin. A thread that would snap with the slightest bit of tension.

She opened her mouth to apologize to Peg, but the words got trapped in her throat.

"I should go," Peg said. "But I want you to understand one thing. John lives with his guilt every day of his life. If Lennon rigged that trap door, and John's sure he did, he did it to hurt John, not that poor young actor. John can't get past that. He blames himself for that young man's death."

Carly's stomach ached. She felt as if she'd swallowed a jagged rock. "Peg, why did you come here?"

Peg sniffled hard and blotted her eyes with a napkin. "Because, if there's even a miniscule chance of a connection between what happened back then and Lennon's death, I don't want an innocent person—your friend—to pay the price."

Her throat clogging, Carly rose to walk Peg to the door.

"And Carly," Peg said, buttoning her coat, "don't worry about your order. John will do a fantastic job and it'll be ready in time for Christmas. That I can promise."

Carly started to give her a hug, but Peg flew out the door so quickly she never got the chance.

• • •

Valerie was loading the commercial dishwasher when Carly shuffled into the kitchen. "You look like you've seen a ghost," Valerie said with concern. "What's wrong?"

"That bad, huh?" Carly rubbed her cheeks, hoping to infuse some color. "Nothing to worry about. It's just a headache. I have some ibuprofen in my tote."

She dug her tote out of the coat closet and fished around the bottom, where every small item seemed to have gone into witness protection.

Valerie coughed slightly, then came over and took her arm. "Seriously, you don't look that great. Sit down and I'll get your ibuprofen."

Carly dropped onto a chair at the small table, her chest tight and her head throbbing. By the time Valerie handed her a glass of ice water and her ibuprofen bottle, she felt her eyes brimming with tears.

With a worried look, Valerie sat down opposite Carly. "What is it, sweetie? Anything I can help with? I saw you talking to a woman before. You both looked pretty serious."

Carly blotted her eyes with her fingers and then swallowed the ibuprofen. "I did everything the chief warned me against. It was one thing when I was giving him real information. I mean, then I was actually helping. But this time I've hurt people who didn't deserve it. All to pursue a crazy theory that got stuck in my stubborn head."

She gave Valerie a shortened version of her encounters with John and Peg Winslow.

For a long moment, Valerie was silent. She ran her finger absently around a coffee stain on the table. When she finally looked up, she said, "Carly, I think it's time I talked to Fred about this. I know I promised you both I'd never take sides in these . . . investigations. But let me tell you something. If you think Fred doesn't value your input, you're wrong."

Carly groaned. "I know he does, Val. I'm just not sure how seriously he takes all my, you know, theories."

Valerie shifted on her chair. "Keep in mind," she reminded, "the state police have the lead on homicides. Fred doesn't turn over any information to them unless he feels it's verifiable. He's a stickler for facts." She smiled and jiggled Carly's hand. "You know that, right?"

"I do." Carly sighed. "So, what do you suggest?"

Valerie folded her hands on the table. "I'd like to ask him to come over here. You can talk privately right here. Nina and I will handle the dining room."

It sounded like a plan to Carly. "Do you think he has time? I know he's been slammed."

Valerie smiled and pulled her cell phone out of her pants pocket. "Let's find out."

CHAPTER 23

"HEY, CHIEF. THANKS FOR COMING OVER."

Carly sat at the kitchen table, motioning for him to do the same.

Holloway pulled out a chair and sat opposite her. Dark circles rimmed his lower eyelids. The stress of the past several days was taking its toll.

"Truth be told," the chief said, "I was glad to take a break. I've had my head buried so deep in this investigation I can barely see daylight anymore."

Carly understood the feeling, but she knew it was worse for the chief.

Valerie came in with two mugs of peppermint tea and set them on the table. She gave her husband a quick kiss and scooted out of the kitchen.

A flush in his cheeks, Holloway sipped his tea and smiled. "Val knows exactly how I like my tea. Nice change from coffee, isn't it?"

Carly knew he was stalling, making small talk before deciding where to begin. In truth, she'd take coffee over tea any day, but the peppermint tea was a welcome treat, especially during the holiday season.

"Carly, why don't you go first," Holloway said. "Val told me a little about what happened, but I want to hear the entire story from you."

Taking in a slow, calming breath, Carly told him everything. She started with Don Frasco finding an obscure article about Lennon's role in *Sins of the Rich*. She described her jaunt to North Adams with Gina, and John Winslow's furious dismissal of them. She ended with her conversation with Peg Winslow, and the guilt she felt for causing distress to both husband and wife.

To her surprise, Holloway reached over and patted her hand. "Carly, you are being way too hard on yourself. You followed your instincts so you could help Gina, and it backfired. Period. Cops go through it all the time. You think everyone they interview welcomes them with open arms?"

Carly quirked a half smile. He was trying to ease her pain by putting her on a par with the police. Unfortunately, it didn't erase the torment she saw in John Winslow's eyes, or the sadness reflected in his wife's.

"If it eases your mind," the chief continued, "the state police have investigated Lennon's background to the nth degree. They know about the play in Massachusetts. They've spoken to the local authorities. Turned out Lennon was a disgraced nephew of the family that owned the theater. They'd disowned him years earlier, but his actions were still a blight on their family heritage. Aside from all that, there was no proof of anything. If Lennon had anything to do with the accident that killed that actor, he didn't leave a trace of evidence. Bottom line, it's a dead end."

A dead end.

An odd sense of relief washed over Carly. She didn't want to follow that trail any longer. She'd treat it as a dead end, too.

The answer to Lennon's demise had to be closer to home—home being the Flinthead Opera House.

"Chief, I know there's so much about this case that's still confidential," she said, "but I'll ask anyway. Is there any word on Curt Blessings's condition?"

The chief gave her a rueful smile. "Ah, Carly. I'd like to tell you, but it's so easy to slip up. Even for you, who I can always trust to keep my confidence."

She sat up straighter. "I promise, anything you tell me will go no further. I won't even tell Ari this time." She squirmed at the thought of keeping it from Ari, but it was a police matter, not a personal one. At least she told herself that.

After a long silence, Holloway said, "All I'll say is that he's going to survive. In a very short interview with the police—the doctors wouldn't allow a longer one—he claimed he didn't recall what happened, or why he was in the hospital."

"So he never saw who shot him?"

"Claims he saw nothing. The shooter got him from behind, so his story is believable."

"I guess," Carly said.

Unless he was only pretending not to remember.

Unless he was afraid his attacker might make another attempt to finish off what they started.

"At least he's recovering," Carly said, feeling relieved. "I'm glad to hear that. Chief, I know you need to get back to work, but I have one last question. Can you tell me what poison was used to kill Lennon?"

Holloway drained his mug. "Again, this is strictly between us. It was tetrahydrozoline."

"Tetra . . . what?"

"Tetrahydrozoline. Remember that tiny cap you found in the snow behind the opera house?"

She nodded.

"It came from a plastic bottle of good old-fashioned, over-the-counter eye drops."

• • •

After the chief left, Carly googled tetrahydrozoline. It was a chemical used in many common brands of eye drops. Used in tiny amounts, it helped relieve redness in the eyes by constricting blood vessels. Googling further, she found an actual case in which a woman killed her husband by adding eye drops to his food.

Yikes. Who knew eye drops could be deadly?

The killer, apparently.

But how were the eye drops administered to Prescott Lennon? Nate had said the actor drank several sodas every day. Could the taste of tetrahydrozoline be disguised in one of those drinks? How much was needed to be fatal?

Nina poked her head into the kitchen. "Hey, there's a guy out here who wants to see you. He says he has something to show you."

"Did he say who he was?"

"Nope. He's an older fellow, very debonair-looking. His chauffeur pulled up in a big black limo and dropped him off out front. You'll remember him when you see him. He was in here once before."

Carly smiled. It had to be Barry Grimble. After his previous visit, she remembered a driver helping him into a shiny black limousine.

As she'd guessed, Barry was seated in a booth near the entrance. He's just taken a sip of his tomato soup when he saw Carly approaching his booth. He dabbed his lips with his napkin and beamed at her.

"Barry," Carly greeted him. "It's great to see you again."

"Ah, just who I wanted to see." He smoothed back his thin wisps of white hair. "Can you sit for a moment?"

"Sure." She slid into the booth across from him. "No grilled cheese today?"

"Not today. I've been indulging far too much these past few days. But I do have something to show you." His blue eyes practically danced.

Barry pulled out a carefully folded newspaper from the inside pocket of his wool coat. "This is the Burlington newspaper. Their theater critic called my performance *brilliant* and *unparalleled*."

Carly took the paper from his bony fingers and scanned the review. Barry had, indeed, been lauded as a "well-loved actor who'd emerged from hibernation to give his fans the most sterling performance of his career."

In a short paragraph farther down, the critic also praised Malachy Foster's performance. "The most startling portrayal of Marley I've witnessed in my lifetime," the critic had written. "Foster is a sparkling talent who's destined to go far."

With a smile, she returned the paper to Barry. "That's high praise, Barry. I'm so delighted for you. How did you like working with Malachy?"

"Oh my, Malachy was a joy to work with," Barry gushed. "Such a gentle, respectful young man. I'll tell you, the world of theater could use more like him."

"I met him a few times. I felt the same way."

Barry's initial glow faded, and he shook his head. "I only wish the performances hadn't been marred by Prescott's death. I'd hoped the police would've arrested his killer by now."

"I think we all hoped for that." Carly folded her hands on the table. "Barry, before he . . . died, did you find Mr. Lennon difficult to work with?"

Barry's gaze shifted to his soup. "I'm afraid I did. He wasn't the actor he was touted to be. I'm not sure why dear Hannah chose him for Marley, but she must have had her reasons."

"Yes, she must have." Carly chose her words carefully. "On a personal level, did you get along with him?"

He gave out an amused chuckle. "My dear, you are shockingly transparent. I know how you young people are. You google everyone to see if they harbor any deep, dark secrets." He wiggled his white eyebrows with a shrewd smile.

Carly felt a flush creep into her cheeks. She'd done exactly that.

He reached over and touched her hand. "I'm sorry. I've upset you, haven't I?"

"No, not really," she fibbed. "I guess you caught me off guard. I did google you. My friend Gina is still a suspect in Lennon's death, and I wanted to help her."

"How can I fault you for that? You did what any good friend would do." He pushed aside his soup bowl, which was still half full. "I'm sure you know," he said softly, "that my first wife left me for Prescott."

"I . . . heard that," Carly admitted.

"Was I angry?" Barry went on. "You bet I was. I could easily have strangled him with my bare hands. But, after a long period of grieving, I realized something. Prescott didn't steal Fiona from me. She left me willingly, of her own accord. I was so in love with her that I failed to recognize her crucial flaw—she was always on the lookout for the next best thing. Did you know she married three more times after Prescott dumped her?"

"I didn't know that."

He glanced at his wristwatch. "I need to dash. My driver will be along in a few minutes." He pulled a money clip from his shirt pocket.

"Barry, please, your soup is on me. Will you be staying in town all week?"

He slipped his money clip back into his pocket. "Thank you. And no, I'm going home today. But I'll be returning on Friday for the last two performances. You will be at one of them, won't you?"

She smiled, relieved that he wasn't annoyed with her. "Yes, my fiancé and I, plus my mom and stepdad, have tickets for Sunday's performance. I can't wait to see it."

"I hope you won't be disappointed," he said with a playful laugh. He rose and tucked his scarf around his neck.

"No chance of that."

In the next moment, the limo pulled up in front of the restaurant. Carly bade Barry Grimble goodbye and thanked him for stopping in.

After his limo pulled away, she sat for a moment and went over their conversation in her mind. A tiny voice told her that Barry had nothing to do with Lennon's death. His story about his first wife had sounded genuine.

Then again, she reminded herself, Barry Grimble was a consummate actor.

133

CHAPTER 24

ON TUESDAY, THE TEMPERATURE TOOK A SUDDEN DROP. EVEN WITH A bright sun, the mercury hovered at five degrees.

Ari ate breakfast in a rush and left home earlier than usual. A broken water pipe at the high school had caused electrical damage, and his services were urgently needed. Carly took Havarti outside for his morning constitutional, which consisted of quickly doing his business and racing back inside to his cozy warm home.

Nina arrived at work early, but Valerie was a few minutes late. Valerie's voice was hoarse from coughing, and her eyes were watery.

"Val, you need to go home," Carly told her. "You can take some lozenges and lie down under a warm blanket, at least."

Her hand on her throat, Valerie shook her head. "No, it's from the dryness, that's all. I always cough a lot in the winter. I'll put a mask on."

Carly was doubtful. If it got any worse, she'd insist that she go home.

They began their daily chores, Carly doing the bathroom. Gina texted to let her know she wouldn't be stopping in for her weekly biscuit. She was finishing up the New Year's Eve invitations she was working on. The customer wanted to pick them up by noon.

It was shortly after nine when someone banged on the front door. A face that looked half frozen peered through the glass around the massive wreath.

Nina hurried to unlock it. "What are you doing here so early?"

Don Frasco, dressed as if he was leading an expedition to Denali, rushed inside the restaurant. "It is so freakin' cold out there. I'm leaving my jacket on."

"It's Vermont!" Nina said cheerily. "Instead of root beer today, how about a nice hot chocolate? It'll warm your bones."

"That sounds good. Thanks." He pulled off his knitted beanie, which sported penguins waddling around the cuff. Then he plunked onto a stool and waved at Carly as she walked toward him from the back of the dining room. "Got something you're going to want to see," he said slyly. "Let me get my hot chocolate first."

Carly raised her eyebrows. "Hot chocolate? For Mr. Root Beer himself?"

He shrugged. "Why not?"

Nina set the hot chocolate down in front of him. Enticed by the aroma of cocoa wafting around them, Carly asked Nina to make one for her, too.

"You got it, boss."

A few minutes later, Carly and Don were seated in their usual booth at the rear. Don sipped from his mug, coming up with a whipped cream mustache.

Carly couldn't help laughing. "I should take a picture of you like that." She stirred her own hot chocolate to dissolve the cream.

He wiped his mouth with a napkin. "You'd better be nice to me. Someone you will be *very* interested in speaking to agreed to video chat with us this morning." He gave her a smug smile.

"Oh? Do tell." She tried to sound casual, but she was itching to know who it was.

He took another sip from his mug, more slowly this time. Carly felt like kicking him under the table to speed him along, but she forced herself not to react.

"Okay," he said finally, "remember yesterday I told you about the actor who got food poisoning? The one who Malachy Foster replaced in *Streetcar*?"

"Yesss. Don't tell me you found him!"

"Okay, I won't tell you." He took another slow sip from his mug.

This time Carly gave his leg a light kick under the table.

"Okay, okay. Don't maim me," he grumped. "One of the feelers I put out came through. I found the actor, and he's willing to go on a video chat with us. He's making himself available in"—he consulted his cell phone—"right about five minutes from now."

"Good green Grinches! Then let's finish our hot chocolates so you can call him." She swallowed a large gulp from her mug. "Will I like what he has to say?"

"Depends," Don replied. "Do you like Malachy?"

Carly swiped a napkin over her lips "I do." *Or I did.*

"I'll call my contact in a few minutes. Meanwhile, do you have any news to share on your end?"

Carly pondered how much to tell him. She wanted to put the Winslow debacle as far behind her as she could.

"I'm not sure if it's news," Carly said, "but I had a visit late yesterday from John Winslow's wife."

Don's ginger-colored eyes widened. "Oh ho! Hiding things from me, are you?"

"Don't be dramatic. I'm not hiding anything. I decided the Winslow angle was leading us nowhere, that's all." She gave him a painful recap of Peg's heart-wrenching disclosures.

After mulling it, Don said, "I agree. It probably is a dead end. Can you send me that copy of the playbill, anyway?"

"Sure, just don't show it to anyone. Peg felt she was being disloyal to her husband by bringing it to me in the first place."

Carly had saved a copy of it on her cell, so she texted it to him.

Don's phone pinged. He looked at it. "Thanks. By the way, you probably won't see me tomorrow," he warned her. "I'll be putting together the paper, and the photos from the play are awesome. The center layout is going to kick butt, if you'll forgive my bragging. And wait till you read my review of *A Christmas Carol*."

Carly glared at him. "Hasn't it been five minutes?"

"Geez, you're impatient." Don pushed aside his mug and tapped at his phone. Moments later, a face filled the screen. "Hey, Orson? It's me, Don." He held up the phone so Carly could see. "I'm here with my bud Carly."

Carly peered at Don's cell phone. A young man with wild-looking blond hair and a scruffy beard stared back at her. Carly waved at the phone, not sure if he could see her. "Hi, Orson."

"Hey," Orson said, "nice to meet you, Carly. My man Don said you wanted to know about the day I got food poisoning and couldn't perform in *Streetcar*."

"Yes, I'd like to hear what happened," she said. "If you're okay with sharing."

Orson scrubbed his hand over his face. "Man, that was a crazy time. The play was a Sunday matinee, and I had a really minor role. Even so, the night before I came down with a super-bad case of early stage fright. Like, I didn't even think my legs would carry me onto that stage, you know? I kept picturing myself collapsing while everyone in the audience jeered at me. Anyway, I'd decided to back out of the play, but a few of my buddies said I just needed to relax."

Carly exchanged glances with Don, but his face was unreadable.

"So the night before, they took me out barhopping. I drank *way* too much. On the way home, we stopped at a place that had chicken wings. All that booze had made me hungry, so I ate about twenty of them."

"They were *driving*?" Carly asked.

"One of them was a teetotaler, so he was the DD—the designated driver."

"Okay, go on," Carly urged.

"So, like, when they finally drove me back to my apartment, they nearly had to carry me inside. I woke up the next morning with a hangover like nothing I ever had before. On top of that, I had a bad reaction to the chicken wings. I won't describe it—it'll turn your stomach—but let's just say I couldn't leave my apartment all day."

"Orson, that's quite a story," Carly said. "Were you mad at your friends for taking you out drinking?"

"Not at all. They really thought they were helping. I guess they over-estimated my capacity for alcohol." He laughed. "And I haven't eaten chicken since that day."

"I can understand why," Carly said, feeling a twinge of nausea herself.

Orson's expression turned serious. "Look, Malachy Foster had nothing to do with what happened to me that night. I know everyone said he did, but they were lying. You know how it is. One idiot starts a rumor, and then it spreads like wildfire."

"I do know," Carly acknowledged.

"One more thing," Orson went on. "I saw Malachy perform in *Streetcar* a week later. He totally rocked that part. Yeah, sure, it was small, but he was larger than life. He's a good guy, so don't believe any crap about him, okay?"

"I won't," Carly said. "Thanks for chatting with us, Orson. Do you still want to be an actor?"

"No way. I love drama, but I'm looking at directing, now. I think that's more my speed."

Don turned the phone back to himself. "Thanks, man. I owe you one."

"Later, Don."

After he disconnected, Carly sat for a moment and thought about the conversation. Orson's tale was completely believable. What reason would he have to lie?

Even if Malachy had no part in sabotaging Orson, did that mean he was innocent of poisoning Prescott Lennon? One didn't necessarily wash away the other.

"What do you think?" Don said, putting away his phone.

"I might end up regretting it," Carly said, "but I'm crossing Malachy off my suspect list."

• • •

Nina had just turned the *Closed* sign to *Open* when Suzanne burst through the door. Suzanne glanced at the wall clock, then tugged off her outerwear as quickly as she could. Her dark blond hair stood on end when she pulled off her knitted hat.

"Sorry to be almost late," she blurted, smoothing her hair with her fingers. "My kid couldn't find his homework, so he had to go to school without it. But I kept searching for it, and I found it buried under a pile of comic books." She blew out an exasperated breath. "I figured I'd better drop it off at his school, and then I got stuck behind a plow driving three miles an hour."

Carly, who was fussing with the ornaments on the faux tree, smiled at her. "Suzanne, you're not late, and it would be okay if you were."

"Yeah, yeah." Her jacket over her arm, she went over next to Carly and stared at the tree. "Hey, aren't those new?"

Someone had hung five red felt mittens on the tree. Each was about two inches high, with a name stitched at the top.

"Yep. But I don't know where they came from. It's a mystery."

Nina shrugged. "Hmmm. Maybe Santa brought them."

Carly had spotted the mittens that morning while she was restocking the beverage case. They were so adorable they'd immediately caught her eye. Had they been there when she first came in? She honestly couldn't remember. Something—a folded paper?—was tucked inside each one.

Suzanne pointed at each mitten with her finger. "Carly, Valerie, Suzanne,

Nina . . . and Grant!" She tapped her lips. "You seriously don't know who did this?"

"I have my suspicions," Carly said. "By the way, I sent Val home. She's coming down with something and she needs to rest. The way she was coughing, we were all going to get sick before long."

"Poor gal," Suzanne said. "She hates missing work, too. She's so devoted to this place. Well, I'd better get cracking. Sounds like we're gonna have our hands full today."

"We are, but here's the good news—" Carly started to say. "And here it is now!"

Flashing a huge smile, Grant sailed through the front door. "Hey, guys. You can't imagine how happy I am to be here."

"We are, too!" Suzanne squeezed him in a hug.

He laughed. "Then let me take my jacket off, okay?"

Suzanne gave him a playful swat on the arm.

He unzipped his puffy jacket and pulled off his hat and gloves. "I gotta tell you, Carly, you saved me, big-time. If you hadn't called me, I'd have been stuck taking my mom Christmas shopping this afternoon." He made a face.

"You bailed on your mom?" Suzanne chided him. "Oh, the poor woman."

"She's not a poor woman when she's shopping," Grant said wryly. "She's more like a power mower, barreling through the mall at the speed of a jet. I can't even keep up with her! Meanwhile, I'm juggling a thousand shopping bags and sweating under my jacket. If I even suggest stopping for a snack, she tells me I can have one when I get home." He gave them a pitiful look. "It really is awful."

"My heart bleeds," Carly teased him.

"No sympathy, huh?" He smiled. "Oh, well, let me put my stuff away and grab an apron."

"I'm right behind you," Suzanne said, following Grant into the kitchen.

Nina went over to where Carly was still examining the tree. "It's sweet that Grant's willing to help out, isn't it?" Her voice was softer than usual.

"It's sure going to be a huge help today," Carly replied. "Nina, you're okay with him working here, aren't you?"

"Oh, sure." She scratched her arm. "I mean, Grant helped train me when I first came on board. He's one of the nicest guys I've ever met."

"I can't argue with that," Carly agreed, but something in Nina's tone set off a vibe she couldn't put her finger on.

Three teenaged boys came in just then, their ears bright red from the cold. Nina smiled and grabbed some menus, then seated them in a booth. "Don't you guys have hats?"

"Nah," one of them said. "Hats are lame."

"Okay, but why aren't you in school?" she said sternly, her pencil poised over her order pad.

Another one offered a toothy smile. "No school today. They had to close the high school because of a busted water pipe."

"I can testify to that," Carly said. "Ari's there now doing some electrical repair."

Nina winked at the boys. "Okay, you're off the hook. What'll you have?"

More customers came in. Grant hurried back into the dining room and started working the grill.

Like old times, Carly thought with a twinge of nostalgia.

The next few hours proved busier than Carly anticipated. She suspected it was partly due to the high school being closed. When Grant had to remind her twice that he needed more sliced tomatoes, she knew her mind was elsewhere.

She pushed through the swinging door into the kitchen. Nina had already sliced a dozen more plump tomatoes and sealed them in a container. Carly removed the container from the fridge and returned to the dining room, setting it down on the cutting board next to Grant.

"You okay?" he asked, his eyes searching her face. He flipped over a Scrooge's Redemption, which was fast becoming a favorite.

"I'm fine," she assured him. "Kind of tired this week."

"Do me a favor," he said quietly. "Take twenty minutes for yourself in the kitchen. I'll bring you a grilled cheddar and a cup of soup. Nina's going to take over for me in a few minutes, so I'll be in to talk to you."

"Grant, we're too busy right now," Carly protested.

"Suzanne doesn't leave until three, and Nina can handle the grill. That woman is a phenom."

"Okay," she relented. "But only half a sandwich."

"You got it. Now go."

Carly turned and went into the kitchen. She poured herself a glass of cider and sat down at the kitchen table.

Why did she feel so scattered? Why couldn't she focus on any one thing for more than a minute?

In the past, she'd depended on Gina to help her figure things out. Their brainstorming sessions always yielded new trails to follow, new theories to pursue.

But Gina hadn't been herself since Lennon's murder. Aside from being a murder suspect, their jaunt to the framing shop on Sunday had thrown her further into the doldrums.

"I come bearing gifts," Grant announced, striding through the swinging door.

He set down half a grilled cheese oozing with cheddar, and a small bowl of soup. The aroma was so tantalizing, Carly dug in immediately. Grant observed her silently as she ate.

After she scraped up the last spoonful from her soup bowl, she said, "Are you just going to stare at me while I eat?"

His eyebrows dipped toward his nose. "I'm seriously worried about you, Carly. I want you to tell me what's going on. And I don't want a sugarcoated version. I want the real story."

"Am I that transparent?" When he didn't smile, her shoulders sagged. "Okay, I'll admit I've had a few rough days."

She began with her disastrous visit with Gina to Winslow Framing, explaining every awful detail. And then Peg Winslow's heartbreaking story about her husband, and how she'd left the restaurant in tears.

"Then I found out from the chief that the state police already knew about John Winslow. They'd looked into it, but decided it was a dead end."

"But you can't accept that?"

She gave out a noisy sigh. "No, I do accept it. But I caused both Winslows unnecessary pain. That's what I can't accept. Plus, I made Gina feel worse than ever. I mean, like she didn't have enough on her plate, right?"

Grant puffed his cheeks and blew out a breath. "I'm sure Gina understands that you were trying to help. I gather you're not going to pursue the Winslow angle anymore?"

"Definitely not. It was half-baked in the first place." She picked up her sandwich and set it down again. "I'm still bothered by one thing. Nothing to do with the Winslows," she added quickly.

Carly explained her feeling that she'd missed something on Friday when Ashley Blanchard had given her a makeover.

"You think Ashley's a possible?" Grant asked.

"That's just it—I don't know. But if I can figure out what I missed that night, maybe I can cross her off my list."

Grant shook his head. Carly could see he wasn't happy with her answer.

"Why do you feel this is your job?" he said finally. "You know the police will find the killer. Why do you always have to be one step ahead of them?"

Carly stared at him in shock. "Is that how you see me? Trying to outsmart the police?"

He gave her an apologetic look. "I'm sorry. I worded that badly. That's not what I meant. I'm only trying to understand—"

She held up a hand. "It's okay, and I hear what you're saying. But listen to me. When people talk to me, they don't feel intimidated. They open up. They reveal details they wouldn't tell the police because they don't see me as a threat. But when the police question them, they hold back. They're afraid that anything they say will make them look guilty, so they only tell them what they think they should know. That's the big difference."

Carly realized she was generalizing, that it didn't apply to everyone. But there'd been times when people had shared information with her that they hadn't divulged to the police.

He gave her a reluctant smile. "You're as smart as you are nosy, you know that?"

"I prefer the word *inquisitive*, thank you very much." She gave his arm a playful smack.

"So, what you're saying is that you want to go to Ashley's salon again?"

"I do."

"During the day?"

"Absolutely. And only when other people are around."

"On what pretext?"

Carly thought about it, and the perfect answer came to her. "To give her a gift card in return for the free makeover."

"Hmmm." Grant pursed his lips. "You could always mail the gift card to her. Would you go alone?"

She shifted on her chair. "I don't really have a choice. Taking Gina with me is out of the question."

Grant sat back and clasped his hands over his chest. "I'd go with you, but it might look strange. You need a woman."

"You mean . . . you're okay with my going there?" Not that she needed his permission. But having his blessing gave her a comfort level she wouldn't have had without it.

Grant leaned forward over the table. "It's not my first choice. But I know you—you'll do it even if I beg you not to." His eyes suddenly widened, and he snapped his fingers. "What about Norah? Maybe she'd go with you."

Norah? Carly hadn't even considered her.

Yet, when she thought about it, she realized Norah would be perfect. She was outgoing, stylish, and she could schmooze with the best of them. And when it suited her, she could be a bit of an actor herself.

"I like that idea," she told Grant. "Only one problem. She thinks I cavort with killers."

"Well . . ." Grant grinned at her.

"Okay, okay." She glanced at the clock. It was already after three. Suzanne had left to pick up Josh, which meant Grant and Nina would be alone.

"Would you and Nina be okay if I went there now? Assuming Norah's available."

"We'll be fine, and Pownal's like, not even a fifteen-minute ride. And we're on winter hours now so we'll be closing at six."

Carly smiled at the "we." Grant still thought of himself as part of the restaurant. As did she.

Grant nodded at her plate. "You haven't even touched your grilled cheese. Eat it and then call Norah. I'll let Nina know your plan."

He started to get off his chair, but Carly grabbed his sleeve. "Thanks for being so positive about Nina. She really looks up to you."

"You don't need to thank me. She's an amazing woman. And I was impressed with the sandwich she created. I didn't know if it would fly, but customers are going nuts over it."

Carly picked up her grilled cheese half. "Would you tell her that?"

"I will. Now eat and call Norah."

She gave him a mock salute. "Yes, sir."

CHAPTER 25

"I CAN'T BELIEVE I'M DOING THIS," NORAH QUIPPED FROM CARLY'S passenger seat. "You're lucky I didn't have any appointments this afternoon."

Carly slid a glance over at her sister. The upward curve on Norah's lips told a different story.

"You love it, and you know it."

"Well, it's something to do," Norah said airily. "At least this way you won't be alone with a killer."

"I'm sure Ashley's not a killer," Carly defended, though she wasn't totally sure.

"Oh? Then why are we going there? Other than to figure out what you missed the first time around, even though you don't have a clue what it was."

Norah's tone irked Carly, but she did have a point. She tried to dream up a response that would satisfy her sister. Unfortunately, Norah knew her too well.

"The main thing is," Carly said, "you need to keep Ashley occupied while I examine that collage. Something tells me that's where I missed whatever it was that I noticed. I need to take a photo of it."

"That's my assignment?" Norah said, feigning horror.

"It is. But don't be obvious about it."

"No worries. I can handle it." Norah pulled down the visor in front of her. She examined her face in the mirror, then snapped the visor back up. "You'll notice I'm wearing minimal makeup. I want Ashley to think I need help doing my face."

Carly rolled her eyes. "She's seen you at the opera house with Nate, remember?"

"That doesn't mean I'm happy with my current makeup. Don't worry, I'll think of what to say when I get there. She does know we're coming, right?"

"She knows *I'm* coming. I texted her to be sure she'd be there this afternoon. She's psyched that I'm making a return visit."

For a while they rode in silence. At one point Carly glanced over at her sister, who was staring out the passenger-side window. A sudden surge of love for Norah grabbed her by the heart. It struck her how comforting Norah's presence was, and how rarely they rode together in a car. She was glad she'd asked her to make the trip to Pownal with her.

"Gina told me you're helping her find a new assistant," Carly said.

"Well, good heavens, Carly, if you'd told me how much trouble she's had keeping her employees, I'd have had the right person in there months ago." She threw up her gloved hands.

"I'm sorry. I thought you only recruited for large companies."

"Not true. I help small businesses as well. Not often, but when I do I'm darn good at it."

"I will remember that for the future." She grinned at Norah, who in turn stuck out her tongue.

The parking lot was about half full when Carly reached the spa. She was grateful to see that the lot had been thoroughly plowed. A wall of snow lined the back of the parking lot where the plow had pushed it out of the way.

Inside the historic building, the door to Ashley's rental space was open. Carly and Norah paused in the doorway, but Ashley was nowhere in sight.

Carly knocked lightly on the doorjamb.

An instant later, Ashley came from around the back corner so fast that Carly jumped.

"Wow. You got here fast," Ashley said. "Come in!"

Norah stepped into the room behind Carly. Wide-eyed, she bounced her gaze all around. "Wow. Your décor is amazing, Ashley. The use of contrasting colors is awesome."

Carly shot her a warning look. *Don't overdo it.*

Ashley beamed at her. "Thanks, Norah. I didn't know you'd be coming over with Carly, but I'm so glad you did. Now you get to see my home away from home."

At the back of the room, a door opened abruptly. Out stepped Honey Lennon, her expression stark, her mouth curved into a fierce scowl. She wore a calf-length coat that brushed the tops of her black boots, her purse strap slung over her shoulder.

Carly tried not to gawk, but Honey was the last person she'd expected to see. She started to say something in the way of a greeting, but Honey marched over to Norah instead. "What are you doing here?" she demanded.

Norah gave her an innocent smile. "Oh, just tagging along with my little sis. Ashley did such a marvelous job with her makeover the other night that I wanted to check out the salon for myself." She looked all around again, as if entranced by the ambiance.

Ashley quickly piped in. "Honey's leaving for California tonight on a late flight from Albany. The police have released her husband's body. She can finally go home and give him a proper burial."

"Yeah, and I thought you were driving me to the airport," Honey snapped.

Ashley blanched. "I am. I'm picking you up at your hotel at five, remember?"

"Okay, well, don't be late."

Honey started to sweep toward the door when Norah grasped her by the arm and pulled her back. "Honey, Nate and I are both so very sorry for your loss. Please call on us if there's anything we can do."

Honey jerked her arm away. "You want to do something? Tell the cops to arrest Prez's killer. They know freakin' well who it is. They just don't want to make waves in this one-horse dump of a town."

With that, she stalked out, her boots clattering on the marble floor of the lobby.

Ashley closed the door behind her. "I'm sorry about that. I've got to be honest, I'm glad she's leaving. She doesn't have a kind word for anyone. Not even the people who tried to help her."

"Like you?" Carly said gently.

Ashley nodded. "I tried to be her friend, but I don't think she knows the meaning of the word. She still believes Gina is the killer. It's ridiculous, and we all know it, but—" She gave a half shrug.

Carly didn't press her. Instead, she pulled an envelope out of her tote. "This is for you," she said. "A small gift in return for my facial and makeover."

Ashley took the envelope from her and opened it. When she peeked at the gift card, her eyes glistened. "Carly, this is so generous. You didn't have to do this."

"I know, but I wanted to. I hope to see you in the restaurant before the holidays are over."

"You will. I promise." She gave Carly a squeeze, then noticed Norah surveying the makeup choices on the counter along the wall.

Ashley strode over and stood beside her. "Is there anything you'd like to try?"

Norah looked thoughtful. "Possibly. I've been using my current brand of makeup forever." She tossed out the name of a high-end brand. "I'm really getting tired of it, especially since they never offer anything new. Same old, same old, you know?"

"I sure do. It's a shame because you have such beautiful skin." Ashley peered into Norah's face. "I'd like to use a different color palette on you. Would you like to schedule a makeover? We can experiment with different shades that will bring out those stunning eyes."

While Norah kept Ashley occupied, Carly strolled over to where the photo collage hung on the wall next to the mirror. There were so many photos jumbled together. It was hard to take them all in. She reached into her tote and quietly pulled out her cell phone.

Carly glanced over at Norah. Her sister was still chatting up Ashley, asking for her opinion on various shades of blush. Carly centered her phone over the collage and snapped a few pics. She quickly slipped the phone back into her tote.

Something in the collage had caught her eye. She needed to see an enlarged version, but she'd have to wait until they were out of there.

She ambled over and slipped her arm through Norah's. "Find anything you like?"

"I did, but I know you have to get back to work," Norah said, sounding disappointed.

Again, Ashley urged her to make an appointment for a makeover.

Norah rummaged through her purse. "Oh, no. I left my appointment book in my car. Can I call you after I check it?"

"Of course you can." Ashley looked pleased at landing a new customer. She gave Norah a business card. "You can text or call, whichever is easier."

"That's great. Thanks," Norah said. She pointed at the door from which Honey had emerged earlier. "Um, is that a bathroom?"

Ashley smiled and held out her arm. "It is. Be my guest. Oh, and don't mind the bags in there. I'm donating some of my clothes to the women's shelter."

Norah scooted into the bathroom and closed the door. A few minutes later she came out, and she and Carly said their goodbyes to Ashley.

They bundled their coats up to their chins and pulled on their gloves. Carly's mind was fixed on the collage as they hustled out to her car. The moment she slid onto her driver's seat and closed her door, she tugged off her right glove and pulled out her cell.

Norah snapped her seat belt into place. "I have something to show you," she said. "But get the heater going first before my teeth start chattering."

"Sorry." Carly started the engine and blasted the heat. On her cell phone, she enlarged the last photo she'd taken of the collage, then moved it around with her finger. Her heart banged in her chest like a thousand drums.

In the photo of Ashley as a child in which she was applying blush to a woman's cheek, her pinky finger was in clear view—and it was distinctly crooked.

Carly's stomach throbbed. Her ears pounded. She handed the phone to Norah.

Norah looked at the screen and then at Carly, her face whiter than the fallen snow. "It . . . it's just like Lennon's finger," she stammered, giving the phone back. "But I think I can do you one better." She extracted her cell from her own purse, tapped it, and showed it to Carly. "This was in one of the clothing bags Ashley said were for the women's shelter. The bag was on the floor next to the sink."

Carly stared at the photo and nearly choked. In a brown paper grocery bag, a clump of bright yellow fabric with a flowered pattern rested at the top of a stack of clothing.

"When I was washing my hands," Norah explained, "I caught a glimpse of yellow that looked disturbingly familiar. It was stuffed about halfway down in the bag. I pulled it out . . . and there it was. And underneath it was a wig. A gray wig." She held up a hand. "Don't worry, I put them both back exactly the way they were. Ashley will never know I saw them."

Carly couldn't speak. All she could do was gape at Norah's phone—at the photo of the missing costume that was supposed to be Mrs. Fezziwig's.

Norah finally took her cell back from Carly and slipped it into her purse. She reached for her sister's hand and grasped it hard, as if it were a lifeline. Carly gripped hers in return.

"I don't even know how to process this," Carly said bleakly. "What if that crooked finger is hereditary? What if Ashley is Lennon's biological daughter? What if she wanted revenge on him for abandoning her and her mom? What if—?"

"Carly," Norah said, shaking her sister's arm. "We'll figure it out. But right now, we've got to get out of here."

CHAPTER 26

THE SKY WAS BEGINNING TO DARKEN. DAYLIGHT WAS FADING FAST.

They'd been gone for over an hour. Carly knew that Grant would be starting to worry if he didn't hear from them soon.

"Can you grab my cell and text Grant that we're on our way back?" she asked Norah. "Remind him that I have to drop you off at your condo first."

"You don't have to drive me home," Norah said, reaching into Carly's tote for her cell. "Nate can always pick me up later. Right now, you and I need to put our heads together. Why don't I go back to the restaurant with you, and we can try to make sense of what we found?"

"You mean . . . you want to help?" Carly was surprised and elated at the same time.

"My gosh, of course I do!" Norah looked at her as if she'd sprouted antlers. "After what I saw today, there's no way I'm letting you do this alone. I'm beginning to see now how you get pulled into these . . . investigations, or whatever you call them. You're so sharp that you keep noticing things—things that would slide right past most people. And once you see them, you can't unsee them, so you have to take action. Am I right?"

"That pretty much sums it up," Carly acknowledged. "I'm also a tad nosy."

"A tad?" Norah huffed. "I can still see you peeking over the staircase railing the night I was curled up on the sofa with Petey Wellman. Mom had gone out for dinner with a friend, and I was supposed to be babysitting you."

"I was twelve!" Carly squeaked. "I can still see your faces when you realized you'd gotten caught. I only wish I'd had a camera back then."

"We weren't really *doing* anything," Norah defended, crossing her arms over her chest. "I had to give you credit, though. You didn't tattle on me."

"No, I didn't."

"You blackmailed me instead. I had to do the dishes every night for three weeks. *And* treat you to a movie."

Carly giggled. It felt good to relieve the stress that was building inside her. "Mom knew something was up, but she didn't ask. She figured whatever it was, we'd already worked it out between us." Tears prickled at her eyelids. "She's a great mom."

"The best," Norah said, a catch in her voice. "Carly, what are we going to do? About Ashley, I mean."

"I don't know, but we'll figure out something. I'm glad I have you to brainstorm with."

• • •

148

In the restaurant, business had slowed to a near halt. Two booths were occupied, but the counter stools were empty. The decision Carly had made the previous year to close at six from December through February had been a good one. It saved energy and gave everyone the chance to go home early.

The downtown stores were still open, but only a scattering of shoppers prowled the sidewalks.

"You guys need coffee," Grant said the moment they entered through the back door. He pointed at a rear booth, inviting them to sit.

"You're a lifesaver." Norah smiled at him and plopped into the booth. "I'm leaving my coat on till I warm up."

Carly went into the kitchen and hung her things in the closet. She returned holding her tablet.

Grant set down their steaming mugs and spoke quietly. "Did you find out anything?"

"We did." Carly gave him a short summary of their discoveries.

"That's pretty wild," he said, running a hand over his dreadlocks. "But there could be an innocent explanation. Are you going to tell the chief about it?"

Carly looked at her sister, who nodded her consent. "We are, but I want to do some googling before we set off any alarms. Like you said, there might be a simple explanation that has nothing to do with the murder."

"I'll leave you two alone then," Grant murmured. "Wave if you need anything."

He went back behind the grill and spoke briefly to Nina, who'd just realized Carly had returned. Nina scuttled over to their booth. "I'm so glad you two are back! Did everything go okay?"

"Everything is fine," Carly assured her. "Norah and I need to check out a few things. We think we have information that'll help the police, but we don't want to send up any red flags unless we're sure."

Nina's lips formed an O. "Is there anything I can do to help?"

Carly smiled at her. "You already helped by holding down the fort with Grant while we were gone."

Nina looked pleased at the compliment. "He sure is great to work with. Anyway, I'll let you two put your heads together. Yell if you need anything."

After she was out of earshot, Carly booted up her tablet. It wasn't that she didn't trust Nina. But until they had a better idea of what they were dealing with, she didn't want to share their findings with anyone else.

"Let's go back to the beginning," Norah began. "What's the deal with the pinky finger? How did you even know about it?"

Carly took a sip from her mug, then pulled her tablet closer. "Honey mentioned it the day she and Ashley came into the eatery." She described their visit, and the way Honey had sobbed about her husband's "poor crooked pinky."

"Okay," Norah said, "but how did you connect it with Ashley?"

"I wouldn't have," Carly said, "except that the day I went there for my makeover, I asked her about it."

Norah looked stymied. "Why?"

"I was trying to get her to talk about Lennon, how well she knew him, what she thought of him, stuff like that. I mentioned the pinky finger mainly to keep her talking about him, but I was also curious about it."

"Nosy Carly does it again!" Norah bleated.

Carly ignored her. She repeated Ashley's story of being raised by a single mom—a wannabe actress—who refused to reveal the identity of Ashley's biological dad.

"Whoever he was," Carly said, "he refused to acknowledge his child."

"Creep," Norah spat out.

"Ashley's mom, Willow, died three years ago," Carly continued. "She never told Ashley who her father was."

"But maybe Ashley found out," Norah suggested.

"That's what I thought." Carly took another sip from her mug, which she'd barely touched. "What was weird about the pinky finger is that she knew exactly what the condition was called—clino something. It rolled right off her tongue like it was an everyday word."

"And now we know why," Norah said. "She had a crooked pinky as a kid. So why doesn't she have it now?"

"Good question." Carly tapped away at her tablet. "Ah, here it is—clinodactyly."

She clicked the link to an article by a top-rated children's hospital. "Okay, here we go. Clinodactyly is an abnormal growth in the middle bone of the finger, usually the pinky finger. As the child's hand grows, the finger becomes more curved. Over time, it can interfere with the normal use of the hand. In those cases, corrective surgery can be performed."

"So, Ashley must've had the surgery," Norah said. "You know, I watched her apply makeup to some of the actors before the dress rehearsal that day. I'd have noticed if she had a crooked pinky. She definitely did not."

"You watched?" Carly smiled at her sister.

"Yeah, it fascinated me," Norah said. "And I've got to say, Ashley really impressed me. She's a talented cosmetician. I mean, old Mr. Fezziwig's eyebrows were a work of art in themselves!"

Carly laughed. "I can't wait to see the play on Sunday. You know, Ashley wants to do the makeup for my wedding party."

"She does?" Norah looked surprised. "What did you tell her?"

"I didn't commit to anything."

"Maybe you won't have to," Norah said soberly.

Norah didn't have to explain her reasoning. If Ashley killed Prescott

Lennon, she'd be wearing prison garb by the time Carly and Ari exchanged their vows.

Carly continued skimming the article, skipping over some of the medical terminology. "It says here that the condition is fairly common."

Norah shrugged. "I don't know anyone who has it."

"Nor do I. But here's the kicker. Clinodactyly can be passed from a parent to a child." Carly looked at her sister.

"So, there *is* a hereditary factor."

Hereditary.

Why did that word trigger a memory?

Nina came up to their booth. "Sorry to interrupt. Grants wants to know if you guys would like any tomato soup before he puts it away."

"Not me, thanks," Norah said. "Nate and I are eating at Canoodle the Noodle tonight. I want to be good and hungry."

"Ari and I love that place," Carly said. "I'll pass, thanks, Nina."

She hadn't even thought about dinner for herself and Ari, but there were plenty of leftovers to work with in the fridge at home.

Wait a minute. Tomato soup.

Tomatoes.

The day Ashley and Honey came in for a sandwich, Ashley mentioned that she was allergic to tomatoes. Prescott Lennon threw a plate of penne marinara at the wall, claiming he'd ordered his meal with Alfredo sauce. Marinara sauce was made with tomatoes.

Was there a connection? Was it possible he was allergic to tomatoes? Was that why he'd had the meltdown?

It was a stretch, for sure. And even if he'd had a tomato allergy, it didn't mean he was Ashley's father.

From the depths of Norah's purse, a rich tenor voice belted out an aria from a famous opera. Her eyes lit up. She dug out her cell and tapped the answer button. "Hey, sweetie. I'm at Carly's restaurant. Can you pick me up?"

Carly was relieved to hear Norah speak so sweetly to Nate. In her heart, Carly felt sure they were meant to be together.

Norah put away her phone. "Nate's coming over," she said with a huge smile. "Can we share what we found with him?"

"I don't see why we shouldn't," Carly said. "The crime happened in his opera house. He wants the murder solved as badly as we do."

Norah's smile faded. "You know, everything we just talked about is kind of circumstantial, don't you think?"

Carly had to chuckle. Norah was fast becoming an amateur detective.

"It is," she agreed. "But we haven't talked about the dress yet. I think that's far more troublesome. If she's hiding a stolen costume and a wig, what else is she hiding? I meant to ask you—when you asked to use Ashley's bathroom, did you suspect you'd find something?"

"Nope," Norah said. "It was a happy accident. Before you called me, I'd been working on some new client profiles. I'd also had about fifty cups of coffee. I really did need to use the bathroom."

A sudden wave of gloom crashed over Carly. She genuinely liked Ashley. The thought that she might be a killer was overwhelmingly sad.

Then again, what did a stolen dress and wig mean? It made her a thief, but not a killer. Had she disguised herself to protect someone else? To incriminate someone else?

Maybe she and Norah should leave it alone. Forget what they discovered about Ashley. It was the job of the police to find the killer, wasn't it?

In the deepest chamber of her heart, Carly knew she couldn't do that. The crooked pinky might be a fluke, but the missing dress and wig were not. It didn't mean Ashley was a killer, but it was proof that she'd stolen something that didn't belong to her.

Gina was still a strong suspect. As for Lennon, he might have been an unbearable ogre, but he deserved justice.

And if Ashley was the person who poisoned him, she needed to be held accountable.

CHAPTER 27

NATE ARRIVED ABOUT FIFTEEN MINUTES LATER. HE SLIPPED INTO THE BOOTH next to Norah and gave her a light kiss.

Grant immediately went over and set down a mug of coffee in front of him.

"Thanks, man." Nate gave him a grateful smile.

Carly and Norah gave Nate a recap of their afternoon. Norah showed him the photo she'd taken of the flowered yellow dress and the wig.

Nate's jaw hardened. "I'm one hundred percent sure that's Mrs. Fezziwig's costume. It was the only one with that bright yellow background. Jess Terwilliger said yellow was her favorite color."

"But why would Ashley steal it?" Norah said, looking perplexed. "That's what I don't get."

Nate squeezed her hand. "My best guess is that she used it as a disguise. Anyone passing by might think she was Jessica without even a second look. With that dress and wig, who would look twice? She could have slipped into Lennon's dressing room after he went onstage and poisoned his drink."

Carly was doubtful. "But if someone *were* to recognize her . . ." She let the thought finish itself.

"I know, I know," he said wearily. "It was just a theory. I'm at a loss myself."

Carly finished the last dregs of her coffee. Nina came by and offered to top off everyone's mugs, but Carly shook her head.

"Okay, how about this?" she offered. "What if Jess reported the dress stolen, then wore it to sneak into Lennon's dressing room to poison him. Nobody would think twice about seeing her in her own costume."

"It's . . . a possibility," Nate said, but he didn't look as if he believed it.

For a few minutes, they all sat quietly. Carly felt as if her stomach was scraping the floor.

"Nate," she said suddenly, "did you know that your maintenance guy, Jeff, helps out Jess in the donation center for the food bank?"

His eyes rounded. "No. How do you know that?"

Carly told him about her excursion to deliver gift cards to the donation center, and how she'd discovered Jeff stocking shelves.

"That's interesting," he said, "but I don't see how it points to anything. Jeff's a great guy. He does a lot of nice things for people." Nate looked mildly annoyed.

"I'm sorry I mentioned it," Carly said. "I just thought it was an odd coincidence."

"Carly," Nate said, this time with a smile, "I know for sure Jeff didn't go near Lennon that day. He was helping the technicians with some staging that morning when he got a call from his mom. His younger brother had broken his leg skiing, and Jeff had to rush off to the hospital. He was gone the rest of the day."

Carly felt her breath leave her. Now she knew why the chief had said Jeff wasn't a serious suspect. The police had already confirmed his alibi.

She'd hoped her trip to Ashley's salon would prove the cosmetician wasn't a viable suspect. Instead, it had added more questions—and provided no answers whatsoever.

Nate looked at his watch. "It's almost five thirty. We can toss this around forever, but I think it's time we called Fred."

• • •

Chief Holloway looked more tired than ever when he came into the eatery. His eyes were sunken, his lids heavy. Closing time was five minutes away and Grant and Nina had left, so they all sat in a booth.

"Thanks for sending Val home this morning," the chief said to Carly. "I couldn't talk her out of going to work. She was so afraid of leaving you shorthanded. I'm glad you realized how sick she was."

"She sure didn't sound good," Carly said. "I hope she's resting now."

He gave up a faint smile. "She is. I bought her all sorts of cough and cold medicine, so she's in bed. I'm heading home as soon as I leave here." He tapped the table with his fingertips. "So, what's up?"

Carly and Norah pitched in to describe their visit to Ashley's salon. Norah showed him the photo she'd taken of the Mrs. Fezziwig costume and wig.

Holloway stared at it, then rubbed a hand over his face. "Nate, you're sure this is the missing costume?"

"One hundred percent, Fred." He placed his hand over Norah's. She was starting to look drained. Their discoveries at Ashley's salon had taken a toll on her.

"The crooked finger angle—I don't know what to make of it," the chief admitted. "I'm tempted to dismiss it altogether. But for the sake of argument, let's say Ashley is Lennon's biological daughter. It doesn't make her a murderer."

"I know," Carly agreed. "That's why we wanted to discuss it with you." She texted him the pic she'd taken of Ashley's photo collage. "It's in your hands, now."

Holloway let out a guttural sigh. "I'll take it up with the state police investigator tomorrow. We don't have enough to ask for a warrant, but maybe we can bring Ashley in for a chat."

Carly's insides clenched. She knew that was shorthand for *interrogation*.

The chief went on. "I think we need to take another look at the footage from that day. A lot of the people who were going up and down the main hallways were wearing costumes. Maybe this one slipped by us." Holloway rose from the booth. "I'm sorry to leave you hanging, but my wife is sick and I need to take care of her."

"Give her our best," Carly said. "Let us know if we can bring her anything. And tell her Grant is happily filling in for her, so she doesn't need to worry."

He touched Carly's shoulder lightly. "Thank you. I appreciate that."

Then he turned on his heel and left.

Nate slipped his arm around Norah. "Ready for Canoodle the Noodle?" he asked her.

Norah looked at him, the love in her eyes so stark it made Carly's heart twist. "I sure am. The first thing I'm going to order is a glass of my favorite Chardonnay."

"Yeah, me too." Nate looked at Carly and smiled. "Hey, do you and Ari want to join us?"

On a normal day, Carly would've jumped at the chance to dine out with Nate and Norah. But at that moment, her heart—and her stomach—were in a deep funk.

"Thanks, Nate, but we had takeout from there last week. We'll join you another time, for sure."

Norah mouthed the words *thank you* to Carly. After the afternoon they'd spent traipsing to Pownal in search of clues about Ashley, Norah obviously wanted to wind down her evening alone with Nate.

Carly didn't blame her.

Ari was waiting for her at home. And that's exactly where she wanted to be, too.

CHAPTER 28

THE MERCURY MADE IT ALL THE WAY TO FOURTEEN DEGREES WEDNESDAY morning.

Carly let herself into the restaurant through the back door, only to find the lights already on. The dining room felt toasty warm. The aroma of fresh-brewed coffee made it feel even warmer.

"Hey." Nina waved at her from the front of the restaurant.

Carly walked down to the front to greet her.

She'd slept well the night before, choosing not to dwell on the murder. Instead, she made "breakfast for dinner" for her and Ari—pancakes, scrambled eggs, and hot chocolate. They'd watched a classic holiday movie with Havarti snugged between them, and then called it an early night.

Nina was standing in front of the table tree, adjusting some of the ornaments. Carly noticed her fussing with the red felt mitten stitched with the name Grant.

"You got in extra early today," Carly said with a bright smile. She removed her outerwear and stashed it all in one of the booths.

"I wake up super early, even in the winter months," Nina said, then smiled. "A habit left over from my childhood, I guess. Plus, the heat wasn't working too well in my apartment. I figured I was better off coming to work."

"Did you contact your maintenance office?" Carly asked her. "You can't go without heat in this cold."

"No worries," Nina said. "I texted my landlord. He said he'd try to get to it this morning."

It sounded pretty vague, but Carly fixed herself a coffee and ambled over to stand next to Nina. Unless she was imagining it, the handmade mitten ornaments had grown a bit fatter.

"Nina," Carly said, "it's okay if you don't want to tell me, but did you make the mittens?"

Nina kept her gaze on the tree. "I did, but don't tell the others, okay? I want them to be surprised."

"Sure." Carly squeezed her shoulder. "It'll be our secret. Do you have a tree at your apartment?"

She shook her head. "No, it's just me, and I don't get too many visitors."

"Doesn't any of your family live close by?"

Nina paused to relocate a tiny reindeer to a different branch. "I don't really have family."

An awkward silence fell over them. Nina's attention was still fixed on the tree.

"Nina, is everything okay?" Carly asked her.

"Everything's good," Nina replied. "But . . . I felt terrible when Grant served us those wonderful biscuits and I told him I didn't eat meat. I was afraid I might've hurt his feelings."

"Oh, Nina, that's not true at all. He felt bad that he forgot, but he certainly wasn't upset with you. Grant respects everyone's food choices."

"Really?"

"Really," Carly said.

Nina sagged. "Thanks. That makes me feel better. I'd hug you if you weren't holding your coffee."

Carly laughed. "Come on. Grab your coffee and let's sit."

Mugs in hand, they slid into the booth where Carly had stuffed her things. Something was definitely troubling Nina. Carly had a feeling she knew what it was.

"Nina," Carly began, "are you worried because Grant's been filling in here?"

Nina stared into her coffee and gave a half shrug. "Not worried. More like, I mean . . . what if he wanted to come back full-time?" Her voice cracked.

"Oh my gosh, Nina. Is that what's been bothering you?"

"Kind of." She wrapped her slim fingers around her mug. "I love it here so much. But if Grant wanted to come back, you wouldn't need me, right?"

Carly looked at her assistant manager. "Nina, listen to me," she said firmly. "Hiring you was one of the best decisions I've ever made. You, me, Val, Suzanne—we're a tight-knit team. We balance each other, we support each other, and we care about our customers. For as long as you want to be here, I will always need you. Aside from all that, I value your friendship more than anything."

Nina snatched a napkin from the metal dispenser. She blotted the tears perched on her eyelashes. "Thank you, Carly. You're all like . . . family to me, you know?"

Carly smiled. "I do know."

Nina sniffled. "You're probably wondering why I made those mitten ornaments."

"Well, for one thing, I sense that you enjoy crafting."

"Oh, I do, for sure. When I was growing up, the other kids and I gave each other homemade gifts at Christmas because we couldn't afford real ones."

"Well, I think they're lovely," Carly said. "I'll take a homemade gift over a store-bought one any day."

Nina's face brightened. "Some of us made some pretty cool stuff. One year we all got paperweights made from painted rocks."

"I would've loved that," Carly said. "Who made those?"

"Rowan did. He had a real knack for artwork." She took a slow sip from her mug.

"Rowan's your brother?" Carly asked.

Nina's voice softened. "Not a real brother. But he was one of the best kids there."

Carly thought she understood. Nina had grown up with foster children. Had she been a foster child, too?

"This one Christmas," Nina went on, "I decided to make special cookies for everyone. Of course, they weren't as fancy as the ones I make now, but they sure tasted good. They got me in some trouble, though." She ducked her head and took another sip from her mug.

"How come?"

"I didn't realize I was using up a whole week's supply of butter. With money as tight as it was, that was not cool."

"You were a kid," Carly said gently.

A knock at the glass front door interrupted their conversation. Carly looked up to see Grant's smiling, frozen-looking face.

Nina swung her head around. "Darn! I meant to leave the door unlocked." She dashed over and unlocked the front door for Grant.

He pulled off his knitted beanie and his dreads sprang up. "Hey, Nina. Hi, Carly." He hung his things on the front rack and poured himself a mug of coffee. "Can I join you guys?"

"Of course you can," Carly said. "We're happy to see you."

"Yeah, likewise." He set a small insulated carrier on the seat next to Carly and slid in beside it. "I figured Val would be out again, so I got here as early as I could."

"She will be," Carly confirmed. "The chief called me this morning. She's feeling better but she's still pretty weak. She needs to stay home and sleep."

The chief had also given Carly an update. The state police planned to review some of the footage from the day of the murder. This time, they'd be searching specifically for the bright yellow Mrs. Fezziwig costume. He promised to keep her informed of their findings but emphasized, as usual, that it was highly confidential.

"Maybe we can send Val some tomato soup later," Grant said, unzipping the carrier with a mysterious smile. "But right now, I have goodies."

For a moment, Nina looked alarmed. Then Grant brought out still-warm homemade cranberry scones, along with a tub of whipped cinnamon butter. "I made these this morning."

Nina clapped her hands and grinned. "Yay! I'll get us some plates."

She scooted out of the booth and returned with plates and knives. They all helped themselves. Nina ate two scones, while Carly and Grant stuck to one.

When they'd finished, Nina gave Grant a silent look of gratitude. He nodded in return.

They began their daily routine, Grant taking over for Valerie.

Carly and Nina went into the kitchen. While Nina sliced several kinds of cheese, Carly prepared enough tuna fish to get them through the day. As she worked, her earlier conversation with Nina kept drifting into her mind.

If Nina had grown up in foster care, it might explain her saying that she didn't have any family. But that was only an assumption. Carly didn't know for sure. And it wasn't her business, really. All she could do was offer Nina her friendship, and that was something she'd already done.

Suzanne came in around ten thirty, complaining bitterly about the cold. She went into the kitchen and removed her winter wear in layers—two scarves, mittens, gloves, a pair of earmuffs, and a knitted hat with a pompom on top. Her jacket came off last.

Nina giggled. "By the time you get all that clothing off it'll be time to go home."

"Yeah, but I stayed warm." Suzanne smiled and hung her jacket in the closet, piling the accessories on the shelf. "Well, I'll start wiping down the tables, unless you need me for something else."

"No, the tables'll be fine." Carly smiled at her. "You seem happy today. It must be something Josh did, right?"

"Nope. In fact, Josh ticked me off royally this morning when he couldn't find his boots. We spent ten minutes hunting for them, and all the time they were under his bed. Kids," she said, putting on a fresh apron.

"Then why the smiley face?" Nina asked her.

"I'm glad you asked. Last night I had an epiphany. With all the sad news I see on TV every day, I realized something. I am a very lucky woman. Jake and I are doing better than ever. We have a decent home and a wiseacre kid we both adore. And I couldn't ask for better friends than I have here, not to mention a fun job. What else is there?"

Carly and Nina both stared at her.

"That's . . . quite a revelation," Carly said.

"Anyway, back to the salt mines," Suzanne quipped, and pushed through the swinging door.

The moment she was gone, Carly and Nina burst into laughter. "You gotta love Suzanne, right?" Carly said.

"Totally," Nina agreed. "She makes this place rock."

• • •

Business was slower than it had been the day before. Thanks to Ari and the crew from the public works department, the high school was up and running. The teenagers would be eating in the school cafeteria instead of invading the eatery en masse.

Around four o'clock, as nightfall began to darken the sky, a solemn face peeked through the glass door. Carly happened to be wiping one of the tables near the front and spotted her immediately. She rushed to open the door.

"Ashley, please come in. Can I get you a hot chocolate or a coffee?"

Ashley shook her head. "No, I don't want anything. Can I talk to you for a minute? Alone?"

"Sure."

They went to the back of the restaurant and slipped into a booth. Ashley's face was drawn and pale, and her lips were chapped. She left on her heavy clothing, removing only her gloves. She didn't appear to be wearing any makeup, which Carly took as a bad sign.

"I got a call from the police this morning," Ashley told Carly. "I guess they took another look at the video footage from the day of . . . Lennon's murder." She swallowed, and her eyes filled.

Grant brought over two glasses of ice water and set them in front of the women. He glanced at Carly as if to say, *"I'm here if you need me."*

Ashley immediately took a gulp, then wiped her lips with her fingers.

"As I was saying," she went on after Grant was gone, "they were watching the footage from that morning when they spotted the costume that one of the actors had reported missing—the Mrs. Fezziwig costume. They enlarged it to like, a thousand times. Even though I had a wig on, they decided it was me wearing the costume."

A slew of responses popped into Carly's head. The one that emerged from her lips was, "Was it you?"

Ashley blinked several times. "It was me," she said in a ragged voice. "But I didn't kill him. I would never do that. I'm not that kind of person."

"Did they show you the video footage?" Carly asked her.

She nodded. "I was walking fast and looking down most of the time. But for a split second I looked up. One side of my face was clearly visible."

"What time of the day was it?"

"The time on the video said eleven twenty-seven a.m. I'd just done the makeup for Bob Cratchit. Mrs. Cratchit was next on my list. But there was something I needed to do first. Something important—" She shook her head and choked back a sob.

Carly waited while Ashley pulled herself together. Just then, Nina came out of the kitchen carrying an empty plastic tub. She stopped short when she saw Carly and Ashley.

Nina set down the tub, then went over to them and smiled. "Can I get either of you something hot to drink?"

"Ashley?" Carly asked.

"No, but thanks. My stomach is too sick even for coffee."

"I'm all set for now," Carly said. "Thanks, Nina."

Nina nodded and retrieved her tub, then began clearing dirty dishes from the tables.

"Go ahead, Ashley," Carly said. "Tell me about the costume."

Ashley pulled in a shaky breath. "I'd taken the costume earlier. I have an oversized cosmetic bag and I stuffed it in there. Without all the padding, the dress wasn't as bulky as you'd think. But I didn't intend to steal it. I was going to put it back after I—" Again, she didn't finish her sentence.

"Around what time did you take it?" Carly said softly.

"Earlier that morning. Around ten, maybe? I grabbed the first one I saw, which was so dumb of me. If I'd known Jess Terwilliger was going to wear it for the dress rehearsal, I'd have taken another costume."

"I'm guessing you were on a mission," Carly said.

Ashley looked down. "I wanted to speak to my father. My birth father."

Carly's pulse jumped. "I thought you said you didn't know who he was."

"I didn't, until Mom learned she was dying. She didn't want me to go through life wondering anymore, so she told me everything.

"She met Prescott Lennon during summer stock, when she was trying to be an actress. He charmed her, wooed her. Back then, I guess, he was super good-looking. Booze and hard living must've caught up with him," she said bitterly. She took another drink from her water glass.

"And he never knew about you?"

"When Mom told him she was pregnant, he said it couldn't possibly be from him. A simple paternity test would have proved it, but he left town so fast she never saw him again."

Carly couldn't even imagine how abandoned Willow must have felt. Single, about to have a child, deserted by the biological father. No wonder she didn't want Ashley to know who her real dad was.

"I had a good life with Mom," Ashley said, smiling for the first time since she'd walked in. "She sacrificed everything for me. But . . . I still wanted to know my father. I wanted him to know who I was. I wanted him to know about the loving, caring woman he tossed away like so much trash." She covered her eyes and began crying softly.

Carly reached over and rubbed Ashley's arm. She saw Grant and Nina both look over at them. "Is that why you applied to Hannah to be one of the makeup technicians? So you'd have a chance to meet him?"

Ashley nodded.

"But why did you need a disguise?" Carly asked her.

She looked incensed at the question. "Because I didn't want anyone to recognize me, okay? I didn't know how he'd react when I told him who I was. I thought the costume and the wig would be a distraction—just in case it all went south."

It made little sense to Carly, but evidently it did to Ashley.

Her tears spent, Ashley swiped at her damp cheeks. "Let me finish because I'm starting to lose it, okay?" She sniffled hard. "I put on the costume in the bathroom, then I hurried to Prescott's dressing room. It was a miracle no one saw me. It was early. Most of the actors hadn't arrived yet. Of course I didn't think about the cameras. When I got to his dressing room, I almost lost my nerve. I finally knocked on his door. He didn't answer, so I knocked again. When he still didn't answer, I took it as a sign. It wasn't meant to be."

"So, you never got inside his dressing room?"

"Never. I started to rush back to the bathroom so I could take off the dress and wig, but I heard footsteps coming down the hall. There was a closet right next to Prescott's dressing room, so I went inside. It had cleaning equipment, stuff like that. I took off the dress and rolled it around the wig into a ball, then raced back to the makeup room and shoved it into my carryall."

"Not to the costume room?"

"No. By that time, a few of the actors were starting to go in and out for their costumes. I couldn't risk someone seeing me put the dress and wig back."

Her eyes held such misery that Carly wanted to cry herself. Was Ashley a killer? Carly didn't know. She was finding it hard to believe that Ashley was guilty of anything except wanting desperately to meet her father.

But Carly had been fooled before.

"Ashley, I am so sorry for everything you've gone through. But I think it's a good sign that the police didn't detain you."

Her face went taut. "They requested a DNA sample, so I gave it. I don't have anything to hide. I told them I was sure that the deceased was my father, but I had no way to prove it. I also offered to take a lie detector test, but they said they'd let me know." She looked coldly at Carly, then gathered up her gloves. "I'm leaving now, but I need to ask you something first. When you were at my salon, I noticed you spending a lot of time around my photo collage. Did you take a picture?"

Carly felt a flush crawl up her neck. "I did," she admitted. "It was an invasion of your privacy and I'm very sorry."

"The pinky finger, right?" Ashley sniped at her. "That's what made you think I might be Prescott's daughter? That's why you showed it to the police?"

"I'm sorry, Ashley. I felt I needed to bring it to their attention. I don't blame you if you're angry with me."

"I'm not angry. I'm hurt that you didn't ask me about it first. I'd have told you the truth." She pulled her gloves on, her gaze lingering on her right hand before she did so. "When I was eleven, my mother took me to an orthopedic doctor. He straightened out my finger with surgery."

Ashley grabbed her purse and stalked past the booths, then went out into the freezing night.

Carly sat, speechless, her heart drumming in her chest. She'd wanted to run after Ashley and try to explain, but Ashley had already nailed it.

Carly had spied on her. And she'd recruited her sister to help.

She was grateful Ashley hadn't mentioned Norah finding the dress and wig. Norah had assured Carly that she'd put everything back in the bag exactly as she'd found it.

Thank goodness for small favors.

It was nearing five o'clock. They hadn't had a customer since the take-out order someone picked up several minutes earlier.

Her legs shaky, Carly went to the front of the restaurant.

"Are you okay?" Nina asked her.

"I am. I was thinking maybe we should close early. It's so cold out, people will probably go directly home from work."

Grant came over and stood beside them. "Are you sure? I'll be happy to stay and close up, if you still have an extra key."

Carly smiled. On the official last day of Grant's employment with her, he'd insisted on turning in his key, despite Carly wanting him to keep it.

"I appreciate that, but I think you should both go home. In fact, I'll drive you to your cars so you won't have to trek across the street to the parking lot."

"You're the boss," Grant said lightly, the concern in his dark eyes obvious.

After shutting everything down, they piled into Carly's Corolla. The parking lot was only a few minutes away, but it would've been a bone-numbing walk.

Grant thanked her and hopped out of the backseat, promising to return the next day. Nina hesitated, and then opened her door. And then it struck Carly.

"Nina, wait. Do you know if the landlord fixed your heat yet?"

Nina hesitated, then said, "I'm pretty sure it's fixed. See you in the morning!" She scooted out of the car and into her own vehicle. Within seconds, she'd started her engine.

As Nina eased out of the parking lot, Carly waved at her. She hoped Nina was telling the truth about her heat having been fixed, and not just trying to allay Carly's worries.

CHAPTER 29

DON HAD BEEN RIGHT ABOUT THURSDAY'S EDITION OF THE *BALSAM DELL Weekly*. Although Carly's knowledge of photography techniques was almost nonexistent, she thought the photos he'd taken at the play on Sunday were impressive.

The center spread was an assortment of shots taken at the performance. In one picture, Scrooge is on his knees, beseeching mercy from the Ghost of Christmas Future. The terror in the old skinflint's face had been captured with incredible detail.

Don had also penned a review of the performance that glowed like a bowl of sunshine. He praised the actors, specifically mentioning "young Malachy Foster" and his epic transformation from "fresh-faced drama student" into the shadowy, dust-colored ghost of Jacob Marley.

The paper was thicker than usual. Ads for local shops and restaurants abounded during the holiday season. For Don it meant some extra money, which Carly knew he could use.

As for the murder, there was only a short paragraph about the investigation being "stalled." Don was no doubt biding his time until the killer was caught so he could write an explosive article.

"So, you got your heat back?" Carly asked Nina.

They sat together on adjacent counter stools, perusing the paper while they enjoyed leftover cranberry scones. Grant had texted to say he'd be a little late. Once again, Valerie was taking a sick day—her last one of the year, she vowed.

"Yes, thank goodness," Nina said, her long candy cane earrings brushing her shoulders. "The heating register is noisy, but I don't mind that. I just want to be warm. Hey, since Val isn't here, I'll do the bathroom today."

"Fine by me," Carly said.

By the time Grant got in, it was after nine. He'd had a few errands to run for his dad but was eager to get back behind the grill.

By lunchtime, the eatery was buzzing.

Carly had just set a container of cooked bacon on the worktable next to the grill when Nina grumbled, "Can you believe it? We're almost out of Sara's fruitcake. Our Scrooge's Redemption will end up being Scrooge's Downfall!"

"Yikes," Carly said. "I didn't think we'd go through it so quickly. I'll check with Sara to see if she has any more loaves."

Carly hustled into the kitchen and pulled her cell from her pocket. She was about to tap the number for Hardy Breads when she noticed she'd missed three calls—one from the Balsam Dell Inn and two from Don Frasco. She played the inn's voicemail first.

"Hi, Carly. It's Kelsey, the event planner from the inn. Hey, I've got kind of a sticky situation. I'm going to need your deposit sooner than I told you. Like, today. Give me a jingle as soon as possible? Thanks."

Carly gawked at her phone. The inn needs the deposit *today*? She and Ari had been told it wasn't due until the first week in January.

They'd reserved the elegant Grand Versailles Room, a portion of the inn that hosted weddings only. The venue had been hailed in bridal magazines as "one of the most surprising wedding experiences in New England." With its own entrance and parking lot, the room boasted a massive stone fireplace, an indoor waterfall, and seating for up to sixty.

Carly jammed her finger on the call-back number. Kelsey answered right away.

"Carly, thanks for calling back," Kelsey blurted into the phone. "I was so afraid I wouldn't reach you in time."

"What's happening?" Carly asked with concern. "I thought we had until January to give you the deposit."

"Yeah, technically you did. But the owner got a call late yesterday from some big-shot buddy of his. I'm talking, a *serious* big shot. You'd know the name. His son is getting married the same day as you and Ari. He insists on having it in the Grand Versailles Room."

"But we reserved it in September," Carly reminded her. "You said we could give you the deposit the first week of January."

Kelsey groaned. "I know, but the truth is we typically require the down payment upon booking. The owner made an exception for you two because Ari has done so much work for the inn, plus he doesn't price-gouge the way some suppliers do."

Carly blew out a frustrated breath. "Kelsey, this is really short notice. Any chance you can wait till early next week?"

"I'm sorry, but the owner's getting extreme pressure from the other party, so he's between a rock and a hard place."

Carly fumed. She definitely didn't need this right now.

"Here's the thing," Kelsey went on. "If we can tell this guy you've already put down your deposit, we can still save that date for you. He'll squawk, but there won't be anything he can do. Unfortunately, it has to be today. Like, really quickly." She quoted Carly the amount. It was hefty, twenty-five percent of the total. But they'd checked out two other places that required fifty percent, so she considered herself lucky.

Carly thought for a moment. "Can we use a credit card? I might have to split it between two."

"That's not a problem," Kelsey said, sounding relieved.

"Okay, give me a few minutes and I'll call you back."

Muttering to herself over the glitch, Carly called Ari to give him the bad news.

"Well, that's a bummer," Ari said, sounding annoyed. "But that room is ours and we're not letting it go. Honey, can you get over there? I'm in Readsboro, up to my ears in a project. I wouldn't be able to get there for another few hours."

"Don't worry. I'm on it. I have both credit cards with me. Or do you think I should hit up Mom for part of it?"

He sighed into the phone. "That's up to you, but I'd rather we take care of it."

"Okay, I'll head over there now."

After they disconnected, Carly called Kelsey to let her know she was on her way. She went into the dining room to tell the others she had a wedding emergency but would be back as soon as she could.

"Don't worry about us. We're doing fine," Suzanne said, adding three new slips to Grant's order wheel. "We're busy, but not crazy busy."

Carly threw on her jacket and gloves, grabbed her tote, and dashed outside to her car. She started the engine, then remembered she hadn't called Sara. She pulled off a glove and made a quick call to the bread supplier.

"You're in luck," Sara said. "I had so many requests for more fruitcake that I made another dozen loaves."

"Great," Carly said. "Can you set aside three for me?" She didn't want to deplete Sara's supply by asking for a half dozen.

"I can, but you'll have to pick them up. If you want delivery, I'm afraid it'll have to be tomorrow."

"Okay," Carly said. "Set them aside for me and I'll try to get there today."

"You got it."

• • •

Carly swung into the parking lot of the Balsam Dell Inn, her thoughts flying in every direction.

Originally, she and Ari had talked about a small quiet service in their own backyard, followed by a catered dinner. They'd chosen July 12 in honor of Ari's deceased mom, Ari wanting it to be a birthday gift to her.

It was only after they saw the inn's stunning Grand Versailles Room that they changed their minds. Carly knew her mom would be over the moon at seeing her daughter married in such an elegant setting. The wedding date was in honor of Ari's mom, but the venue was a gift to Carly's.

Inside the lobby, the tree was lit up. The white velvet doves nested serenely among the strands of dark red berries. It was such a peaceful scene that Carly couldn't help smiling.

She didn't bother checking her coat. She was there only to put down the deposit, after which she'd head to Hardy Breads for the fruitcake loaves.

Kelsey's office was on the second level. As Carly strode toward the foot of the wide staircase, she saw a woman stumble over a chair leg and fall to her hands and knees on the plush carpet. The bags she'd been carrying landed on the floor, and she cried out.

Carly rushed over. She dropped her tote on the floor so she could help the woman, then suddenly realized who it was.

"Oh my gosh! Hannah, are you okay?"

Hannah Collier, wearing a black woolen coat and a dark pink cloche, looked somewhat dazed. "I-I think so." She gave an embarrassed smile. "At least I didn't hit my head."

She got to her knees and brushed her hands over her coat.

A black-suited service attendant wearing a sparkly red bow tie rushed over to assist. "Ma'am," he said anxiously, placing a hand on her shoulder, "would you like me to call an ambulance?"

"Absolutely not, I'm fine," Hannah insisted, straightening her hat. "I just need help getting up. And don't worry," she said with a reassuring chuckle, "I'm not going to sue. I tripped over my own klutzy feet."

After Carly and the attendant helped her to a standing position, Hannah gave her arms a little shake. "Well, I guess I'm in one piece," she said with a laugh.

Once assured that she was steady, the young man gathered up Hannah's numerous shopping bags and Carly retrieved her own tote. She heard the ping of a text from her cell, but she'd have to check it later. She first wanted to be sure that Hannah got safely to her room. After that, she'd hustle to Kelsey's office to pay the deposit for the wedding.

"Wait." Carly glanced around at the floor. "Hannah, did you have a purse?"

Hannah patted the left side of her coat and winked at Carly. "I keep my wallet inside my inner pocket. Getting my purse snatched in the city twice taught me a valuable lesson."

"Ah. You're a seasoned shopper." Carly smiled and slid an arm through Hannah's. As anxious as she was to give her deposit to Kelsey, she wanted to be sure Hannah was settled first. "Come on, let's get you up to your suite."

The Colliers' suite was even more exquisite than Carly had imagined. Along one wall was a stone fireplace, an electric fire burning inside. The knotty pine walls boasted paintings of old New England. Two plush sofas flanked a glass coffee table, on which rested a massive bouquet of red roses, white carnations, and winter greens.

Hannah unbuttoned her coat and tossed it over one of the sofas, plunking the cloche on top.

The attendant set Hannah's shopping bags carefully on the floor. "Is there anything else I can do for you, Mrs. Collier? Perhaps send up a tray of tea and pastries, courtesy of the inn?"

"No, thank you," Hannah cooed, "but perhaps later."

He nodded and wished her a good afternoon, starting for the door.

"Wait," Hannah said, "before you go—" She held up a finger and grabbed her wool coat, then reached into the lining and pulled out her wallet. A square slip of paper, like the kind torn from a notepad, fluttered to the floor.

While Hannah gave the attendant a tip, Carly retrieved the note. She started to set it down on the coffee table when her eye caught the short message scrawled on it.

I know what you did.

Let's talk $$$

CB

Carly felt her knees weaken. Her heart began racing so fast it could have entered the Indy 500 and won.

CB. Curt Blessings?

The attendant thanked Hannah for the tip and closed the door.

Hannah turned to Carly. When she spotted the note Carly was staring at, she sucked in a sharp breath. "Where did you find that?" she hissed, snatching it from Carly's fingers. Her gentle gray eyes morphed into roiling storm clouds.

"I didn't find it," Carly said as calmly as she could. "It fell out of your coat when you took your wallet out."

Hannah licked her lips. Her fingers were clutching the note so tightly that her knuckles had gone white. For a beat or two she stared at it, then she crumpled it in her fist. "I'm sorry," she said with a bland smile. "I didn't mean to snap at you. My nerves are a wreck these days." She lifted her wool coat off the sofa and fumbled around in the lining's inner pocket.

"That's all right. Totally understandable," Carly said evenly. "Hannah, I'm really glad you're okay, but I do have to dash. The event planner here at the inn is waiting for me. If she doesn't receive our deposit very shortly, our wedding will be toast."

Her tote on her shoulder, Carly sidled toward the door. When her cell rang, she jumped. She reached into the tote and pulled out her phone. Don Frasco was calling her. She swiped the answer button.

"Hey, Kelsey, I'm at the inn," Carly said, her voice too loud even to her own ears. "I'm heading to your office right this moment."

"Carly, what the heck are you talking about?" Don griped. "I called you three times. I googled the names on that playbill, and I have a thought about who killed Lennon."

"Yes, I know I'm late, but please hold that date for us. I promise I'll be there in two—"

"Shut off your phone and put it away. You're not going anywhere."

Carly swerved around to see Hannah leveling a gun at her. The gun was so small and dainty that it might have been a fake, or a prop.

168

It wasn't a chance Carly was willing to take.

Her heart lodged in her throat, she tapped the phone, then slid it back into her tote. "It's off," she said. "Hannah, I . . . don't understand. What are you doing?"

"You figured it out, didn't you?" Hannah's words came in ragged spurts. "You know who wrote that note."

Carly felt tiny beads of sweat coating her upper lip. "Actually, I have no idea what you're talking about. Now, will you please put that gun away so I can keep my appointment with Kelsey?"

Hannah waved the gun toward the opposite sofa. "Sit. Down," she commanded. "I'm going to tell you a story. I'll warn you, it's not a pleasant one, but it's one you need to hear."

Her mouth dust-dry, Carly did as Hannah instructed. She set her tote on the floor and folded her hands in her lap. Hannah sat on the other sofa.

"Once upon a time, there was a family. Mother, father, three kids. After the father died—far too young—the mother remarried. The new husband was a widower, a kind man with two children who missed their mom desperately. They were all like that TV show, you know? The one with the blended family where everyone got along?"

Carly knew the program she was referring to, but she let Hannah continue.

"Then, at thirty-seven years old, the mother learned she was pregnant. She had a boy, a sweet, angelic little boy. She named him Evan." Her eyes narrowed and her gaze clouded. "I was five at the time, and I adored that baby. We all did. I helped Mom feed him his bottle, sang to him when he cried, walked him endlessly in his stroller. Evan and I . . . we couldn't have been more bonded if we'd been twins."

The name Evan sounded vaguely familiar. Where had she seen it before?

Her eyes glassy with emotion, Hannah continued. "Then we all grew up. Some of us married. A few married and divorced. I married late, but to a wonderful man." She paused to swallow back a sob.

"What about Evan?" Carly asked softly.

Her gun hand remaining steady, Hannah pulled in a long, shaky breath. "Evan graduated from college with a bachelor's in art, but all he ever wanted was to be an actor. I think he got that from me," she said with a sad chuckle. "In high school, he starred in *The Crucible*. Mom and I sat in the audience with tears in our eyes. At the end, Mom cried at how brilliant he was—she literally sobbed with pride. She loved all her children, but Evan was her treasure."

A sick feeling clawed at Carly's insides. She remembered, now, where she'd seen the name.

"Years later, after graduating college, he heard about a playwright who was recruiting actors for a play he'd written. The venue wasn't much, a small theater in Arlonville, Massachusetts. Evan got to the auditions a day late because his bus broke down. The lead role had already been cast, but he was overjoyed just to get a minor part. They started rehearsals, but after a few days the lead actor was cut from the role. He was arrogant, couldn't take directions, showed up to every rehearsal with beer breath."

"Prescott Lennon," Carly murmured.

"Yes." Hannah's damp eyes blazed with fury. "Imagine Evan's elation when Lennon was cut and he landed the lead role. Mom wanted desperately to see him perform, so I drove us there and we got a room for a few nights. She was so excited when they told us we could sit in on a rehearsal."

"Hannah, listen to me," Carly said in a quiet tone. "You don't have to finish the story. I know about the accident—"

"It wasn't an accident!" she shrieked. "That horrible Prescott Lennon rigged it to look that way. My mother . . . she came close to dying herself that day. She watched her son plummet through that stage floor, only to learn that the fall had killed him. She was hysterical with grief. She had to be taken out by ambulance. After we got back home, she didn't eat for a week. Not even a speck. She was never the same after that. Day after day, I watched her die slowly . . ."

Carly felt herself choking up. "Hannah, I can't even imagine your pain, or your family's. Is that why you asked Lennon to try out for the play? So you could get to him?"

Hannah's chin quivered. "Yes. I knew he was a lousy actor. But this way I could finally make him pay for what he did. Everyone told my mother she should forgive and move on. How do you forgive someone who cruelly took your child without an ounce of remorse?" Her face crumpled, and she broke into sobs, the gun lowered to her lap.

Carly closed her eyes and breathed a sigh of relief. After a few moments, she rose and sat down next to Hannah, slipping her arm around the woman's quaking shoulders. "I don't know, Hannah. I'm not sure I could, if it were me."

Hannah raised her tear-streaked face to Carly. "Those people, the ones who owned the theater, they sent Mom a large check. A *very* large check, no questions asked. As if that could compensate for the loss of the most beautiful human being I've ever known."

Carly recalled the chief telling her that Lennon had been a disowned relative of the owners. Although no evidence of Lennon's tampering had ever been reported, the family no doubt wanted to sweep the tragedy as far under the rug as they could.

Hannah wiped under her eyes with her fingertips. "Before Mom passed, she . . . she made me vow that I would punish him for what he did, for taking our Evan from us. Don't you see? I . . . I had to promise, so she could die in peace. It was the only way."

But you didn't have to carry out the promise, Carly thought soberly.

Very quietly, her heart thrumming, Carly moved the gun from Hannah's lap to the coffee table.

"How did you manage to poison him?" Carly asked.

"After I ordered him off the stage, he stormed away to his dressing room. I fetched my purse and removed the eye drops. My poor Douglas, he thought he'd misplaced them. I'd read about eye drops being toxic if swallowed, and that's what gave me the idea. I knocked on Prescott's door. When he let me in, his attitude had changed. He was meek, scared. I told him to pull himself together or he was out of the play. He went into his private bathroom, and that's when I saw my chance. His energy drink was sitting on the table next to the sofa, about half full. I squeezed every last ounce of those eye drops into it. When he came out of the bathroom, I ordered him to drink it so he'd have the strength to go back out there and face his audience."

Carly was stunned at her audacity. It could've gone wrong in so many ways, and yet she managed to poison him.

"So he drank it?" Carly said.

"Every last drop." Her lips trembled. "I didn't expect it to work so fast. But then his eyes turned glassy and his face got bright red. He stumbled toward the bathroom, but he didn't quite get there. He made a terrible sound and then he dropped behind his mirror."

Carly couldn't imagine what was going through Hannah's mind in that moment—watching her long-awaited plan for revenge play out right in front of her.

"For a moment, I felt elated. I'd waited half my lifetime to see him suffer. The prop—the chain—was on his dressing table. Some pencils were there, too, so I used one to lift the chain. Somehow, I managed to wrap the chain around his neck without touching it. It was loose, but I didn't care. I meant it to be symbolic . . ."

"Symbolic?"

Hannah's gaze fogged. "Yes. Of the prison my mother wasted away in until the moment she passed."

Carly felt bile rise to her throat. She took slow, deep breaths until she could speak again.

"Hannah, what happened with Curt Blessings?"

Hannah frowned. "He . . . he saw me that day, coming out of Prescott's dressing room. I was shaking so hard my legs barely supported me. The pantsuit I was wearing didn't have any pockets, and I still had Douglas's eye drop bottle in my hand."

"But he couldn't have known you poisoned Lennon with it, could he?"

"Of course not," she huffed. "But he clearly knew something was up. After that creature's death was made public, he put two and two together. He wanted money."

"How did you dispose of the bottle?"

"After Curt went around the corner, I opened one of the exit doors and tossed it outside. It was windy and cold. I'd hoped the bottle would get carried away. I . . . guess I didn't think it all the way through, did I?" she said bleakly.

The bottle itself, as far as Carly knew, had never been recovered. It was sheer serendipity that she'd found the tiny cap in the snow when Nate had given her the tour of the opera house.

Something else occurred to Carly. "Hannah, were you the person who flushed Lennon's prescriptions?"

Hannah stared at her in shock. "How did you know about that?"

"The plumber who fixed the clog told a friend of mine."

She swallowed. "I thought, maybe if I got rid of his prescriptions, he'd die from a heart attack. Then I wouldn't have to—" Her slender form sagged like a deflating balloon. "I was going to flush the contents and get rid of the bottles later. But Douglas was outside the door calling my name, worried about why I was taking so long in the bathroom. I panicked. I tossed the whole bag into the toilet, praying it would flush all the way. Those commercial toilets are pretty powerful."

It flushed, all right, but then it clogged up the works, Carly thought.

"I couldn't very well use my gun to kill Lennon," Hannah said. "The noise would've been deafening."

"Yes, for sure," Carly agreed. She glanced at the gun resting on the coffee table. "Hannah, where is Douglas?"

"Douglas? He's out Christmas shopping." She pressed her hands to her pale cheeks. "Please, I don't want him to know what I did. You won't tell him, will you?"

"No, I won't," Carly promised.

And then, as if she'd closed a door on a particularly bad odor, Hannah skimmed her dewy gaze around the room. It landed on the shopping bags the attendant had left on the carpet. A ghost of a smile on her lips, she jiggled Carly's hand. "Do you see all those bags over there?"

"Yes." Carly forced a smile. "It looks like you did some serious shopping."

"I did," she tittered. "I'm putting together gift bags for everyone in the cast, to thank them for their fabulous performances."

"Hannah, that's a lovely gesture."

"I . . . I just don't know if I can get them all done before the final performance. There's an awful lot of them to do." She squeezed Carly's fingers eagerly. "You'll help me with them, won't you?"

Carly nodded over a lump in her throat the size of a plum pudding. "Of course I will."

Out of one corner of her eye, Carly saw the door to the suite slowly open. A man and a woman stepped in quietly, paused to take in the scene, and then walked over to them.

"Good afternoon," Chief Holloway said to both women. He pocketed the cell phone he was holding, then stared meaningfully at Carly. She nodded to signal that she was okay. Then he turned to Hannah and smiled. "Hannah, this is my good friend Officer Cindy Little. She came here with me as my helper."

"Pleased to meet you, Hannah," Cindy said kindly. She removed the gun from the table and placed it in a bag.

"Be careful with that," Hannah cautioned. "It has a powerful kickback. I found that out the hard way."

"Yes, ma'am, I'll be very careful."

Carly rose from the sofa, and the chief sat down in her place. "Hannah, I'm going to drive you to the station now so that I can ask you some questions."

Hannah looked stricken. "Oh, dear, that won't do at all. My husband will wonder where I've gone. I can't—"

"We've already notified him," Holloway assured her. "He's going to meet us there."

Hannah nodded slowly, looking vastly relieved. "Thank you. You're very efficient, aren't you?"

The chief smiled. "I try."

Cindy helped Hannah with her coat and hat. "Do you have gloves?" Cindy said brightly. "It's getting chillier out there by the minute."

Hannah pulled a pair of dark pink gloves from her pockets and smiled. "Of course I do. And they match my hat!" She slipped them over her fingers.

Holloway took charge of the gun, while Cindy slipped a firm arm through Hannah's and escorted her to the door.

Protocol, Carly knew, would have been to place Hannah in handcuffs. Instead, Cindy led Hannah out of the suite as if they were old friends going out for lunch. Carly silently thanked both officers for ignoring the rules.

Hannah turned suddenly to Carly. "You'll come back later and help me with the gift bags, won't you?" she pleaded.

"Yes, I'll be happy to," Carly said, a quaver in her voice.

After Cindy and Hannah left, Holloway spoke to Carly. "That was smart thinking, leaving your phone on. Don could hear everything, loud and clear. The second he realized what was happening, he called me on a different phone so I could hear it, too."

Carly nodded, barely able to speak. She felt numb, so heartsick for Hannah that she wanted to sob. In a short space of time, she'd watched Hannah's mind shift sideways and fracture. Hannah was no longer the refined woman who'd invited Carly to tea barely a week earlier. She was more like the child who sang to her little brother and took him for walks in his stroller.

Or had the whole thing been an act? Realizing she was trapped, had she already been practicing for an insanity defense?

The chief squeezed her shoulder. "You sure you're okay?"

Carly aimed for a smile that she was sure came out like a scowl. "I will be," she said.

"Be prepared," the chief cautioned as they moved toward the door. "I tried to keep the police presence minimal, but there are a few uniforms in the lobby."

"Thanks for the warning."

"And don't worry about driving. I'm going to take you home. You and Ari can pick up your car tomorrow. Right now, you need to go home and have yourself a glass of wine and a good cry."

And she would, too. In the privacy of her home—with her fiancé and her dog for solace—she'd have herself a glass of Chardonnay and one doozy of a cry.

CHAPTER 30

"THIS IS GOING TO BE MY BEST CHRISTMAS EVE EVER," NINA ANNOUNCED, the tip of her elf hat dangling over one pointy elfin ear.

Carly smiled. She'd had the same thought about herself.

Her life had seen a lot of change over the past year. She and Ari had gotten engaged. They'd successfully rehabbed their two-family dwelling into the beautiful one-family home it had once been. Adding items chosen with care to reflect their individual tastes, they'd made the house their own—although they'd kept a few of Joyce's vintage pieces as a tribute to her generosity.

And now they had a wedding to plan. *Gulp.*

After the new year, it would be pedal to the metal to finalize all the details. Carly was grateful to have so many hands working to help—her mom, Norah, Gina, and her team at the eatery.

She had a lot to be thankful for.

Because it was Christmas Eve, she'd shortened the restaurant's hours from eleven to two. It gave customers a chance to enjoy a quick meal, along with complimentary cookies, before rushing off to do last-minute shopping.

As for the staff, they'd all agreed to wear costumes. Carly had chosen a Mrs. Santa outfit, sporting a knee-length red dress with fuzzy white trim and a pair of red leggings. Suzanne disliked costumes, her only concession to the rule being a set of reindeer antlers and a shiny red nose.

Valerie had used a massive cardboard box to transform herself into a gaily wrapped gift. Her head stuck out the top, and a bright green bow was clipped to her topknot.

Grant, who was home for the holidays, went all out. He wore a Santa costume with all the trimmings, including a pillow stuffed into his shirt.

Nina was snapping pictures like crazy, determined to capture every second of the festivities.

Gina and Zach were also invited. Gina had refused at first, unwilling to "barge in" on the eatery's get-together for the staff and their plus-ones. But the gang had insisted, and she'd happily relented. After all, she *did* live in the building.

Although Don wasn't an employee, everyone had begged to include him in the festivities. His fast thinking had enabled the police to arrest a killer quietly, without any fanfare.

It was Don who'd figured out Hannah's connection to Lennon. Googling the names of the male actors from the *Sins of the Rich* playbill, he found Evan Calloway's obituary from twenty-five years earlier. Although it didn't cite the cause of death, the obit named Hannah Fergus, Evan's half sister, as a surviving family member. After doing a quick google search on Hannah, Don realized Hannah Fergus was now Hannah Collier.

Before the others got there, Nina removed the felt mittens from the tree. "Do not open these until Christmas," she said sternly, handing out each of the mittens to the named recipients. "That is a direct order."

Everyone mumbled their agreement and slipped their namesake mittens into whatever pockets they had.

"I wonder what Don's going to wear," Carly mused, setting a tray of utensils, holiday napkins, and paper plates and cups on the counter.

"He claims he's dressing as himself," Nina said. "We'll see."

Nina glanced at the clock. "Hey, it's almost two. Can we close now?"

The last customer having left, Carly turned the *Open* sign to *Closed*, leaving the door unlocked. "Done!"

A glance around her eatery told her that everything was as it should be. The tables had been wiped clean. Holiday music floated from Suzanne's old boombox. The combined aromas of cinnamon, lemon, and cloves wafted from the kitchen, where Grant was preparing his special holiday punch, among other treats.

The chief and Ari arrived first. Neither had been thrilled about wearing a costume, especially the chief, but they'd each agreed to a headband. Ari's was a plaid snowman hat, a sprig of holly tucked into the brim. The chief wore a coiled Christmas tree with a gold star at the top, a tiny set of handcuffs its sole decoration. Valerie had found the trinket at a dollar store and thought it made the perfect ornament.

Everyone froze in place and stared when Don Frasco arrived. Sitting atop his head was the face of a snarling green Grinch. A lime-colored headband clamped over his ears kept it securely in place.

Don looked at everyone and scowled. "This thing looks ridiculous, doesn't it?"

Carly couldn't resist a chuckle. She loved Don to pieces, but the Grinch was the perfect costume for him.

"It's not ridiculous, it's adorable," Nina said with a giggle. She went over and planted a kiss on his cheek, so fast he barely saw it coming.

His freckles deepened with color. "Something smells good," he said, removing his outerwear.

"Grant's in the kitchen whipping up some yummy treats," Valerie explained.

"I hope they don't all have cheese," Don declared.

After the final performance of *A Christmas Carol*, Don had issued a special edition of the *Balsam Dell Weekly*. He hailed the production as a "rip-roaring, holiday-themed, tear-the-roof-off success." A bit hyperbolic, in Carly's opinion, but she enjoyed reading it nonetheless.

In Hannah's absence, Nate had taken charge, directing the production in his easygoing creative style. He'd been so impressed by Ashley Blanchard's talent at makeup application, he'd asked if she'd take on the most challenging character of all—the ghost of Jacob Marley. She did such a marvelous job that Nate intended to request her services for his next opera production.

For Carly, *A Christmas Carol* had been the best performance she'd ever seen. The costumes, the makeup, and the superb acting kept the audience clapping for a full ten minutes after the final bow was taken. Both Carly and her mom had left the theater with tears in their eyes.

A few days earlier, Ashley had visited the eatery. Carly was pleased that she'd used her gift card to order a grilled cheese. She'd shared with Carly that the DNA test had proven Prescott Lennon was her biological father. Although Ashley had never gotten to meet him, it was a form of closure for her.

"Ho ho ho! Wassail for everyone!" Grant sailed into the dining room carrying a large glass punch bowl and a ladle. He set the bowl on the counter next to the cups and napkins.

Suzanne leaned over the bowl. "What the heck is wassail?"

"Ah, my dear lady, it's a delightful holiday drink. Kind of like apple cider but more intense. It has apples, lemon, orange, ginger, cloves—"

"Okay, I got it," Suzanne said, waving a hand. "Now I want to drink it."

Grant ladled out cups of wassail for each of them. "Aren't Jake and Josh coming?" he asked Suzanne.

She made a face. "Unfortunately, no. They both waited till the eleventh hour to do their Christmas shopping, so now they're stuck at a crowded, overheated mall. Serves them right." She took a swig of her wassail. "Hey, this stuff is good."

Grant grinned. "I was hoping you'd all like it. I've got some other goodies coming out next. Be back in ten!" He dashed back into the kitchen through the swinging door.

While Ari chatted with Don, the chief took Carly's elbow and led her out of everyone's earshot. They paused near the door to the restroom.

"I wanted to give you a quick update," Holloway murmured.

"Thanks," Carly said. "I've been wondering."

"Hannah Collier is being held for a thirty-day psych eval. Her husband hired a crackerjack New York lawyer to defend her. He's hoping the extenuating circumstances will work in her favor."

Carly sighed and took a sip of her wassail. "I guess only time will tell."

Since that day in the Colliers' suite, Carly had been thinking a lot about Hannah. The more she turned it over in her mind, the more she believed Hannah had never wanted to kill Lennon. Flushing his prescription bottles in hopes he'd have a heart attack? Not exactly an efficient method of murder. And using her husband's eye drops to poison his drink seemed like a last-ditch effort to carry out her plan. It was almost as if she was sabotaging her own intentions to do away with him.

Unfortunately, the eye drops in his beverage had done the trick.

"By the way, Chief," Carly said, "do you know what that gun was? It looked like an antique."

"It was a lady derringer. Despite her husband's objections, she said she wanted it for protection. She'd insisted on buying a 'ladylike' gun—not something a thug would carry, is how she put it. Even worse, she never got a permit for it, or learned how to use it. She bought it from an online antique arms dealer. They even supplied a complimentary amount of ammo."

"That's terrible," Carly declared. "How is that even legal?"

Holloway shrugged. "It's not. The state police have tracked down the dealer, so they might be in some trouble. But that's a problem for a different jurisdiction."

"So," Carly said, "was the derringer the gun she used on Curt Blessings?"

The chief nodded. "She tried paying him off, but he said it wasn't enough. She decided, before the situation snowballed, to end the blackmail. In a way, though, Blessings was lucky. That derringer is designed only for close-range use, and it's louder than thunder. That's probably why she only grazed him from about ten feet away."

Carly mulled that over. How odd it was that Curt's surname turned out to be an *actual* blessing.

"But how did she know where to find Curt?"

Holloway swirled his drink in his cup. "He'd listed his aunt's address as his, since he'd planned to bunk with her for the duration of the performances. Hannah sneaked out early that morning while her hubby was still sleeping. She didn't know how to use the GPS on her phone, so the day before, she bought an actual street map of southern Vermont at the Balsam Dell visitors' center."

"Unbelievable," Carly murmured. "She certainly did a lot of planning just to get Curt Blessings out of her life. But what about Curt? I'm glad he's okay, but aren't the police filing charges against him for attempted blackmail?"

Holloway blew out a sigh. "Nope. The evidence just isn't there. The DA decided not to pursue it. Oh, one good thing. He admitted he lied about Gina handling the chain of cash boxes. She'd helped him untangle it, just as she said. He didn't want to get in trouble for letting her into the prop room."

Carly shook her head. "Then he should be charged with lying to the police," she said crossly. "Look at the torment he put her through."

"Can't say I disagree," Holloway said, "but the DA wants to focus on Hannah."

"You know, Chief, I can't help feeling bad for Hannah. She was so misguided. Even after marrying a man who was devoted to her, she was still determined to carry out her mother's dying wish for retribution. Maybe if Hannah had gotten some help earlier, it could've gone differently."

"Maybe," the chief said soberly. "I guess we'll never know." His expression softened. "Carly, if this case goes to trial, you know you'll be called to testify."

"I know," she said glumly. "I've been down that road before."

Valerie padded over and wrapped both her hands around the chief's arm. "Hey, you two," she teased, "are you still talking about murder?"

Carly flashed a smile. She saw Ari grinning at her and waving her over. "Nope. We're joining the party."

Grant came out of the kitchen carrying a large tray of appetizers. "This is a new recipe for me. I want you all to try these first."

"Ooh, what are they?" Valerie trailed him over to the counter.

"They're naan breads covered with a feta cheese mixture, oven-baked and then drizzled with balsamic glaze. And they're vegetarian. I cut them into triangles to make them easier to eat."

Everyone except Don reached for a sample.

"And for Don," Grant said with a wicked smile, "I'll be back in a minute."

Grant returned with another tray. "Taco filling and guacamole baked in mini phyllo cups. Not a speck of cheese."

Don's eyes popped. "Whoa. Thanks, man. These look awesome." He lifted three onto his plate.

Grant kept the snacks coming, some being recipes he was trying for the first time. As the wassail ran low, he prepared more.

It was after three when Gina and Zach burst through the door. "Hey, everyone, sorry we're late," Gina said breathlessly. "We didn't have time for costumes, but we stopped at Sissy's Bakery."

His grin a mile wide, Zach held up a large white bag. "She made dozens and dozens of cinnamon-sugar donut rounds. They were only a dime each while they lasted. And these are still warm!"

After removing their coats, they were greeted warmly by the gang. The combined aroma of sugar and cinnamon was like a siren song, drawing everyone to the donuts.

Gina hugged Carly, her brown eyes beaming. "I'm so glad you invited us. I've been looking forward to this all day."

"Me too. Have some of Grant's wassail. And wait till you taste his appetizers!"

"I'm sure they're to die for," Gina said excitedly.

At the word *die*, Carly flinched. "No," she amended with a smile. "They're to live for."

With everyone having arrived, the chatter grew louder. The men, except for Don, talked football, while the women discussed their plans for Christmas Day.

Carly and Ari would be hosting dinner for her mom, Gary, Norah, and Nate. Carly was supplying the main course, a baked ham, Nate and Norah the sides, and Rhonda the dessert. Carly had invited Nina and Don to join them, only to learn that they'd both accepted an invitation from Suzanne to dine with her family.

"Suzanne's adding a vegetarian pasta dish to her menu, just for me," Nina had squealed with delight. "Isn't she the sweetest?"

"Yes, she is," Carly had agreed. Suzanne was, indeed, far sweeter than she liked to pretend.

True to his word, John Winslow had finished framing her and Ari's engagement photo well in advance of Christmas. He'd been cordial, if not friendly, when Carly picked it up. She'd already wrapped it and tucked it under the tree. She couldn't wait to see her mom's face when she unwrapped the gift Christmas morning.

As it drew closer to four o'clock, it was time to wrap up the festivities. Carly had already given out bonuses to her staff. All that needed to be done was the cleanup.

She excused herself and went into the kitchen. Grant followed behind her.

Carly looked around in amazement at her spotless kitchen. "What the—"

"All done," Grant said with a big smile. "I washed everything as I went along. There weren't many leftovers, but they're covered and in the fridge. You just have to run the dishwasher. I'll take my mom's punch bowl home with me."

"Grant," Carly said, barely able to hold it together. She went over and hugged him, holding on for a long moment.

"Have a merry Christmas," he said, sounding choked up himself.

"You, too. And your mom and dad."

In the dining room, Ari was collecting the trash into a large compostable bag. Hugs, handshakes, and "Merry Christmas" wishes were making the rounds. Nina dashed over to Carly and pulled her aside. "Ignore what I told the others," she whispered. "You can peek into your mitten after they're gone."

"Thank you again," Carly said. "Have a wonderful day tomorrow."

After they all trickled out into the cold December night, Ari swept Carly into his arms. "Do you know how lucky I am to be engaged to you?"

She laughed. "That works both ways, partner."

A gleam in his eye, he gave Carly a quick kiss. "I'm getting excited about our wedding."

"Me too," Carly murmured. "I can't believe it's only seven months away."

"Only?" Ari quipped. "That seems like a lifetime to me."

Given what Carly had gone through at the inn, the owner had been kind enough to accept their deposit a day late, and at a ten percent discount off the total cost.

"Believe me, it'll go by faster than you think. There's a lot to do in those seven months."

"I suppose," Ari said grudgingly. "By the way, since the chief drove me here you'll have to give me a ride home."

"I think that can be arranged," Carly said with a flirty smile.

She double-checked the kitchen to be sure everything was in good shape, then shut off the lights and locked the front door. They started to leave through the rear exit when Carly stopped short. "Wait. Nina said I could open my mitten." She unzipped her jacket and pulled out the mitten from the pocket of her Mrs. Santa dress. Inside the tiny decoration was a folded sheet of paper that read:

Carly, I am going to bake all the cookies for your wedding. And I promise, they'll be gorgeous. Love, Nina.

She showed it to Ari, her heart swelling. "Am I the luckiest person on earth?" she asked him.

"Second luckiest," Ari replied in a husky voice. "Now, let's go home and celebrate Christmas Eve in our cozy new digs."

RECIPES

Scrooge's Redemption

Nina had so much fun creating this very simple recipe that she wanted to share it with others. While not everyone is a fan of fruitcake, this dense, moist treat (at least in some people's minds) seems to pop up in supermarkets and specialty stores as soon as the holidays roll around.

Fruitcake is filled with dried fruits, candied fruits, nuts, and spices. Often it is soaked in liquor, but that part is optional. Because of its consistency, fruitcake can be tricky to slice. If you can buy it pre-sliced, that would be your best choice.

With Grant's help, Nina came up with the perfect cheese to pair with fruitcake, resulting in a grilled cheese that appealed to most everyone—even those who normally turn their noses up at fruitcake. Here is the recipe for Nina's "Scrooge's Redemption."

2 slices of fruitcake, sliced thin or pre-sliced
spreadable Brie cheese
softened butter

Butter one side of each of the two slices.

On the unbuttered side of one slice, spread a generous amount of the spreadable Brie.

Top with the remaining slice, butter side up.

Grill in a pan on medium heat, about three or four minutes on each side, or until the Brie looks melty.

Enjoy this treat with a steaming cup of tea, or even with a glass of eggnog. And raise your cup to Ebenezer Scrooge, the founder of the feast!

Grant's Festive Feta Appetizers

Christmas Eve at the eatery was the perfect place for Grant to test his Festive Feta Appetizers. They're easy to whip up in a short time, and a crowd pleaser at any event at which you serve them.

⅓ cup extra-virgin olive oil
3 plum tomatoes, finely diced
3 or 4 scallions, chopped
8 ounces of crumbled feta cheese
2 packages of naan bread (or one package of 12 naan rounds)
1–2 teaspoons Greek seasoning (less is more)
Shredded fresh basil
1–2 tablespoons balsamic glaze

Preheat the oven to 350 degrees.

Combine the olive oil, diced tomatoes, chopped scallions, and crumbled feta in a bowl and mix thoroughly.

Top each naan bread with the mixture; sprinkle *lightly* with Greek seasoning.

Top with bits of shredded fresh basil, to taste.

Place on a cookie sheet and bake for 8–10 minutes, then remove from oven.

Drizzle with balsamic glaze.

Cut into halves or triangles for easy eating.

The feta mixture can also be served cold as a dip along with crispy crackers. Just remember to remind your guests—no double dipping!

ABOUT THE AUTHOR

As a child, Linda Reilly practically existed on grilled cheese sandwiches, and today they remain her comfort food of choice. Raised in a sleepy town in the Berkshires of Massachusetts, she retired from the world of real estate closings and title examinations to spend more time writing mysteries. Linda is a member of Sisters in Crime, Mystery Writers of America, and Cat Writers' Association. She lives in southern New Hampshire with her two feline assistants, both of whom enjoy prancing over her laptop to assist with editing. Visit her on the Web at lindareillyauthor.com or on Facebook at facebook.com/Lindasreillyauthor. She loves hearing from readers.

Made in the USA
Monee, IL
27 December 2024

75491379R00114